FULL CIRCLE

Dyanne Davis

WD

||PUBLISHING||

Manufactured in the United States of America
First Edition : ISBN: 978-0692217146
Cover Design: A.M. Wells

Acknowledgements

As always, I give thanks to the Creator.

To A.M. Wells, thank you for all that you do. I am assured that you will become a well known writer and cover designer.

To Honey, may God continue to bless you. I look forward to the day when your own story of life after….life…is published.

To my family, friends, and readers, thank you for your continued support.

And bringing up the rear, the most important two people in my world. Bill, my love, my hero, my romance story come to life, you are loved by me, and you have my heart. But you always knew that, didn't you? To our son Bill Jr. I'm glad you rejoined us in this life, hoping to meet you again in the next…though not too soon.

Acknowledgements

<u>Dedication</u>

Full Circle is dedicated to **ALL** who believe, or have wondered if,
REINCARNATION, is not only possible, but whether they are living proof of it.
I personally know of many such persons, and I thank them for sharing their
thoughts with me.

And to the muse who thought to bring the trilogy to me: Thank you.

Dyanne Davis TITLES:

The Gift (Book II in the Undying Love Trilogy)
Giving It Up
An Imperfect Life
Hitting The Right Note
The Affair (Book I in the Undying Love Trilogy)
The Critic
Another Man's Baby
Many Shades of Gray
Two Sides to Every Story
Forever And A Day
Let's Get It On
Misty Blue
The Wedding Gown
The Color of Trouble

Novellas:

Santa Baby
Taming the Bad Boy
Forget Me Not
It's The Little Things
Rebound Love
Flight 22

Anthologies:

Continental Divide (Lotus Blossoms Chronicles 11) Anthology
On My Knees (Destination Romance) Anthology

Titles under F.D. Davis:

In The Beginning
In Blood We Trust
Lest Ye Be Judged
The Good Side of Evil (Carnivale Diabolique) Anthology

ᚠ	fehu	f	fire, wealth, material needs, goals, promotion
ᚢ	uruz	u	house, desire, inner feelings, unconscious
ᚦ	thurisaz	th	thorn, hardship, pain, introspection, focus
ᚨ	ansuz	a	air, leader, justice, teacher, intelligence, communication
ᚲ	kenaz	k	knowledge, wisdom, insight, creativity, inspiration
ᚷ	gebo	g	gift, love, marriage partnership
ᚹ	wunjo	w,v	joy, success, recognition, contentment
ᚱ	raido	r	ride, journey, change, destiny, travel
ᚺ	hagalaz	h	hailstorm, loss, destruction, change
ᚾ	nauthiz	n	need, poverty, hardship, responsibility, frustration
ᛁ	isa	i	ice, block, stagnant, patience, rest
ᛃ	jera	y	year, change, cycle, rewards, motion
ᛇ	eihwaz	j	junction, endings, transformation, death, rebirth
ᛈ	pertho	p	pawn, magic, mystery, prophecy, chance, work
ᛉ	algiz	x,z	protection, assistance
ᛊ	sowulo	s	sun, strength, positive energy, activity, conscious, male
ᛏ	tiwaz	t	truth, struggle, duty, discipline, warrior, justice
ᛒ	berkana	b	birth, growth, health, earth
ᛖ	ehwaz	e	equality, duality, change, love, partnerships
ᛗ	mannaz	m	man, human, self, family, humanity
ᛚ	laguz	l	water, emotion, fears, female
ᛜ	inguz	ng	energy, sex, work, grounded, balance, land
ᛞ	dagaz	d	day, happiness, success, time
ᛟ	othila	o	goddess, property, home, permanence, legacy, moon

FULL CIRCLE

Reincarnation was real. No one knew that better than Doctor Chance Morgan. Perhaps that wasn't altogether true. In the past three years, the forty-eight-year old cardiologist had reunited with several people from his past: a wife, son, and father in law. If not for the shared experiences perhaps he would have thought he was losing it.

Chance sat across from Blaine MaDia, world- renown psychic medium and the son Dimitra and he had given life to in their previous incarnation. He took a moment to study Blaine, noting there were no familial similarities to indicate he was any relations to either Dimi or him. Damn it. He had to remember that his Dimitra was dead, and though she remembered her past life she was now Michelle and preferred that he call her that.

Where Michelle had almond shaped eyes and skin the color of warm honey, Blaine was almost translucent, he was so pale. His eyes were a vivid blue and his hair was now ash blonde. He was taller than Chance by an inch. He was 6' 3" and all sinewy muscles, where Chance was a bit more compact more than likely from all the hours he'd spent keeping his body in shape. But his eyes were hazel and his hair brown with a minimal of graying around the edges. Michelle said it made him look distinguished. He wasn't sure about that. But he wondered how anyone could believe that three vastly difference people could claim to be family. He laughed softly. It took faith was all he could say, and as for the three of them not only had they gone on faith they'd had it proven to them that their souls were connected. For on meeting Blaine their souls had been psychically linked and together they'd seen their past in bright, blood red colors—, Dimitra's life blood as she'd lain in his arms, dying, and caressing the baby-soft skin of their son. Imbuing him with her psychic gifts. And because of their psychic link they'd witnessed Dimitra's passing.

Their truth, however, wasn't the norm, and he and Blaine sat contemplating the odds of that happening. He was a man of science-- not prone to flights of fancy at all--but he'd taken a twenty plus year journey to find his wife from a past life and that made him different. Finding her made him lucky, or it would have if she'd not already had a husband in this lifetime that she refused to leave. Now he could only sit here in frustration talking to the one person that should know exactly how he was feeling, but so far hadn't shown the proper compassion for Chance's situation. What did it matter? Compassion would not fill the void in his life; neither would going over and over the details. Still, something in him forced him to press on. He needed to understand how he'd searched half his life for a woman, thereby proving he wasn't insane, only to lose her.

The losing of the other part of his soul was the burning issue, not learning that he was a powerful psychic able to help end a psychic war. That was only an afterthought, for with that knowledge came the question. What had he done to deserve this? What was his karmic debt? And why the hell must it be repaid in this lifetime?

Disbelief tightened his jaw. "Find someone to love. Was she serious?" Chance peered over the rim of his soda can, his look questioning, and his eyes unable to hide the pain in his heart.

"Michelle just wants you to be happy. She doesn't want you to worry about her. I promise you in your next incarnation you'll find her again."

Chance studied Blaine for a moment, this son of his he'd known for nearly three years in this lifetime. He took a drink before sighing. How could anyone understand the torment he was going through?

"I've spent a lifetime searching for her. How am I supposed to just give it all up and go on as if I'd never found her?"

"Because, if you don't, neither of you will be happy," Blaine answered.

"Is that the psychic in you talking, or is that the son?" Chance halted his question for a moment allowing a smile to touch his lips. "And if it's the son, whose interest are you looking after? Mine or Michelle's?"

He watched Blaine's face as his features appeared to shift and change. For such a young man he took everything so seriously, even thinly disguised jokes, but then of course, Chance had known he would. He didn't deny that at times he got pleasure from teasing Blaine.

"I want you both to be happy," Blaine, answered at last. "But I don't want to see Michelle hurt, if that's what you're asking me."

"So, I guess we know where your loyalties are." Chance got up from the overstuffed chair and began pacing around the desk in Blaine's office.

He stopped, something catching his eye, making him pause, then keeping him rooted to the spot staring at a photograph of himself with Michelle and Blaine.

"I don't remember our taking this picture."

"That's because we didn't. It's something I got a friend of mine to do. Michelle and I were together. I wanted you in there too, the whole family."

Again Chance smiled at nothing in particular, just the irony of the situation. "It looks like you've got an abundance of family now. My son, the twenty-first generation psychic, who will no doubt produce the world's greatest psychic. How does Cassandra feel about that?"

"We're taking it one day at a time. She's not fighting the idea of the two of us fulfilling the prophecy any longer, and she's not fighting having fallen in love with a psychic. So I guess we're making progress."

Chance laughed out loud. "I can't imagine the bias one psychic has against another. That whole thing is ludicrous." His eyes narrowed. "Then again so is fighting psychic vampires. God, I don't believe any of that happened."

"Yeah, I agree." Blaine answered with a laugh of his own. "If I hadn't lived it, I would not believe any of it. Who in the hell would believe I would find my true parents?"

"Soul parents," Chance teased.

"Soul parents," Blaine amended and laughed again. "Who would believe that not one of us, but all three of us would remember our past lives, and that we would find each other in this one? What are the chances of that happening?"

Chance looked down on Blaine for a moment with pride, remembering the infant he'd raised into adulthood in a previous lifetime, and the young man he'd found once again in this life.

At last he answered. "I think the odds on that happening would have to be about a billion to one. All of us not only believing in reincarnation, but remembering our lives together."

"And your finding not just your son, -- but your wife, what do you think the odds are on that happening?"

A stab of pain pierced Chance to the quick. "I don't know."

"It's truly hard to fathom that she would not only remember you, but still love you. I would think that would be darn near impossible. You have to have some kind of idea about this. Come on, stop playing coy. What do you think the odds would be on that?"

Again Chance answered, "I don't know."

"Well, I'd say it's damn near impossible. But you did find her. She remembers you, and she loves you. She damn neared destroyed her marriage because of her love for you."

"Stop. That's enough. I don't want to talk about this anymore."

"Why not?" Blaine continued, "I think this is just what you need. My God, you're the luckiest man in the universe. You found your soul mate time after time, after time. You're blessed."

"I'm alone."

"You don't have to be. She doesn't want you to be."

"She wants me to have someone to wipe out her guilt at having Larry."

"He's her husband."

"I don't give a damn!"

"Chance, she has no reason to feel guilty. She didn't know about you. She didn't have any memory of this, not until she met you."

"And you think that matters to me? She should feel guilty that she's sleeping with another man, that's she making love with someone other than me. That she…," he stopped unable to go on.

"Do you want her to be unhappy and miserable? Do you want her marriage destroyed? She didn't remember. You, yourself said the odds are a billion to one that two people would find each other again, let alone remember. Why are you being so hard on her?"

"Because I remember," Chance thundered, "because she haunted my dreams for twenty years. Because I love her, and I can't just stop." He slammed the can on the coffee table paying little heed as the brown liquid sluiced out over the top and landed on Blaine's papers placed there for his clients.

His eyes followed Blaine and slid over to the ruined flyers. "I'm sorry," he muttered. "I just thought when you called…I wanted to believe she'd changed her mind, that she wanted me, wanted to be with me. Had I known you only needed me as a missing part for some psychic triad," he sighed. "I probably would have come regardless."

"I sincerely wish I could tell you that I'm sorry I called. She begged me not to, she didn't want you involved."

"You mean she didn't want to see me."

"No. She didn't want you hurt, not by the battle nor by seeing her again."

"Why did you call me?" Chance stopped in his sloppy clean up and glared at Blaine. "She was right I would have been better off."

"We needed you."

"Yeah to fight a damn psychic, turned magician, turned demon. If your little hunch hadn't worked, we would have all been dead."

"Yeah, but it did work. Besides, you have some of the facts distorted. Norman Yates was not a demon, just delusional. Even Sal didn't have a demon in his body; he was just stupid and arrogant enough to allow another entity to use him."

"How did you know it would work?" Chance challenged. "What if it hadn't?"

"It had to, because of the power of three. You, Michelle, and I are the triad, the psychic trinity. Three souls linked throughout eternity."

For a moment he remained silent watching as Blaine rubbed the bracelet on his wrist, the bracelet that was identical to his own. His lids fluttered and closed and for a moment as he remembered. He saw Norman Yates in the room throwing energy bolts at them, slamming Blaine into the wall. He saw the fear etched on Michelle's face, but her fear had been for her husband Larry.

With little effort he saw the three of them, himself with Blaine and Michelle on either side forming a triangle, Blaine saying some incantation and the psychic turned wizard falling to the floor.

Even now the tremendous surge of energy that flowed through their bodies touching all in the room had not dissipated. He'd not known any of them possessed such powers, but thankfully Blaine had figured it out. It was what had been needed in order for them to link with Salvatore, entering his mind, unbinding him and freeing his soul to battle for possession against the entity he'd invited in.

Perhaps, Blaine's claims that the three of them formed a psychic triad was true. When he thought about it the facts spoke for themselves. The three of them had performed three feats requiring incredible psychic strength honed through the ages. With pride he remembered joining with the wife and son that belonged to him in another life, linking once again to heal the Mystic and return him to life. A Mystic whom it turned out was Blaine's grandfather and Michelle's father. Yeah it had certainly been one hell of a day.

He'd even felt sorry for Larry. The man was a lawyer, he dealt in realities. Hell, for that matter, he himself was a scientist, a trained cardiologist, but he'd long since shelved any preconceived ideas to the back of his mind about what could and couldn't happen.

Many of his patients had lived when by all accounts they shouldn't have. In those rare situations he'd never taken the credit, even though patients had insisted on offering him praise. He'd told them time and again to praise God. So he was one up on Larry as he believed in miracles. And now it seemed he believed in psychic wars, demon possession and that he was one third of a powerful psychic triad. He held his hand out. Even now the palm vibrated with electrical energy. For a moment he wished he could go back in time just a few months, for Michelle had belonged to him then. He glanced toward Blaine not liking that his son could so easily read it. Not liking that he couldn't rewrite the ending but was forced to relive it.

When the smoke had cleared there had been such an adrenaline rush everyone was hugging, crying tears of relief, while he'd stood off to the side watching the woman he loved comfort another man. Damn irony.

Chance rubbed at his eyes, smelling the faint lingering of Michelle's perfume on his skin, feeling her touch on his arm as she came up to him. That's when she'd told him to stop loving her, to find a woman in this lifetime to share his love with. A crushing ache filled him and he turned from Blaine, wishing he were anywhere but in the room with his psychic son.

"She was right, you know."

"Damn it, Blaine, don't read my mind."

"Then put up your shields."

"I shouldn't have to. It's an invasion of privacy."

"You're right." Scratching his cheek, he sighed and had the decency to look away. "It's our connection. You're my father, part of the triad. Reading your mind isn't me trying. It's as natural as breathing. Besides, I'm worried about you."

"Didn't you learn anything with all the mess you got us involved in? Wasn't the point of the Mystic in all of this was to teach you that there are rules you must follow? And not to behave in such an arrogant manner?"

"You forget, I didn't say I read your mind. I don't have to. It's written all over your face. I wouldn't have called, but I got Michelle into that mess and I couldn't let anything happen to her. I couldn't bear to lose her. I'd just found my mother."

Blaine was in pain. That thought alone stopped Chance. He'd forgotten for awhile how much his son had wanted a mother in his last incarnation. A mother who'd died shortly after giving birth to him, a mother who passed him her powers and loved him thorough death was all he'd had in his previous incarnation.

As hard as it was to admit it he had no choice, Blaine was right. They were lucky to have found each other again. He shouldn't be jealous that his son wanted to remain around Michelle; after all he'd never known her.

The mere curiosity alone would propel things in her favor, but it was more than that and he knew it. The unbreakable bond of mother and son was the reason they all remembered their lives and their loves. If not for that love, all three of them would still be wandering, lost, without firm knowledge that the other existed this time around.

"Its okay, Blaine, I understand you did what you had to do to save your mother. I would have done the same thing."

"I didn't want you hurt."

Blaine sounded lost, his voice like that of a small child. Chance walked toward his son and put his arms firmly around his shoulder. "Don't worry about me. I'll be fine. Heaviness filled him. He could only pace in an effort to make the tension dissipate. With sudden clarity he realized the scent of Michelle's cologne wasn't still clinging to him after a year. It was in the room. Crazy. Smacking his forehead softly he turned back to Blaine.

"How often do you see her?"

"At least twice a week."

"How often do you talk to her?"

"Don't do this, Chance. What's the point?"

"I'm just curious."

"It depends.

"Every day?

"Yes?

"Two to three times a day?"

"Where are you going with this? I don't have a schedule for calling Michelle. If I want to hear her voice, I call. If she wants to hear mine, she calls. We go out for lunch, she comes to my home with Larry, I go to theirs. I'm making a relationship with some of her kids. I'm not the one who moved, Chance you are. Even so, I travel to San Francisco every couple of months to see you. We're both too old to play this game. You have no reason to be jealous of the time I spend with my mother." When his father didn't answer, he tilted his head slightly to the side.

"I see the problem."

"I'm glad that you do. It's easy for you to tell me that I can't see her, or talk to her and you talk to her several times a day and see her at least twice a week. You're allowed to be in her life and I'm not. How is that fair?"

"She has a husband."

"You went after Cassandra regardless of what she told you. You loved her and you were determined you belonged together."

"Cassandra was single."

"Was single?"

Blaine couldn't help it, he smiled and continued to smile until Chance understood.

"The two of you got married? When? Why didn't you tell me?"

"We've been married almost four months. We didn't make an announcement, and no, Michelle didn't attend. It was just the two of us, and the Mystic. I couldn't exclude you. And I couldn't have you and Michelle together. So we eloped."

"Women want a big wedding. You cheated her out of that—because of me? Blaine, I'm sorry. Listen, I'll tell you what I'm going to do. You visit me one month. And I'll visit you the next. That way we will see each other at least once a month."

"That works for me. I have more news though. I hope you'll be happy for us. Cassandra's pregnant. I'd love it if you're a part of your grandchild's life."

"I promise. You know I'm not really as dense as I seem. I know the three of us made the right decision but it doesn't stop me from hurting or missing her. It also doesn't stop me from being jealous of Larry or of you for getting to spend time with her. I've been thinking maybe I need to do more, go farther away, where I can't come into contact with her scent. Being here in your office, being with you, I'm on sensory overload. It's as though Michelle were right here and all I have to do is reach out and touch her."

"What are you going to do?"

"I'm not sure. I've been having really strange dreams lately. I think my not being with Michele has something to do with a past karmic debt, but I have no idea what it is or how to pay the debt and make sure we're together in the next life. No offense, but I'm not fully sold on the bracelets bringing us back together. When we die who the hell knows what will happen to them?" Chance closed his eyes allowing his head to roll about on his shoulders. He stretched every limb, giving himself time to think as the kinks uncoiled. "I do believe it's time for a change."

"What do you mean?"

"I mean that I have to go far enough away that I can't smell Michelle's perfume, that I can't feel her touch, somewhere far enough that when I imagine Larry's hands on her body, making love to her, far enough away that I can't jump on a plane and return in order to choke the life out of him." He caught the smile on Blaine's face. "I'm glad to see my pain amuses you."

"It doesn't." Then with more seriousness Blaine asked, "What are you thinking about doing? Where can you go that will make you forget?" Then worry crept into his voice, "You wouldn't...?"

"No, I wouldn't. There are always envoys going out of the country to do humanitarian work. I could go for a time. I think a lot of hard work might be just the thing I need right now."

"Can't you do that in the States? With the mood of the world and the terrorists right now, it might not be the best time for Americans to be traipsing all over the globe."

"Traipsing?" Chance laughed at his son. "I'm thinking I might go to India. They could certainly use my help and they are rumored to have some of the greatest mystics in the world. I can kill two birds with one toss."

"That's stone."

"Yeah I know, but this is my analogy, so I get to change it." He smiled at Blaine warming up to the idea as he talked. "I can study and help others at the same time."

"Chance, I do hope you do your research. Yes, India is rumored to have produced some of the greatest mystics but depending on where exactly you plan to go you're not going to like it. You're too regimented, too disciplined. You're a surgeon used to the best equipment and the absolute best in sanitary conditions. Some of the villages are not up to your standards. I don't want you getting ill. If anything happened to you..."

There was genuine concern in Blaine's puckered features, enough so that Chance decided to stop being flippant in his approach and consider his son might not want to lose him for a second time.

"I'm sorry," he apologized, "I will be careful." However he couldn't resist smirking, "Right here in the states, I ran into a man who could make my heart explode at will, another who turned your arm into a block of ice. I'm not making light of this, but after all that I've been through, men with guns are not my biggest fears. Besides," he said softly and almost to himself. "Michelle promised to wait for me in our next life." He rubbed the bracelet on his wrist feeling the heat.

It was the right thing to do. He could feel it in his gut. Maybe Michelle was right, this lifetime wasn't for the two of them. He understood that, hell he even accepted it, but liked it, no that was a different matter entirely. It would take a lifetime to fix that particular problem. Only when she was his again, in his arms making love to him would he like it.

"How soon do you think you'll leave?"

Chance stared blankly; he wondered what the hell Blaine was talking about. He blinked twice trying to clear his head from thoughts of Michelle wrapped around his body.

"India," Blaine repeated. "How soon do you think you'll leave?"

"I don't know. It might take a few months. I have some friends who've been on missions before. I'll find out as soon as I get back to San Francisco when another group is heading there, or if there's one there that I can join now. And don't worry, I want something remote but I'm not going to take risks. There are many groups there with all kinds of engineers working on providing clean water, sanitation and electricity. I want those conveniences, but I also want a place that will have more work, need more from me. I need to work everyday until I'm too tired to think, too tired to even dream."

"Are you going to tell her?"

"Why?"

"She'll want to know."

"She gave up that right."

"You're still angry with her."

"Disappointed." Chance smiled. "But then I would be disappointed if she didn't love her husband. She would not be my Dimi, would she?"

"You need to stop thinking of her as Dimi. She's Michelle now. So, are you going to tell her?"

"No."

"Are you going to tell me… before you go that is?"

"I'll try."

"Chance, you're not going to do anything stupid are you?"

"End my life? Let's stop beating around the bush on this issue. No, I'm not suicidal. If anything, I feel like I've been the victim of a homicide. I have these swords piercing my heart, my body, my mind and my spirit, and there's not a damn thing I can do about it except maybe crawl away somewhere and lick my wounds before they fester."

"You're being melodramatic."

"I'm being honest. That's how I feel."

"Are you going to at least give another woman a break? I mean if some woman just happens to fall in love with you, will you at least consider that loving someone will not be such a bad thing? You won't be betraying Michelle."

Chance's eyes narrowed and he glared directly at Blaine.

"I didn't. I swear I didn't read your mind. It's in your eyes. You feel you'll be cheating on her if you fall in love."

"I would be."

"You wouldn't. She's married. This is a new life. She's happy, and she wants you to be."

"I'm trying, I swear I am, but I remember every moment of every day we've spent together, every lifetime, including this one." He rubbed his hand across the bridge of his nose going upward to massage at the pinpricks of pains shooting across his temples.

"Blaine, I spent over twenty years of my life, this life, trying to find her. I divorced my wife the moment I remembered Dimitra."

"Michelle."

"She'll always be my Dimi.

"She's Michelle now. You have to start thinking of her as such. Not Dimitra and not Dimi."

"Alright, Michelle. How do you think I can possibly find someone else after knowing for a certainty that the woman in my dreams for my entire life is real, that she's here, that she's my wife and that she loves someone else? How am I supposed to forget how much I love her? You tell me how to do that, Blaine, and I sure as hell will try."

Blaine stared back but Chance didn't back down. He couldn't give his son what he wanted, a guarantee that he would replace the woman he'd loved for a thousand years.

"Just keep an open mind," Blaine almost whispered. "That's all I ask. Don't shove love away."

The conversation had shifted, Chance knew Blaine was talking about himself, his own missed opportunity, but then again those missed opportunities had brought him Cassandra Boozer.

"I promise. I will not shove love away."

"I don't believe you." Blaine laughed softly. "But thanks for the effort. Will you at least wait until my son is born so I can introduce him to his grandfather? "

"How do you know you're having a son?"

"I just do. Will you stay in this country at least until he's born?"

"I wouldn't think of leaving before that. So in the name of equal time how about if we go to your home and pick up Cassandra and I take the two of you out for dinner. The tension between them eased and they both took in a breath and released them simultaneously then glanced at each other and smiled. Their easy, relaxed relationship was intact.

CHAPTER TWO

Ten months later:

Though Chance had tried to get Blaine to forgo accompanying him into the airport, he had anyway. And he'd managed to somehow get permission to go to the gate to see him off. That hadn't been allowed in years. Chance shook his head. Leave it to his son to persuade the powers that be to allow him special permission to see him off. Perhaps it was the glow of being a new father. A smile spread across his face as he thought of Blaine and his family. Michelle and Larry had attended the christening. He'd done his best to behave, act as a grown-up. He'd said hello and then pretended they didn't exist. Because of the baby it hadn't been bad. He'd held on to him as though he was his lifeline. Perhaps others thought that was what he was doing because no one came to take the baby from him. Or perhaps the fact that he was leaving the country they all thought to give him the time as a sort of goodbye gift.

By the time he boarded the plane doubts assailed him. A bit of melancholy, unease about his decision to leave, and profound loneliness. Taking his seat in the first class section he was glad he'd splurged. The flight would be unbearably long. Still he wouldn't have thought to do it if it hadn't been for Blaine's nagging and then threatening to pay for the ticket himself. With a laugh, Chance knew his son was trying to let him know he was important in his life. That he already knew. It was strange but this relationship with Blaine felt natural, as natural as the one he'd had with him in their previous incarnation.

Taking a look around the cabin of the jet, something felt different. He closed his eyes and concentrated, hearing the different dialects spoken in razor sharp quickness. Awareness of the difference came swiftly. Not a word, not one blasted word did he understand. A shiver touched him. Had he done the right thing? Leaving all those he loved as though he wasn't taking them in his heart. And what about his grandson? Again he shivered before he heard Blaine's voice in his mind and for once was happy about the invasion. "I'll make sure you stay connected. Don't worry."

After the mental message from Blaine, Chance had relaxed reading a book he'd bought just for the trip on his new Kindle Cassandra had given to him. He searched his pocket for the small spiral bound notebook he carried. Some friends of his had taken the time in the past months to teach him some much needed words. He'd promptly forgotten each and every word he'd been taught. He wished he hadn't. He needed that knowledge now. He'd left his home and his culture, not sure he was ready for this, but it didn't matter. Now he didn't have a choice. He'd made a commitment.

Exhaustion claimed him. The journey would have been less taxing if not for the change in planes and the five hour layover. But it was what it was, there was nothing to be done about it. Mercifully the last leg of the extremely long journey was almost over. The plane taxied into position for them to disembark. As soon as the other passengers began to stand and open the overhead compartments he did likewise. . Stretching his six feet two inch frame in hopes of loosening the kinks he reached for his overhead bag and walked away from the doors of the jet, following the mass of people, and trying hard not to feel lost in the throng of bodies pressing in around him. There was no order like he was used to in the States, no sense that there was someone he could go to for directions. Through the grace of someone, God, his guardian angel, he wasn't sure, but Chance managed to make his way through the lines. Mostly he just followed the crowds. Suddenly he heard a voice yelling his name.

"Dr. Morgan, Dr. Morgan."

Looking over the over the sea of heads wrapped gaily with different strips of cloth he was trying hard to spot the English sounding voice that beckoned to him. "Yes," he screamed. "I'm Dr. Morgan, over here."

It was another two minutes before he connected the voice with a face. He grinned broadly at the man. Not having heard anything but his voice, the man's appearance was not what he expected. The man's color and skin texture reminded him of an unshelled pecan, brown, hard and sort of leathery from the sun.

"Dr. Morgan, thank you for coming. I'm Sabu, assistant to Dr. Trammel."

"Come," the little man ushered him along. "Let's retrieve your luggage."

The large musty room reeked of perspiration and body odor.

Chance's stomach lurched. He needed to get outside the door, and smell the fresh air if only for a moment.

"Sabu, how about a peek outside? Do you think I can do that without causing a lot of trouble with Customs?"

With a knowing grin, his guide turned and walked several paces in the opposite direction. Chance watched as Sabu walked up to an official. He saw the little man hand over several bills and point to Chance before returning to join him.

"You may wait out here if you like. How many bags did you bring?" he asked, holding out his hand.

"Three bags, but about fifty boxes of supplies." He smiled at the questioning eyes. "I brought medical supplies. Just give me a moment and I'll be back to help you."

Chance hurried out the door, wishing like hell he hadn't offended Sabu or his country, but if he'd stayed packed in that room he was going to vomit and that would sure as hell be a lot more offensive.

He burst through the door, preparing to take a deep gulp of air but found himself coughing instead. The air outside was not much better.

What the hell have I gotten myself into? He took a good look around. Taxies lined the street, but not enough, for there were people pushing and shoving each other out of the way to get to the waiting vehicles.

For the first time in his life, he missed the familiar order of the Chicago police, though he and his friends had secretly called them Nazis. They were so fond of order, not allowing a person a moment to retrieve waiting passengers. Now he thought this town, this place, this country could use it.

Well Chance, you made the decision, now suck it up and go give Sabu a hand. A smile crept across his face and he pulled a packet of gum from his pocket. If it was strong enough to repel onions, it should be strong enough to allow his nostrils to breath until he had his luggage.

He walked back into the crowded building, wondering if he would ever again spot Sabu. His small stature made it hard to be spotted over a crowd.

"Dr. Morgan, Dr. Morgan, over here."

Chance grinned. *Looked like Sabu was good at his job.* He walked gratefully toward the voice and to the carousel. His knowing what his own luggage looked like made the job go smoother. Twenty minutes and five filled carts later he grinned at Sabu. "I think this might be a little more than your car can handle."

"That's why I brought a truck. Doctor Trammel warned me you might have brought packages. We have a long ride ahead of us. If you didn't have so much to bring we could have taken the train and you would probably have been able to sleep."

"Most of the things I brought with me are medical supplies." Sabu gave him the oddest look, one he couldn't decipher.

"Dr. Trammel is most grateful to have you here."

"Speaking of Dr. Trammel, can you tell me a little about him, Sabu? For instance, how long has he been here?"

Sabu smiled and remained silent, causing Chance to wonder if he'd done something wrong. He'd not asked the man to divulge any dark secrets, just a simple friendly question. But he was patient; he'd outwait him if necessary. Lifting his brow and giving just the slightest tilt of his head, he indicated he was still waiting for a reply.

"Dr. Trammel has been here forever."

Chance stopped in his tracks, his eyes narrowing, "Isn't Dr. Trammel an American?"

"Yes."

"In that case why did you say he's been here forever?"

Again with the smile and no answer. Chance halted behind Sabu, waiting as four young boys, teens judging from their size, rushed out to help load the packages.

Okay he'd come to India in part because of the mystery of the country. Well it doesn't seem I'll be disappointed, he thought as he helped to load the boxes.

It had taken him a bit longer than he anticipated to find a place he really wanted to work, a place that wasn't already swarming with Americans. He didn't want to leave one America to enter another smaller one. He wanted the rawness and judging by his first view of the country, that was exactly what he was getting.

As soon as he'd found a group, he'd set about getting doctors from that part of India to teach him little things he needed to know. Then he'd haunted the offices of every doctor he knew begging them for their samples, using guilt when they didn't want to hand them over.

All the medical sales reps were probably holding a party right about now—glad he'd left the country. He'd badgered those poor souls to distraction, trying to lay his hands on any and all medications he thought would be useful. Now he was here, and looking at all the boxes filled with samples his mind went to Michelle.

He'd gotten a thank you card from her and Larry for taking part in the psychic war Blaine had tumbled into. The mentioning of them as a family unit being the needed force, the triad, barely a footnote. That one gesture alone filled him with anger and hurt. To think the woman he loved, and her husband sending him a thank you for helping to save her life.

He wanted to hate Larry but he really couldn't. He couldn't blame him for loving Michelle; after all, Chance had loved her forever. With all the boxes loaded, Chance climbed in the truck besides Sabu. Closing his eyes he did his best to keep his promise to his son. No remote viewing of Michelle, no sending his spirit to be with her. Taking in one deep breath after the next he fell into a deep sleep and remained there until he felt a hand on his shoulder trying to rouse him.

"We're here, Dr. Morgan," Sabu said, pulling the truck up with a lurch in front of a run-down, crumbling building made of loose stones.

He had no idea how long they'd driven. A quick glance at his watch told him it had been for hours. Opening his eyes fully, he glanced at the building they were parked in front of. The safety of the building left a lot to be desired. Chance was trying hard not to be judgmental. He'd never thought of himself as such. Then again he'd never faced the amount of decay he was seeing before him. How the hell was he expected to work in this place? He shivered; glad he'd gotten every shot he could, hoping they would work to keep him healthy.

He finally got out of the truck and stretched, turning for a better view. As he looked at the surroundings, he barely heard the honk of the truck's horn until a swarm of teen boys rushed out and jumped about throwing his boxes and luggage down as though they weighed nothing.

He stood and watched them, awed at their agility, their youth, wishing he had thought to bring more treats for the children. He did have dozens of lollipops, but he had a feeling they wouldn't last very long.

"Dr. Morgan, come on. Dr. Trammel is probably waiting for you.

This way. The boys will take your things to the room you will be using."

Reaching for the handle of his carry-on. Chance followed Sabu, thinking he was being lead to tea or some such room that accepted visitors. Instead he was lead to a washbasin of some kind, with a putrid smelling green liquid lining the bottom.

"Wash your hands," Sabu instructed.

"I don't think so," Chance replied, "What is it you want me to do?"

"Dr. Trammel needs help. He's been taking care of patients for hours. He's shorthanded. He told me to get you back here as soon as possible so you could assist."

Chance's head tilted upward, surely this was a joke. "Sabu, do you know how many hours I've gone without sleep?"

"You slept the three hours while I drove."

"That doesn't count."

"Didn't you sleep on the plane?"

This was insane. Surely George Trammel did not expect him to arrive and jump into caring for patients, short handed or not. He decided to try again. "I'm in no condition to do heart surgery."

"I don't think that's what Dr. Trammel has in mind for you." He took a quick glance at his watch. "I think he should be in the middle of a skin graft. That is what it says on the schedule. That takes awhile."

"I know nothing about that."

"You're a doctor, right?"

"Yes, but I'm a cardiologist."

"That's okay, no need to apologize, we can still use you. Now please wash your hands. That solution is disinfectant. We change it daily."

"No offense," Chance muttered, "But when I work I will require fresh water to wash my hands, and fresh disinfectant." He noticed the smile disappeared from Sabu's brown face. He was aware the man's estimation of him had plummeted. He didn't care. He wasn't about to plunge his hands into that slime. He didn't think any of the shots he'd received would cover such an exposure. Besides, that, he didn't much care for that crack Sabu made that his being a cardiologist would be acceptable, as though he was less qualified than Dr. Trammel.

"I need you to take me to my room so I can at least wash off the grim and change. I have no plans on stepping into an O.R. or even a patient care room with no sleep."

"Are you not planning on speaking to Dr. Trammel?"

"I can do that later."

"Now would be better."

Things were not getting off to a very good start. "Sabu, I need to change. Then I will do as you ask and tell Dr. Trammel I'm here. I will not however, be assisting him, until I've rested." Following behind Sabu he ignored the surliness of his guide. Sabu merely pointed at a room containing little more than a narrow bed. Chance eyed the bed suspiciously.

"The linens are clean."

"And the bathroom?"

Pointing to another door in the small room Sabu sighed. "Please hurry."

Opening his carry-on and removing one of the plastic containers, Chance wiped down the small bathroom did the same with the bed and every surface he could reach then and only then did he give the bed a look of longing and immediately fell down on it without changing. It seemed he'd just fallen asleep when someone was waking him. "What the…?"

"You're needed."

"How long did you let me sleep?"

"You're needed. Please come."

"Give me a moment to undress." At first it didn't seem Sabu was planning to leave the room, probably thought he'd fall back to sleep, and more than likely he would have. Chance finally stood, not making a move to follow Sabu, instead he stared at the man, determined not to leave until Sabu gave him a chance to undress. Grabbing for his bag, he opened it and retrieved a pair of the surgical scrubs he'd thought to pack near the top of the bag. In a couple of moments he was following Sabu. "Is Dr. Trammell still working on the graft?" They walked again to the place where the basin with the putrid liquid sat. "I told you, I'm not washing my hands in that. There was no way to ignore the long suffering sigh Sabu issued.

"Hold your hands over the basin, sir."

"Sabu, if I am to assist in any type of surgery, I will need a gown and gloves." He pointed toward the sink. "You have running water.

I'll wash my hands first then you can pour your disinfectant over them."

After washing his hands Chance cupped his hands noting Sabu's friendliness was completely gone. He turned his palms over and waited while Sabu poured more liquid over them, refusing to allow the drops to drain from his hands and back into the basin Sabu had indicated but held his hands over the sink instead.

No wonder there is so much disease here, Chance thought, and flung his hands dry refusing to use the towel Sabu offered. Only God knew where it had been. His eyes followed Sabu's movements. He noted the little man stopping at a basin that held gloves apparently being washed in more of the putrid liquid, then Sabu glanced over his shoulders, sniffed his nose in the air and handed Chance a brand new pair of gloves.

"Here you go, sir. Now if you could cover, Dr. Trammel could really use your help."

Rolling his eyes, he opened the sterile gown, slipped it on then donned the gloves. Chance walked into the less than makeshift operating room, making a mental note to contact everyone he knew for supplies and funds to help the group.. How the hell were they expected to treat patients and have them heal without the possibility of an infection? They had to be given a chance at the most basic of medical care and that included using sterile material each and every time. He didn't care what it cost. He would buy supplies with his own funds before he washed his hands in whatever the hell that was.

"Dr. Morgan, welcome, could you assist me please?"

Chance walked forward, this time choking back the stench, going toward the table, not wanting to. *How the hell could they practice medicine in these conditions?*

When he looked down at the table, a pair of luminous, dark brown eyes stared back at him from the body of a little girl of maybe five or six. He glanced over at the woman holding the child's hand, more than likely the child's mother.

"She's awake," Chance said in wonder his glance meeting that of Dr. Trammel.

"Yes. We're not in America, Dr. Morgan. We do the best we can. Now could you grab some of those opened gauzes and mop away the blood, so I can see?"

Chance glanced down at the less than sterile surroundings. Thank

God his gloves were sterile. At least he wouldn't be introducing any
more bacteria to the little girl.

"We're doing the best we can."

Chance glanced up quickly wrapping his hand around a handful of
gauze. The man had answered a question he hadn't asked, but merely
thought. He pressed gently against the child's hip, his eyes searching
her out. He saw the glistening of tears she tried bravely not to show
and he smiled at the girl. "I'm sorry if I'm hurting you honey."

The girl turned her head away, but her mother smiled at him
before she too turned away.

"They don't speak English, Dr. Morgan."

"What happened?"

"She was playing and injured herself."

"Did you deaden the area?" For his question, he received a long
lingering look, but no real answer. He could only hope that the child
was not being sutured without something to deaden the pain being
given. He added Lidocaine to his list of things he would request from
his friends.

For the next hour, Chance worked with Doctor Trammel doing
what he was told, feeling like a chastised errand boy.

His eyes kept searching for the little girl's. He was talking in
soothing tones to her, not caring if she understood him or not. He
glanced every now and then at the progress Doctor Trammel was
making. He noticed he was taking his time, making precise stitches.
The girl would barely have a scar. At least they had that to be
thankful for. Lost in thought it took a moment to realize he was
being given an order.

"Now if you would carry the child into the next room I'll get the
table ready for the next patient."

Chance looked down at the figure of the small child and hesitated.
"You want me to carry her?"

"As I said, this is not America. We do not have transporters
waiting to wheel patients out. Now hurry, please. I have three other
patients waiting."

Chance lifted the child as gently as he could, yet he felt the coarse
fabric of his gown rubbing against the freshly bandaged wound. He
nearly missed the small grimace of pain from the small bundle he
carried. Tears came to his eyes as he laid her on one of the cots in the
joining room.

Returning to Dr. Trammel, Chance proceeded to walk toward a stack of fresh gowns. His attempts to change from his soiled gown had lead to a reprimand from Dr. Trammel.

"We'll contaminate the next patient if they come into contact with the blood."

"Then I'd suggest you don't let anyone come into contact with it."

Glaring, Chance held his ground until George had Sabu show him to the room where patients not needing anything that came remotely close to even a single stitch waited for him. In annoyance, he removed the gown and gloves and began examining the patients. Below the surface, he felt the anger building. But there had been no time to fight. The patients were waiting. He would wait until the last of them had cleared out for the day before he complained. *Hell I'm not being paid for doing this. I came of my own free will. If my help isn't needed then I'll take his ass back to San Francisco.*

It was seven hours before Dr. Trammel called it quits and told Chance they were done for the day. Taking a look around the examination room, he noted that the entire room was illuminated by battery powered lanterns. He'd been assured there were at least some modern conveniences like, electricity. He supposed he should be thankful for the running water. Pausing he waited at the door trying to ignore the poor condition of the building. "Dr. Trammel—" The raised finger from the other man stopped him in his tracks.

"We can become officially acquainted later. I'll come to your room in a few minutes if that's okay with you."

"Of course, I had thought…never mind I'll see you in a few minutes." At the moment all Chance wanted was to sleep. Making his way toward the small room he'd been assigned, he thought of home and glanced at the cot with a mattress less than an inch thick. Chance sat on the unbelievably lumpy thing. A moment later George poked his head in the door. "I want to talk to you," Chance said. Those were the last words he spoke that night. He fell asleep.

CHAPTER THREE

A light tapping on the door woke Chance from his dream. Glancing around the room at the crumbling mud walls, he groaned. He'd hoped the past day had been a horrible nightmare. What business did he have in India? Why hadn't anyone talked him out of coming? Deciding not to answer, he turned his face back toward the wall and ignored the tapping.

"Would you like a cup of coffee, Dr. Morgan?"

Chance rolled over on the small cot toward the voice beckoning to him and the smell of strong freshly brewed coffee. He squeezed his eyes together, wishing for a moment that he was home, at the very least in the hospital and one of the nurses or orderlies was the one offering the coffee. But he wasn't home and he knew the voice belonged to none other than Dr. Trammel. It appeared the man had no concept of privacy.

He allowed his eyes to open slowly, the gritty feeling alerting him to the fact that he'd had too little sleep. He tried his best not to glare at the man, but after being in the air over twenty hours then immediately whisked into a makeshift operating room followed by another seven hours treating patients after nothing more than a catnap he found the task damn near impossible. George Trammel had to be insane.

Chance eyed the coffee longing for a cup, but not trusting the contents of the water used to brew the delicious aromatic stuff. God he'd almost kill for a cup right now. He swung his legs over the side of the bed.

"Dr. Trammel, good morning."

"Please call me George. So, Doctor Morgan, would you care for a cup of coffee? We have a long day ahead of us."

Again Chance eyed the cup, looked longingly at the steam and shook his head. "Not right now thank you. I need to unpack and I need to......"

"There is no time for that. I let you sleep as long as possible. We open in ten minutes and patients have already been lined up for hours waiting for us."

Chance stood, stretching his sore muscles. He looked in disgust at the cot. *Damn*, what the hell had he gotten himself into? He'd come to lend a hand, to help and he was being treated like a servant. If George Trammel didn't appreciate his help, maybe he should just go home, back to America with his downy soft, king size bed, and fresh water that he could trust. And he could have a cup of coffee without worrying if the stuff would kill him. *Damn. Blaine was right.* Why hadn't he listened?

"Where are the other volunteers?'

"You and I are it."

"You've got to be kidding me!"

'I'm afraid I'm not."

"When I talked to you on the phone you assured me all conditions were up to standards. Electricity, plumbing and safe water. I have a battery operated lamp."

"But you do have a working toilet."

"Thanks."

"Before you leave here, you will understand what a gift this is."

Chance doubted it. He rubbed at his eyes and ran a hand through his tousled hair. He looked back towards Dr. Trammel and saw the man smiling.

"What's so funny?"

"New recruits."

"Excuse me; but did I join an army that I wasn't aware of?"

"No, but you're no different than anyone else who travel half the world to help. You're no different than I was."

"What are you talking about?" Chance heard the anger in his own voice yet did nothing to conceal it.

"What are you running from Chance? Is it a woman that brought you here?"

Stunned into momentary silence Chance glared. *What the hell was this inquisition about? The man had sounded friendly enough on the phone.*

"Dr. Morgan, I didn't seek you out. You called and asked to help. Why should I be grateful that you gave up your life to come here? Your life awaits you anytime you should choose to return. The people here don't have that luxury. This is their life, not a nightmare they can wake up from, and this hell you see before you is their existence.

"Now I'm sorry if I seem brusque to you, but I don't have time to hold the hands of every do-gooder who comes here running from their own problems, claiming they came to help.

"Frankly I don't give a damn why you're here, you're another pair of hands and that's all I require. Your skills as a surgeon makes you just a little more valuable than the people who scrubbed the floors in your big city hospital. But make no mistake, if they came here to help, I would welcome them with every bit the same courtesy I'm extending to you, and chances are they would be more appreciative."

Chance was angry. The man had no right to question his motives. For a long moment he said nothing as he felt the vein bulging in the side of his neck. Silence was doing no good. If he didn't speak he would explode. "I don't know where we got off on the wrong foot...I came here to help...if my services aren't..."

"Your services are appreciated, believe me, but don't try and fool me about your reasons for being here and whatever you do, don't try and fool yourself. You're here for your own personal reasons that have nothing to do with the people here. And that's okay. Your reasons are your reasons. I'm not judging you."

This time there was a smile and a twinkle in George Trammel's eyes when he spoke. Chance's chin jutted out; there was something he wasn't getting. "It doesn't sound that way to me. Hell, I just opened my eyes and you're attacking me."

"No, I'm trying to tell you how things are. I came in here to offer you coffee, coffee by the way I know you want. I can see your mouth watering for a taste, but you're afraid of catching something, thinking perhaps I may not have used the most sanitary of means to prepare it."

Chance felt a crimson flush cover his face. "I'm sorry. Was I that obvious?"

"Yes, you were, but I've had a long time getting used to it. All the new recruits behave the same way the first few weeks, at least the ones that come from a privileged lifestyle. It seems those who've had less are not as discriminating. No offense, but I've worked many surgeons and I must say they are the worst volunteers, so picky about the conditions, wanting to ensure everything is to their liking. Surgeons are used to be catered to in America, treated as though they were some kind of god. I daresay you more than likely believe as a cardiologist you hold the power of life and death in your hands. Yes, Chance, I do believe you are one of the privileged class."

"If by privileged lifestyle you mean my desire not to contract something from the lack of sanitary means I've seen practiced here, or my desire that I not contaminate one patient with the blood from another. If my being privileged means I would never in a hundred years choose to not scrub between each patient, to don a clean gown and new gloves. And I chose to use fresh disinfectant. I would be sued at home for participating in this madness."

"We both would. I didn't choose to not have enough supplies or too many patients. We do the best we can with the little we have. What would you have us do, turn away patients?"

"Yes, that's exactly what I would have you do. I should never have assisted you with patients after such a long flight. I have need for a certain standard of care for my patients."

"As do I," George said calmly. "We care for the patients and our intentions for them are the very best."

"The road to hell was paved with good intentions I hear." Chance smiled. "I don't doubt your dedication, but I don't want you to doubt mine. I came to help, but I can not in good conscience remain here and work without some basic sterilization technique. I understand your lack of funds. I have a solution if you're willing to listen."

"By all means, Dr. Morgan, continue."

The patronizing tone was hard to miss but Chance continued. "I will purchase my own supplies to use as long as I'm here."

"I think I understand. You will be the one sanitary doctor and the great American hero. Is that what you propose?"

"You didn't let me finish. I will do my best to get as many supplies for your clinic as I can."

"Have you noticed we're in the middle of no where, Chance? There are no medical supply stores around. Are you not planning on assisting until you have what you want?"

"You have to have at least a stockpile of supplies. What you allot for my use until I can get my own, I promise I will replace. Regardless of what you think about my reasons for being here, I do see the need, and I would like to assist you."

"So tell me, what are your reasons for coming here, Doctor Morgan?"

Chance stared at George, mentally calculating his words. He was not condescending in the least, actually his voice sounded down right curious. Well, that was too damn bad, he was not here to titillate with stories of his lost love. He came to work and work only.

"Please call me Chance." His tongue was working again, he could talk. "I'm sorry if I seem to be a bit uncomfortable." He hesitated seeing the other man's smile that told him what he was displaying was a lot more than mere discomfort.

"Yesterday was a long day. You have to admit the plane ride was long; add to that, standing there in customs haggling over the proper amount of bribe. Well, the whole day was a little much. I didn't expect to come here and be thrust right into the middle of things without a moment to breathe." He flung his hands out in front of him pointing at his bags and the stacked cartons of supplies he'd brought with him. "I just need some time to adjust, take a walk around, and get my bearings."

"Are you saying you'd like the day off?" George Trammel let his gaze light on Chance's staked boxes, and unpacked luggage. "You want a day to perhaps sight-see."

"Yes," Chance answered feeling his lips stretch out into a smile thinking, *finally, we're seeing eye to eye.*

"Then by all means take your day off and enjoy yourself, take your time. I on the other hand need to get to work."

He sat the cup he'd brought for Chance on the scarred plywood desk. "There are too many people out there to count, all sick. I'll go help them and I'll explain to them that when my help finishes sight-seeing he'll join us. See you later, Chance." With that, George smiled warmly and exited the room.

An hour later Chance joined him, George's sarcastic retort having burned its way into him. He had taken the time however to eat a bag of dried fruit, raisins and peanut butter crackers he'd brought along, and rinsed it down with one of the bottled waters from his cargo. Still he wished for a cup of coffee. He'd have to find time to unpack his supplies so he could at least have the instant coffee he'd been instructed to bring. Walking into the examine room he grunted and nodded in George's general direction.

"That was a very short sightseeing tour you took."

Chance eyed the man warily and saw immediately that he was teasing. "Oh I guess I took a look around and things are getting into focus." He hadn't noticed Sabu hovering nearby. This time the man was smiling at him.

"Dr. Morgan, these are yours," he said proudly showing Chance a corner in the room and giving him two well worn but clean cotton gowns, an unopened five gallon bottle of disinfectant and two brand new pairs of heavy duty gloves, the kind meant for washing not throwing away.

Chance smiled his thanks, then glanced over his shoulder to see what Dr. Trammel thought of all of this.

"It's okay, Chance, but the gowns and gloves will be all that we can give you. You will have to clean both if you want to have them the way you want them. The disinfectant will be yours alone."

"What about a...?" Chance looked down not wanting to ask for anything more.

"Here you go," Sabu handed him a sealed package indicating the basin was either sterilized or new. Chance poured the liquid in the basin gratefully.

"Not too much, Chance, this is all you will have for at least a month."

At that statement Chance's hand halted in midair, he'd only poured an inch or two in the basin, not enough to do any real good, but when he thought of the alternative he recapped the bottle and handed it to Sabu who promptly wrote Chance Morgan in big bold letters.

They worked for six or seven hours without a break. Chance was determined not to stop until George Trammel himself took a break. He was relieved when the man motioned to him to come with him after they'd both finished their last patients. He noticed after they left that Sabu and several of the teens continued to call in patients.

"Who's going to...?"

"Don't worry," George answered him without allowing him to finish, "They know what they can and can't handle. We can take a few minutes to get some refreshments, maybe some coffee."

Chance grinned.

"Think about it, as badly as I need your help, do you think I would risk your getting ill?"

There was no ready answer, because he wasn't convinced that the ill treatment wasn't meant as some kind of test. Chance eyed his colleague, he wasn't sure what to say, maybe allowing doctors to get sick was George's form of dealing with uppity Americans.

"I'm American, did you forget?" George's booming laughter cut across his thoughts.

"How did you...?" He thought of Blaine, and looked directly at the doctor facing him. This was India. "Are you...?"

"Am I what?"

Chance closed his eyes. He was letting his thoughts get the best of him. "Forget it. It just occurred to me that you always seem to know what I'm thinking. I thought for a minute there, you were reading my mind."

He waited for George to answer him, deny it, call him crazy. But he did none of those things, he simply sat and smiled leaving Chance wondering. This however wasn't a topic he chose to deal with at the moment. He'd barely had a moment to think, now he needed badly to go the bathroom glad for that one modern convenience.

When he returned to the room he was alone. With a slight shrug of his shoulder he realized for the moment he would not be able to question George Trammel further. Instead he went to his room riffled through his boxes and took out several packs of crackers and tins of sardines. He pulled the lid back on the sardines and ate with relish licking the oily substance from his chin. It tasted like a banquet fit for a king. He'd never before tasted sardines, but had been warned ahead of time by friends to bring lots of provisions. He ignored the question trying to take root in his head. This did not make him a snob, he was only trying to stay healthy enough to do the job he'd come to do. He couldn't very well take care of the sick if he was malnourished could he?

As he wiped his lips, a trace of guilt hung on the fringes. He took a long drink from his cache of bottled water and returned to the room to find George Trammel busy at work. He hated feeling like a slacker. Chance glanced at his watch, barely fifteen minutes had passed. A fifteen minute break after working for six or seven hours straight was not a thing to be ashamed of, yet he was.

He worked well into the night again, not stopping until Sabu had dispensed with the last patient and they'd called it a night.

Chance dipped the gown he was wearing into the pan of disinfectant swirling it around and around. It was not clean when he lifted it from the water, but at least it should be germ free. He made a mental note to himself to contact all his friends to send him emergency supplies of gowns, gloves and disinfectants.

When he was done, he poured out the used disinfectant from the basin, ignoring the rumble of voices behind him. He turned in time to see Sabu's look of disapproval and Dr. Trammel's look of amusement. He washed the basin with a tiny amount of clean disinfectant before pouring in more to soak the gloves he'd worn the entire day.

He would make do, if the others could do it so would he, but this was necessary. It was his bottle of disinfectant to use as he saw fit. When he was done he turned having felt eyes on him.

"We have a pot of stew cooking, you must be starved."

Stew. For a moment the thought of a tasty beef stew filled with carrots and new potatoes teased his senses until he remembered that in India cows were sacred. The rumors from his friends back home made him think of the different kinds of things that might be in the stew. Those thoughts filled his head quickly replacing his fleeting desire for a hot meal with dread.

"No thanks, George. I have some rations." Chance noticed the looks that passed from Sabu and the teens then to George.

"As you wish," George answered.

Later in his quarters when he opened another tin of sardines for his supper this time he was unable to let go of the guilt that assailed him. A dozen pair of brown eyes tugged at him until he remembered the boxes he'd packed. Pulling out the medications he piled them on the cot. This should make up for some of the hard feelings he'd caused. When he reached the box containing the cellophane wrapped suckers he smiled.

The next day he handed a treat to every child that he aided, then started handing them out randomly to every child he saw.

For a week his routine remained the same: up, work for six or seven hours, return to his room and eat from his dried food and quench his thirst with some bottled water. He'd even come to tolerate the cold instant coffee he managed to make with his bottled water.

After a week of grueling hours, Chance was feeling pleased with himself. He'd made numerous adjustments, he was getting use to the hard hours, and the smiles on the faces of the children left him feeling elated. It was with the elation that he pulled a bag from his belonging and retrieved a stack of books to go along with his evening meal. His door popped open a crack and George's head popped in.

"The children love the lollipops."

Turning toward George in disbelief, Chance smiled surprised to see something he'd done for once had managed to elicit praise from his colleague.

"Thanks. I thought they would like them."

"They do. Too bad I can't offer them something more. I don't know, maybe something with protein, a bit of dried fruit, some peanut butter, crackers, a tin or two of sardines, something like that. Good night, Chance."

Damn, damn, damn. Chance glared at the lone sardine remaining in his can and shoved it in his mouth. It would probably be the last of his stash he'd get to eat and he was aware of it.

CHAPTER FOUR

Cipro, the wonder drug. Chance held the pill in his hand for a moment before taking it. Shaking his head and sighing softly finally he placed the pill on his tongue and held the tablet in his mouth a moment before drinking from the last of his bottled water, relishing every drop. He had kept his water and only a handful of his personal rations after being shamed by Dr. Trammel into giving them away.

He'd been forced to eat his meals with Sabu and Dr. Trammel and the horde of teenage boys that helped around the place. Chance wasn't taking any unnecessary risks, he'd started taking Cipro with the last sardine he'd eaten. He never asked what he was eating now. He was afraid he didn't want to know.

Two weeks, he couldn't believe it. He'd been in India two weeks. Doctor Trammel had promised that after two weeks he would be able to go into New Delhi and send a message home for supplies, bottled water, anything. For one brief, unguarded moment he'd thought of replenishing his rations, but knew he'd not be able to keep them. Instead he planned on asking for jars of peanut butter, beans and rice, things he could give the children, food that could be cooked for all of them, then he wouldn't have to guess what the hell he was eating.

Suddenly the sound of loud voices, including feminine, soft sounding, American voices reached his ears making him halt his day dream of a good juicy steak and fries.

He stood still a moment longer and listened as the sound of the voices came closer, then a rap on his door and the room filled with twenty people.

"Dr. Morgan everyone."

Chance glanced over toward Dr. Trammel, relieved to have dressed moments before the group descended on him. Waving his hand toward the group assembled in his small room he laughed and said, "And all of you would be?"

"Sorry," Dr. Trammel said hurriedly as he started the introduction of the doctors and nurses. "They've all had a short break."

"Yes," a short redhead smiled at Chance and he found himself smiling back in return.

"You have been weighed," she said.

"And you have been measured," another voice chimed in.

Chance found his stomach suddenly in knots. He'd seen the movie as evidently had everyone in the room. He knew what came next. He felt the smile leaving his face. As the group smiled at him a touch of anger claimed him. He'd worked his ass off, and now that he had more help Dr. Trammel was ready to toss him out on his ear, well to hell with him.

Dr. Trammel stepped forward and Chance braced himself, he wouldn't react with anger, he'd show no emotion.

"Dr. Chance Morgan, as they've said, you've been weighed and you've been measured and—"

"And I have been found wanting."

"You've been found to be an extremely valuable member of our little team. Welcome aboard."

Chance's mouth opened in astonishment. Despite his efforts to close it he couldn't, he was in shock. One after the other, the group filed by shaking his hand thumping him on the shoulder laughing loudly.

"What's going on here?"

"Dr. Trammel likes to play jokes on the new arrivals. Or as he likes to say, 'he sifts the chaff from the wheat"

It was the redhead again. "What are you talking about?"'

"Well, whenever we get word of a a new group, and especially lone doctor that's coming here Trammel test their mettle. He sends the rest of us off for a much needed vacation and he works the poor soul to the bones, making them work double shifts, shaming them into giving up any and all supplies they may have brought with them."

A light was beginning to turn on for Chance. "What if it didn't work? What if the person didn't cave?"

"They wouldn't still be here. We've had entire groups leave after a day or two. If you're here when we return you've passed the test."

Chance glanced at the redhead not sure if he liked the joke or not, but damn sure he liked the idea of more help. "Listen, you're all going to have to give me a little time to learn your names." He turned to the redhead. "What's yours Red?"

"Karen."

"Well, Karen, thank you. Thank all of you for being a part of this little prank."

"Don't worry, Chance, you'll get your opportunity to do it to the next group although it's a lot more fun when there's one person. They have it harder."

She grinned. "Would you like a real cup of coffee?" she asked, eyeing his jar of instant. "You can watch me make it. Or would you like to take a tour of the main building, the one with electricity most of the time, and all the things you've no doubt been missing?"

"Let me guess. It's the building next door, the one that looks as though it was constructed in the last decade." He should have known and would have gone to investigate but he'd been kept so busy day and night that he'd no longer thought about the building. Now he did.

"There's a bed waiting for you in there. Sabu will make sure your personal belongings are moved. Later I'll show you to your new room."

Chance followed the group into the building next door and into the large eating room and watched as Karen looked under a curtained off section and hauled out an industrial size coffee maker and plugged it into a wooden base.. He stood back watching George Trammel lift an unopened five gallon bottle of water and pour it into the machine.

"Have a seat, Chance. I'll bring you the coffee when it's ready."

When he was done George turned toward Chance and smiled as he took a seat at the table. "I did offer you coffee."

"You never told me that—"

"That what? The water I used was clean? What's the matter with you man? I told you I didn't want you to get sick. I didn't want to get sick either for that matter."

"But you knew I thought…"

"And am I responsible for your thoughts or your prejudices?"

"But I'm not."

"You don't think that you are. You came here with preconceived ideas. A lot of them, granted, are true, but not all. You didn't give yourself a chance to distinguish fact from fiction."

"I only came here to help." A huge smile appeared on George's face. Chance swallowed. "Why would I be here if I didn't want to help?"

"Because whatever you're running from is far worse than what you've found here. It's that simple. Now are you ever going to tell me what really brought you here, what's keeping you here? I've thrown more at you than I ever have at anyone and you've taken it all. Your reasons must be extremely powerful to not make you run screaming back to New Delhi and the airport. Is it a woman?"

Chance stared at George, a small smile pulling at the corners of his lips. "Is it usually a woman?"

"Usually that, or someone wants to find the Dali Lama and begin a spiritual journey."

"Do you disapprove of those reasons?"

"It's not that I disapprove. It's just that you don't need to travel anywhere but inside yourself to find spiritual truths. As for coming here to heal a broken heart, look around you, have your heart healed?"

Chance thought of the hundreds of people they'd treated since his arrival. The little girl with the huge, soulful brown eyes he'd helped George with on his first day there and had carried in his arms haunted him still. She'd been so brave. He felt his eyes tearing and blinked them back. He had to admit George Trammel was right about one thing, India was definitely not the place to come to heal a broken heart. Here, he'd had his heart shattered into a million pieces because of the sickness and starvation. Even now he was ashamed of hoarding his food. He shivered.

"You're no different than any of us, Chance. It doesn't make you a bad person. Every person who didn't make it goes back and tells others of their experiences and advises them to bring a ton of food. We know that the stories are different from the ones who stay."

"How long have you been here?" Chance saw a light go on behind George's eyes. He recognized a far away look of longing and he wondered what it meant.

"I've been here forever it seems."

"That's what Sabu said, but I'm asking in term of years. How long?"

"Fourteen years."

"What brought you here, a broken heart?"

"You could say that. Mostly, I just wanted to return home."

Okay, now Chance was truly puzzled. "George, you're American, what are you talking about?" He saw the doctor's eyes swing over his head before he returned his gaze to stare at Chance.

"Another time, I believe I see Karen heading in this direction with a cup of coffee for you." He started to rise, paused then smiled.

"By the way, Dr. Morgan, you have the next three days off. Sabu can take you around sight seeing." The man laughed before moving away.

"Here you go," Karen said moving into the spot George Trammel had just vacated." I didn't know what you wanted in it."

Chance held the cup in his hand inhaling the fragrant aroma before putting in the sugar and powdered cream. He held it another moment in reverence before putting it to his lips and sipping.

"Thanks."

"You're welcome," Karen smiled. "I remember when I first got here, I almost didn't make it. George's guilt trip about my food stash didn't work on me. I refused to give it up."

Chance couldn't help admiring her spunk. "You didn't cave?"

"No."

"I'm impressed."

"Don't be. I behaved like a spoiled little rich girl and a typical do-gooder, help others as long as it doesn't hurt me."

"So what changed?"

"Dr. Trammel actually told me he had help coming in a couple of days and I would be free to leave. I was all set. I packed my things and waited for the end of my sentence. That was five years ago."

"What happened?"

"Dr. Trammel asked me to accompany him to a small village to take care of a sick woman. I went clad in about three pairs of gloves and at least that many gowns. I even wore a surgical mask."

"Really?"

"Really."

"How did that make you stay here?"

"First I had to change my heart and admit the real reason I came here. Then I had to see myself as a part of humanity, not just as an American."

Chance chuckled, Karen was sounding a bit like George Trammel. "He got to you after all, didn't he?"

"Yeah, he did. But it was what he did when we went to the home that confused and amazed me. Here, it's the custom to take at least a token gift when you visit someone in their home, even if it's the doctor. George took a box of saltine crackers, that's all. He didn't give the family the entire box, only half. As people came over to visit he handed them a couple of the crackers. You would have thought he was giving them gold, or at the very least a week's worth of groceries."

"How did that change your mind? It could be seen as just self serving to gain their praise."

"Ahh and that's what I thought in the beginning, then the daughter of the old woman we went to see insisted we eat the evening meal with them. George sat down eagerly and ate with relish praising the woman's cooking, even asking for seconds. Her face was beaming."

"I don't understand. They were poor he shouldn't have eaten at all, definitely not eaten seconds."

"That's what I thought. But by eating with them he'd given them the honor of being one with them, they had no money to pay him. They didn't really have the food, but they had their dignity. That he didn't take from them."

"I see."

"Not yet you don't. Their faces glowed, I mean literally glowed then they all joined hands and prayed. I had to pinch myself. I couldn't believe what I saw. Suddenly the empty bowls were filled to overflowing with food enough to share. I swear as neighbor after neighbor kept dropping in and taking food from the bowl it never emptied, never."

"What happened?"

"I have no idea. I asked George and he wouldn't tell me. He told me only that I may not have seen what I thought I saw. I knew he was wrong. When we got back here he went looking for Sabu and asked me to join them for dinner as he always did. First I was surprised that he could eat more, second he knew I never ate anything but the food I brought."

"I said, 'no thank you' and he answered me, "just remember there is always enough, anytime you chose to join us you will be welcome."

"I looked at my rations as I entered my room. They were dwindling down. I remembered his words. There will always be enough. I remembered the never ending bowls of food. There was something about George Trammel that wasn't ordinary and I didn't want to leave until I found out what it was."

"Have you?"

"No."

"But you're still here."

Karen laughed and Chance found himself liking the sound maybe a little too much. He'd come to India to get over loving Michelle not to find her replacement. Licking his bottom lip with the tip of his tongue he blew out a short breath then asked again. "Why are you still here?"

"I'm still here because the next day I joined them for dinner. I didn't get rid of my rations, but I joined them." She laughed. "That first time I even imagined myself ill afterward until George gave me a cup of tea and told me, '"Karen, you're fine, don't worry."'"

"George sounds more like a guru than a physician."

"It's funny you should say that. One of his favorite saying is, 'physician heal thy self.' I know now he's speaking of a spiritual healing. On my first trip home I got someone to embroider that saying on a wall hanging for him."

Chance took careful note of the way Karen spoke of George Trammel. She was awed. "Are you and he involved?" Better to get these things out in the open.

"No nothing like that. I admire the man."

"Are you married, engaged or in any other way committed?"

"No, and thanks for asking, but I'm not looking for any commitments or entanglements. And I'm definitely not looking to help some guy forget a lost love."

"Why does everyone keep saying that?"

"Because it's usually the main reason that brings a person here. And it's definitely what keeps them here after George pulls his little trick on them."

"Why does he do that?"

"He wants only committed people who don't think they're better than the people they're helping to be here. He wants us to look at each other as extended family members, no egos, no pay, doing what we do because it's the right thing to do, because it's our responsibility. He doesn't want us to ever return to America and think of this as mission work, but simply that we were on vacation, visiting family, lending a helping hand."

Chance smiled. "Are you sure he's not a guru?" He finished his coffee and looked over his shoulder at the sound of eggs being cracked on a bowl. He stared as several of the doctors ripped open packages of frozen vegetables that were sitting in a container of dry ice.

A few minutes later someone plopped an actual vegetable egg omelet down in front of him. His fork was digging into the feast before he could say thank you. It was only after his third omelet that he looked up. "Thank you," he finally managed to say.

The room had suddenly become quiet, the sound of chatter evaporated. Chance stared around the room a second before the laughter met him, then thunderous applause. A flush covered his skin as Karen's soft hand covered his own.

"Don't worry, Chance, they're all teasing you. We were all the same when we finally got a taste of the kinds of foods we were missing."

George stooped down beside him and gave him a fresh cup of coffee." So, you like the food?"

"I like."

"Then I'm glad you enjoyed it."

He moved along toward another table and Chance watched his departure. "Listen, you guys didn't happen to smuggle in any steaks did you?" He knew he'd made a mistake instantly as the appalled look on Karen's face spread to her eyes.

"It was only a joke," he said before Karen or any of the others thought to chastise him. He drank deeply of the coffee. He'd really not meant to offend.

"We're aware of that. But we're also aware that you've been wanting a steak since you've been here."

Chance spilled some of the hot coffee. What the hell was going on? What was the deal with everyone reading his mind? He thought of Blaine. *Use your shield.* Oh hell no, he thought, hell no, enough with this shit. The last thing he needed in this life was more psychics.

"Lighten up. We all had the same thoughts. Sometimes we still do."

The laughter inside his head belonged to Blaine. Somehow the thought of his son's ability to remain connected with him made him feel better. Perhaps George and Karen weren't reading his mind. *Good. He had no use for the psychic world. He wanted to remain blissfully unaware.*

CHAPTER FIVE

The idea of finally being able to see something besides patients nearly had him jumping out of his skin like an eager child. He was finished with breakfast and he'd had as much coffee as he could hold. He was merely waiting for Sabu. He smiled when he noticed Sabu entering the room and making his way toward him. He was beginning to think all he had to do was think of him and he'd magically appear.

"Doctor Morgan, I'll be waiting when you're done with breakfast."

Chance nodded his thanks to Sabu then turned to the assembled group and giving another thank you to the doctors who had prepared the omelets. Turning back to Karen he wondered if he should ask the question uppermost in his mind.

"I have the day off." He attempted to smile.

"Good."

"Sabu's going to take me to see some of the country." He hesitated, not wanting to push.

"I'd be happy to come along."

Chance stared at her for a long moment before turning to Sabu. Awareness was beginning to nudge him out of his self imposed stupor. He had to be careful. It had been almost a year and a half since he'd last made love to Michelle. Since then he'd not had the desire to touch another woman. How could he?

He looked at the quizzical look on Karen's face, sure that she probably could read his mind. For once he hoped she could. The last thing he wanted was to become involved with a woman. He had nothing to offer one except maybe a few hours in bed. He could never offer love. His heart belonged to only one woman.

"Maybe you'd better not," he said softly.

"Chance, I'm not looking to fall in love with you. You don't have to worry."

This time he wasn't surprised, hell nothing else in this lifetime could ever surprise him.

"Karen, listen it's not that I don't find you attractive, it's just that…"

"There is no need to finish that statement, your heart belongs to someone else." She smiled at him. "And you wonder why everyone keeps asking you why you came here. My God, man, it's in your eyes, your voice, anyone looking at you can tell you came here to forget someone very important to your spirit. Did she die?"

Tears sprang quickly to Chance's eyes surprising him. For once he remembered to put up his psychic shields. He didn't want to talk about Michelle with Karen. Without even a moment to prepare for what he knew was coming he was thrust back into their previous lifetime together, when he'd held her in his arms as her life seeped away. The grief so strong that it followed him to this life he lived now.

No, there was no way on earth he wanted to discuss the death of his wife with another woman. Besides, she'd never understand. It wasn't easy to say to people that he was mourning the loss of his wife from another lifetime. And oh, by the way I found her again in this life, but I can't have her. She's married and she suggests I do the same.

For several long moments Chance stood still, unmovable, his attention diverted by his memories, his pain sharp, stabbing the fragility of his moment of joy. This would never work; he could never run from the love he felt. India was not the place, no where on earth would be. He'd know relief only in death. There he would wait for Michelle.

"Doctor Morgan, are you ready?"

It was Sabu staring at him with concern. Chance blinked. "Yes, I'm ready, Karen's coming too if that's all right with you." He turned away from them and walked back toward the building. There was something he had to do.

For a long time he held the picture in his hand remembering his surprise and joy when he arrived in India and found it wrapped among his belongings. The same picture Blaine had of the three of them. He allowed his finger to gently caress the images, his eyes boring into Michelle's image wishing she could know he was thinking about her.

"*She knows, Chance.*"

The picture slipped from his hand and landed with a soft thud on the hard mattress. He spun around looking for the owner of the voice a chill sweeping over him. He knew the voice, but it couldn't be. He'd barely had the thought. How could anyone pick up on that?

He sat on the bed and lifted the picture again, this time rubbing at the images with a purpose. Again he heard the voice, Blaine's voice.

"Chance, we'll both always be with you, now go enjoy India."

"But you're not with me," Chance whispered softly, "this is all just a dream and now I'm sitting here in this room talking to myself."

"Do you really think you're imagining hearing my voice?"

"Yes," Chance answered without hesitation, "I've no doubt come down with something. I don't think your powers are strong enough to reach me here."

Laughter answered him, strong, male laughter, Blaine's laughter.

Chance's gaze dropped down to the bracelet on his wrist, the stones were glowing. In that moment he knew without a doubt it was his son's voice he was hearing. Pride filled him at Blaine's rapid growth.

"Then why can't I hear Michelle? Why can't I feel her love?"

"You know she loves you, Chance. This isn't easy for her, but this is what she has to do. She's married to Larry, she loves him too."

"But she's my wife."

"And she's his. In this lifetime she's his wife, Chance."

Chance rubbed his hand across his forehead. This long distance psychic conversation with his son was just as hard as the real thing. It hurt. Blaine didn't understand that he couldn't give up loving Michelle that easily.

"I didn't ask you to stop loving her. But for all of our sakes you have to get on with your life. It you can't it will only make things harder for all of us."

"Dr. Morgan, we're ready to go."

At the sound of Sabu's voice, Chance's eyes snapped open, his telepathic conversation stopped abruptly. He took one last look at the picture in his hand before he wrapped it back up and tucked it into his bag. This was private. He didn't want people gawking at the picture, asking questions.

He followed Sabu out to the waiting truck. For two weeks he'd looked forward to a day of rest, a chance to go out and see the country. Now all he wanted was to climb aboard the first plane leaving any of the numerous airports in India heading for the Unites States and return home. He wanted to be at least in calling distance of Michelle. Maybe her powers weren't as great as Blaine's. Perhaps that was the reason he couldn't feel her. He needed to go home. When his gaze landed on Karen he saw that she had an odd expression on her face. He watched her, his head tilted, thinking she'd reached some decision. When she opened her mouth and began to speak he knew he'd been right. Something more was going on.

"Sabu, take us to the Grand Trunk Road."

"But."

"No buts, please. Dr. Morgan needs to take his mind off of things. Grand Trunk Road will be perfect."

Chance watched the two of them talking about him as if he weren't there, or as if he were a stupid child they were attempting to entertain, or to make him forget his pain. The thought made him angry. Neither of the people in the truck could ever make him forget Michelle.

For over an hour there was silence. He was determined not to speak to the other occupants and so far it appeared they had nothing to say to him, not one thing was pointed out, not one point of interest. Some sight seeing expedition this was turning out to be.

Not more than thirty seconds after thinking that, Chance felt his lungs closing. He was assaulted at once by the most awful stench he'd ever encountered.

"What the hell is that?" he asked as he hurriedly rolled up the back window and reached to close the other one as well.

"That's Grand Trunk Road," Karen answered. "Here you might need this." She whisked a thin surgical mask from her bag and handed it to Chance who gratefully put it on.

"That smell, it smells like..." *It smells like shit* he wanted to say, but thought better of being so crude.

"Those are cow dung fires." Karen laughed. "Don't worry you're not hallucinating, it smells exactly like what you think it does."

Chance cracked his window just an inch, the smell sickening him. Even with the mask he felt the burning in his throat. He again closed the window and stared straight ahead at the thick bluish pall of the smoke. So much pollution. No wonder there were so many respiratory problems in this country.

"And we came on this road because?" He didn't attempt to hide the sarcastic tone to his voice. This sure in hell couldn't be what he was dying to see for the past two weeks and 'dying' being the operative word, because surely many a person had undoubtedly died from the pollution.

"Chance, try taking in the things you see. Forget America for a moment and look around. When you're able to look at all of this, this entire country with something other than revulsion then you will know that God has touched you."

"And the only way you think God can touch me is to bring me here? I feel trapped in this truck, look at all this traffic," he complained. "We're stuck here. Breathing in all this pollution from the cars is bad, but the smell of shit, that's a bit too much."

This time he didn't worry about offending, they had said themselves that many of the fires were fueled by cow dung.

"Are you going to tell me that I'm to feel blessed because I got the privilege to smell this?" He slammed his body back against the cushions. He could suffer being killed by cow shit smoke, but to think of cutting that cow up and putting it to better use, like a steak in his belly was sacrilegious. He didn't get it.

Karen sighed loudly before reprimanding him. "Chance, look around, please tell me what you see, not what you smell."

"I see cars and trucks, millions of them."

"Okay, what kind?"

Karen's voice was now beginning to irritate him, the tolerance of a mother to a child, or the sane to the insane. He sat back aware he was behaving like a spoiled brat. It was he who'd asked for Sabu to show him around, and he who'd asked Karen to join him. Then he remembered. He hadn't actually gotten around to asking her, she'd volunteered. And he hadn't asked Sabu to bring him wherever the hell he was taking him. He'd wanted to go into the town that was less than a mile away. Civilization was in the town and that was what he'd been after. Now he was stuck. *"Father try." Of course it would be now he'd hear Blaine's voice.* Telepathic paternal guilt. Fine, he'd try to be more patient.

He looked toward the front of the truck, neither Sabu nor Karen seemed bothered by the smells, as neither wore masks, but they had closed their windows and for that he was eternally grateful. He closed his eyes. This time he didn't need Blaine's scolding voice to tell him he was being a jerk, he damn well knew it.

When he dared to open his eyes he glanced out of the left window. There he saw several white vans filled with nuns.

"Who are they?" he asked without bothering to explain who he meant.

"They're sisters from the same order as Mother Theresa."

"Mother Theresa?" Staring at the vans and the nuns inside, a feeling of peace filled him. "But I thought Mother Teresa's work was done in Calcutta."

"The sisters work all over, bringing help to those most in need." Sabu turned his head to stare at Chance. "Just like the United States, India is a big country, we have our rich and then we have our poor. The sisters, of course, help the poor."

Chance couldn't tear his eyes from the van, his lips were slightly ajar. He felt as though he should be in prayer. One of the nuns turned and saw him, she smiled at him and he hoped he smiled in return. He knew he waved. He sat back gazing through the glass not wanting to lose site of the women.

"So you did find something on this tour that you like?"

Karen laughed, but Chance wasn't offended. He had given them a rough time and they were with him only to help. It was not their fault he was missing Michelle. He looked again out the window at the nuns. Looking at the women he realized the constant knot of pain he carried with him had eased just a hair.

"Pull over, Sabu, Karen directed. I'll buy us all a cup of chai, tea." She explained to Chance.

That got Chance's attention; surely Karen wasn't asking him to drink tea brewed over a fire fueled by cow dung. "No thanks," he muttered. "I'm not thirsty."

"Chance, lighten up. I promise the fire they used is not cow dung. Promise."

A huge smile lit her face and Chance wasn't sure if she was kidding him or not. She'd climbed out the truck and was holding the door open for him. He had no choice. He got out of the truck, stretched his legs and looked hard for even a tiny peek at the nuns. He saw them a short ways ahead, and he could swear the same nun was still looking at him and smiling.

He looked at the man selling the tea. Whatever was in it he felt he was blessed by the sister. It would be safe to drink.

With a muttered prayer he finally took the clay cup Karen offered to him. Noticing that she appeared very comfortable with her surroundings, he wondered if he would be there long enough to behave in the same manner.

"What's in this?" he asked curious.

"Just try it," Karen urged.

He sipped cautiously at first. The tea was hot and very sweet. There was something else about it he hadn't expected. It was milky.

He wondered if it was cow's milk but didn't want to make a fool of himself by asking.

"How do you like it?"

He glanced at Karen then down at the last remaining drops in the cup. "It's very good."

And it was, if you could ignore the burning in your throat from the many fires and the pollution, or the stinging of your eyes long enough to enjoy it. It wasn't bad at all. In fact he'd like to try another cup.

Chance walked toward the vendor with his cup outstretched, when the man took the cup from his hand and smashed it to the ground he halted, thinking, *what the hell*. For a nanosecond he was stunned wondering what on earth was wrong with the vendor before looking toward Karen for an explanation.

"Did I just do something to offend him?"

"No, not at all. The cups are thrown away after use."

"Why?"

"Well, one for hygiene and number two to keep another caste from drinking from the cup."

Chance stared at her, not sure now if he wanted another cup of tea. Before he could decide Karen had bought him a second cup and was placing it in his hand.

"Go ahead, it one's of the first things you've liked."

He held the cup in his hand and began looking around at all the different people. A lot of them obviously not from India.

"I thought the caste system had been done away with in most of India. Considering this is supposed to be the country of enlightenment I'm surprised it still exist."

"Chance, you're an educated man. Do you really think that in a country of well over nine hundred million people there would be no classes?"

"But I thought… well I've read that this was a country where all different religions get along together; you know the belief in the sanctity of life."

"That's true for the most part, but you're aware that India like every other country has it wars. And it does have caste systems in many parts."

"I will admit I've only read bits and pieces about the country. I'm not familiar with the customs. I'll plead guilty to what I know about the customs has come by way of other doctors or nurses who visited here."

"The customs in the entire country are not the same."

"Oh. Such as?"

"Take cremation for instance. In many parts of India it's not allowed, because of the desecration to three of their most scared elements: earth, fire and air. While in Banaras, they have a continuous cremation going."

"How do you know all of this?"

"I've been here five years. I've been to many cities here. I've studied the different customs."

Hmm. Chance didn't bother to answer. He looked instead out over the land. He squinted, sure that because of the smoke his eyes were playing tricks, not believing he was seeing people actually living on the side of such a busy road. He walked farther down the road for a better look at the little makeshift village. He could see upon closer inspection the shacks were made from discarded bits of tarpaulin, tin and cardboard. These shack literally lined the roads.

"They're movable."

He looked toward the sound of the voice. Karen had sidled up alongside him and had remained quiet until now.

"Movable?"

"Yeah."

He didn't know what to say to that, instead he pointed toward a long bridge. "What's that?"

"That's the Alllahabad Bridge. From there you could easily go to the Ganges River if you wanted."

Chance felt his brows moving downward in a frown that grew even more as Karen's smile grew wider. It appeared she was enjoying educating him on all that he didn't know about India.

"Remember me telling you about Banaras and their cremation ritual? When they're done...I mean when the body is completely burned they take a heavy stick and crack the skull to release the soul, then the bones and the ashes are throw into the Ganges."

He couldn't have possibly heard correctly, but one glance at the smirk on Karen's face and he needed no reassurance that his hearing was intact. Chance couldn't help the horrified look. He felt the chill of the horror through the marrow of his bones. *More pollution.* He thought of all the dread diseases that would be released in this manner. Again Karen appeared to be reading his thoughts, he could tell from her answer to him.

"Young children, holy men and people with small pox are not cremated."

"There's a hell of a lot more diseases than smallpox." This time it was he who stared at Karen. She was still smiling. This country appeared to make all Americans go mad after being there for so long it seemed. He'd have to remember that and leave before he too was infected with the madness

"There is a wonderful practice that is performed in the Ganges, something you might find a bit unorthodox, but which could help you if you'd allow it."

"What could that be?" Chance paused noticing that Sabu had once again joined them.

"Every twelve years there is a great celebration, one of the holiest times for the Hindu. Kumbh Mela upwards of fifty Million people bathe naked in the water to be purified of all their past life sins. Many take in the cremated remains of love ones. You might want to try that if you're here long enough. Its months from now, in February, I believe." She smiled and stopped talking.

What the? Chance eyed Sabu then Karen. He ignored his impulse to ask them both if they'd bathed in the polluted water. If he had sins from the past that were lingering, they would have to linger with him still. There was no way in the world he was going to bathe with millions of naked people in water polluted by the cremated remains of humans. No, he would just have to hang on to his sins of the past a bit longer.

CHAPTER SIX

The patient's heartbeat stilled and there was nothing he could do. No magic was going to bring life back to the woman Chance had worked feverishly to save.

He stood for a moment looking down at the body, wishing he were not there, not still in India. Maybe in Chicago or San Francisco he would have been able to do more.

Damn. This was his field of expertise. All the other things he'd done since being in India didn't bother him nearly as much. He didn't expect to know about reattaching limbs or skin grafts, but he'd done them and Dr. Trammel had even said he'd done a good job. Now here was something that none could top him at, and he'd failed.

"Chance, are you going to be okay?"

He looked into Karen's worried eyes; she was on his team, if that's what it was to be called. He wasn't the lead doctor by any means. It just happened that this patient was assigned to him because of his acclaim.

"She's dead."

"You did all you could, we all did."

"I'm a cardiologist! You don't understand. I've saved people in much worse shape."

"You saved people, Chance? I didn't know you carried that much power."

"What the hell is that supposed to mean?"

"It means you're not God."

"I didn't say I was, but perhaps if I had some decent equipment I could do my damn job. I could have saved her."

Chance looked around. He noticed that the others had stopped working to stare at him, their expressions telling him of their disapproval.

"What? Are you going to tell me none of you ever question what the hell we're doing here? I thought we came to help, to save lives. How can we be expected to work, to do our jobs in such barbaric situations?"

His voice had become louder with each word and the silence that greeted him from the other doctors and nurses merely made him shout louder. They were looking at him as if he was the only one who didn't get it.

Chance threw the bloodied sponge down on the even bloodier drape. "To hell with your opinions. I'm the one who has to tell that family there won't be a wife or mother coming home to them tonight." With that he stormed out of the room his thoughts on a completely equipped operating room with never ending sterile supplies. It seemed a lifetime ago.

One look into the shimmering eyes of the scantily clothed, ragged children, and Chance couldn't stop the wrench in his heart. He allowed his gaze to slide over to the husband knowing the pain the man would be in. He remembered his own pain at the loss of his beloved from a lifetime before and he shivered where he stood. This was going to be hard.

"I'm sorry," Chance whispered walking up to the husband, "I lost her. I tried but I couldn't save her."

The man glanced back at him, and numbness claimed Chance's limbs. He waited knowing the man had not understood one word, knowing he would have to find someone to tell him what he'd said, wishing he could pretend that what he'd told the man was enough.

"Sabu," Chance called out, his glance never leaving the face of the dead woman's husband. He saw the moment the man knew what he was there to tell him. His eyes dimmed slowly for a long moment then he smiled and laid his hands on Chance's arms.

"Thank you."

"No, don't thank me," Chance moaned. "Don't you understand? I couldn't save her." He turned toward Sabu in agony; grateful he had arrived at last and was translating to the husband Chance's dilemma.

Chance watched as the man's smile still didn't fade. It was only after Sabu pointed toward him that the man's demeanor changed. He also pointed at Chance.

"He asks if you're a great deity."

"Why?" Chance glared at Sabu certain he'd not told the man what he wanted, but something else instead.

"He said you have no reason to feel troubled. His wife is now at peace. There is no pain, no empty belly, and whatever reason she had for having a sick heart she has learned and will not have it in the next life."

Reincarnation. Of course. Still, how could the husband remain where he was, smiling, happy that his wife had made the journey? Tears sprang to Chance's eyes. The last thing he wanted to do was wait for another incarnation to be with the woman he loved. Hell, his heart still hurt from her last death. He'd never gotten over it. and yet this man stood smiling at him.

Chance wiped hastily at his eyes wondering if the man truly loved his wife. If he did how could he want to continue living? He took one last look at the man before him, turning to Sabu he uttered simply, "Tell him I'm sorry." Chance walked away.

For the first time since arriving in India the cot he slept on offered comfort. Chance sat on it holding the picture of himself with Blaine and Michelle. He'd lost her a long time ago, another lifetime, yet his soul remembered as if it were only yesterday and still he grieved. When the expected knock came, he muttered a curse, knowing the door would open even without his consent.

"Chance, may I talk with you a moment?"

With little choice but to acknowledge him, Chance couldn't help wondering what George wanted or what would happen if he said, "No, you can't talk with me." He glanced in George's general direction. The man had too much of the same traits as a bull dog to leave the room graciously without having his say. No, Chance knew the man's request was only meant as a form of courtesy.

"Sure, why not?" he answered at last.

"Chance, I understand that you feel bad that the woman died, but her life was never in your hands. We don't have that power."

"If I had the right equipment things would have been different."

"Maybe not, we'll never know," George interrupted.

"I know I can't continue to work like this."

"Are you saying you're leaving?"

Chance smiled. "You heard correctly, that's exactly what I'm going to do. I can't stay here any longer, not working under these conditions."

"Are you going to honor your three-month commitment or are you going to bail now? If that's the case we can see how soon you can get a plane back to the States. We don't want anyone working here who doesn't want to be here. It doesn't help our patients or our cause. And it doesn't help you."

Chance rolled his eyes. Why couldn't George Trammel for once just get pissed and stop behaving as though every single word he spoke or action taken was somehow meant to enhance Chance's life experience? Thinking this he glanced angrily in George's direction. "Don't try psychology on me, it won't work. This wasn't about me. It was about my not being able to do my job without the right equipment. It's about me not saving a woman that I should have been able to help."

A loud cackling sound came from George and Chance frowned in his direction. The man was mad, everyone in the whole damn country was mad.

"Why, Chance Morgan, I thought there was hope for you, but I see now there isn't. You're an arrogant, conceited, bastard. How dare you think you have the power of life and death?"

He was tired of his colleagues laughing at him as though he were a neophyte. Livid with annoyance he stood, his fists clenched at his side, his anger rising like bitter bile. Though it was a bit childish Chance hated the serenity that surrounded George. He was at peace. Something that Chance wanted, but so far it had eluded him.

"George, I never said that."

"You did. You keep saying that if you had the right equipment you could have saved her. You, you, you. That's all any of us have heard and frankly we're getting sick and tired of it."

"Then I guess it's best I'm leaving, isn't it?"

"What do you think I'm going to do? Fall down on my hands and knees and beg you to stay? Hell no."

They were both angry and it was apparent that neither was backing down as Chance took his bags and began throwing his things in haphazardly. He would have thought that would be the end of it, that George would simply storm out and leave him in peace but of course that wasn't the action he chose. He decided to continue talking and frankly Chance was tired of him.

"You're also a selfish bastard to walk out on your commitment. To do that means you have no moral code. I pity you, Chance, I really do. You've learned nothing," George spat out in disgust and walked from the room.

Chance tried to ignore the muttering inside his soul telling him the same things George was. As he turned to walk away he shoved the thought away from himself. Something was out of kilter, something was wrong with him. That much he knew or he wouldn't be following after the man.

"George, wait a minute." Chance sighed loudly. "I'll stay. I don't back away from my commitments, so I'll stand by my word."

"Good." George smiled, his white teeth gleaming against bronzed skin that was almost as brown as the inhabitants of the country.

"I thought you wanted me to leave."

George shook his head slowly before closing his eyes. "I'm sorry. I keep forgetting how different it is for foreigners. That is one of the things I must work on, my patience with infants."

Had he heard him correctly, had the man called him an infant? And by the looks of things George thought he was not just an infant, but an extremely stupid one. George was still shaking his head while his eyes held a far off look as though contemplating some secret thought.

"Do you believe in reincarnation?" George asked.

Reincarnation? Now it was Chance's turn to laugh. An infant, the hell if he was. He could tell George Trammel a thing or two that would surely blow his mind. *Did he believe in reincarnation?* Hell he was living breathing proof of it. He had a wife that he'd loved for centuries, a son that he'd left behind in the last lifetime, and now...now he'd found them both again in this life. Believe in reincarnation? He was living it.

"Yes," he answered at last. "I believe in reincarnation. Why?"

"Because if you do you should understand why the husband is happy. His heart is broken sure, but he feels that his wife's problems were brought on by something she did in a previous life. He believes she will not have to deal with the same problems in the next life."

Once again irritated with his own behavior, Chance turned away from George. There was a need for him to get control of his emotions. He was being irrational and lashing out at others because of his own pain. He'd had been told on many occasions that his thoughts were transparent. And for now he didn't want George to know what he was thinking. He took a moment to compose himself before turning back to face him.

"Reincarnation has nothing to do with not feeling the loss. It doesn't prevent me from feeling, excuse me, from knowing that if the woman were in the States and I'd worked on her she would be alive." Chance smiled with satisfaction. "That's not a guess, George, that's a fact."

"So you're saying God is less powerful here in India than he is in America?"

The man was being deliberately obtuse, that wasn't what he'd said at all. Chance repeated the words he'd spoken to George Trammel, inside the privacy of his thoughts. He cringed. That was indeed what he'd said. He shook his head. "I didn't mean it that way."

For once George was smiling at him and his smile more than anything reminded him that the man reviewed him as a stupid infant.

"So, you're right and I'm wrong, at least on that score," Chance admitted.

"This was never about one of us being right or wrong, or about winning or losing. I'm simply sharing my philosophy, that's all. Would you like to come to the ceremonial cleansing for your patient?"

Chance peered at the man, sure that more was meant in George's words than the simplicity of merely washing the woman's body with soap and water. Again George smiled leaving Chance with a shiver that refused to go away. The coldness was familiar. George Trammel was reading his thoughts. Immediately his shields went up keeping George out.

"What kind of cleansing are you speaking of?" Chance asked without hesitation.

"The final one. The woman never made it to Mother Ganges in this life to ask forgiveness for her sins. So her husband will take her ashes and give them over to the river. His family will join him, and there they will all bathe, seeking forgiveness for all their past sins."

"You're going I suppose."

"It's an honor. The family requested it. They also requested that you come as well."

Chance shook his head. "Thanks, but I don't think I'm ready to watch children frolicking in the contaminated water alongside the remains of their mother's corpse. No, count me out, too much culture for me."

With that he turned his back on George and the idea of going to the ceremony to watch a million people poison themselves with the polluted water.

Spiritual growth was one thing, insanity another.

CHAPTER SEVEN

For once Chance had the entire compound to himself. Evidently every single member of the staff had decided to go to the ceremonial cleansing. One last half-hearted effort was made by Karen to get him to join, by explaining that it wouldn't be a million people. That wouldn't happen until February and was still over four months away.

What difference did it make-- a million, fifty million, a thousand, even the handful from the clinic? He didn't want to go. Besides, he had other plans. Until recently he'd not known of the dusty computer in one of the more torn down buildings. How such a shabby place could house such a valuable piece of equipment he'd never know.

George's voice still rang in his head. "Does this thing work?" Chance had asked.

"Of course," George replied.

For the first time in weeks hope for a sense of normalcy gripped Chance. "I don't imagine that you'd be hooked to the Internet." He had glanced at the computer.

"Sure."

"Are you serious?"

"Yes, why? Are you into computers?"

"Well, I'd like to send a few emails if that's possible. I'm beginning to feel disconnected with my life." Chance stopped abruptly. "Of course I'll pay for the expense or whatever." He ignored the indulgent look on George's face.

"Chance," he'd said after what seemed a month of silence. "Feel free to use the computer anytime you choose, and the Internet. No one ever uses it, except of course the new people."

Of course, Chance thought, the ones still sane and wanting to go home.

Anyway none of that mattered now. He'd only used the thing sparingly feeling as though he was being judged each time he went into the room and turned on the modern machine. It was his conversations with Blaine that was keeping him going. He couldn't wait to tell him what the entire medical team was up to today.

He typed in the last letter, hit send and waited, hoping that a bell would ring, that somehow Blaine would be on line, that he'd receive an instant message. He needed that now.

Within seconds, he heard the voice on the computer saying, "you've got mail" and he smiled to himself. *Thanks Blaine.*

"That's terrific. I've heard a lot of things about cleansing away the sins of past lives by bathing in the river."

Chance stared blankly at the words on the monitor. Surely Blaine was joking. He wasn't in India, how had the madness infected him?

"Don't you see how unsanitary that is, how dangerous?" Chance again pushed the send key.

"Don't you see how spiritual this all is? What a wonderful opportunity to give up the self and put complete control in the divine to protect you."

Blaine's reply was rapid. This wasn't what Chance needed or wanted. He wanted to talk to someone who understood, someone who felt the same as he did. **"Would you bathe in that dirty water?"** he typed in.

"In a heartbeat," was Blaine's reply.

Chance didn't bother to answer, he powered the machine off and went back to his room. He couldn't be accused of being unenlightened. The last twenty plus years of his life had disproved that theory. Hell, he'd gotten divorced because the voice of his wife from another lifetime kept calling out to him. And he'd actually gone out in search of her. How dare Blaine or anyone accuse him of lacking the desire for spiritual enlightenment?

But for them to not see the illogical flaw of bathing in contaminated water in order to continue to perpetuate a superstition was absurd. Not in a million years would he ever understand that one. Maybe he could understand the people who had been born into that culture, and indoctrinated to believe ritual bathing would purge one of their sins. But to find educated men and women believing in such nonsense was unthinkable. And for them to suggest he participate in the ritual was beyond insane. It just wasn't going to happen. He closed his eyes tightly and lay down on the cot. His dreams would have to serve to amuse him.

"Dr. Morgan, wake up. There is someone here to see you."

His eyes opened just a slit and he peeked upwards at Sabu, wondering when he'd returned. Better yet, why was he waking him? "What is it, Sabu, who's here and why couldn't it wait?"

"There's a little girl here with her mother. They want to talk to you."

"No, not now, I'm too tired to see or treat patients." Chance frowned. "If you're back then surely someone else can handle this."

"There is no problem. They simply wish to speak with you."

Bringing his legs over to the right side of the cot and instantly regretting his quick movement, he sat up. A loose piece of straw jabbed him in the ankle with such force it drew blood. Reaching for an alcohol wipe Chance cleansed the area and sighed, glad he was still taking antibiotics..

"Listen, Sabu, I don't want to see anyone from that family."

"Which family would that be?"

Sabu was being a smart ass, Chance was well aware of that. "The patient who died, the one you all went to the Ganges for the big send off. That patient! I have nothing to say to the family."

For a moment Sabu stood still with what Chance was sure was a smirk on his face. Then he looked Chance straight in the eye, his determination evident. He wasn't about to budge from the room until Chance came with him.

"God, I'll be glad when I leave this place," Chance snapped while jamming his injured foot into his shoe. "Where are they?"

He followed Sabu out of the room and into the tiny cubicle that passed for a visitors' lounge. For a moment he didn't recognize the woman and kids standing there to greet him. The woman was all smiles, the children playing around her legs were screaming in glee.

"Hello Doctor."

"Hello." Chance marveled that the woman was speaking English to him, broken yes, but English. She put out her hand to tap the shoulder of one of her children causing the child to turn around and look at him. First she eyed him shyly.

"Thank you," the child whispered before lifting her dress to show him the barely visible scar on her leg.

The child from the first day, the one he'd helped George with. The one who had undergone such pain while being fully conscious. She was thanking him. He didn't believe he deserved her thanks. He wanted to apologize that they'd worked on her while she'd been awake. Accepting the thanks, he was aware many people in the country could and did die from the type of injury the child had received. He was thrilled she'd healed so nicely. He smiled at both the mother and child, glad she was able to run and play.

The Mother turned toward Sabu, evidently having learned only a few words of English.

"The Divine has a plan for you," Sabu translated. "You have a pure heart and much love."

Chance stared in awe unable to speak, watching the woman mutter to Sabu, not yet trusting that Sabu wouldn't change a message.

"But you have pain also, great pain." Sabu's eyes were intent on the woman. Chance watched them both closely as the woman touched her hand to her heart. "I'm sorry doctor for your pain. Go to the Mother Ganges, she will forgive you."

This had to be a setup. Chance looked at Sabu then the woman, before his eyes looked down on the little girl. His hand reached out to touch the child's hair, enthralled that a child who'd endured so much would now be here smiling at him, thanking him.

"She has a gift for you," Sabu said.

"Why?" He looked at the child's mother as his hand grazed the child's face. "Why are you giving me a gift? It's not necessary."

"For your kindness. You felt her pain and that of her daughter's and she felt yours. She feels a kinship toward you," Sabu translated.

Chance watched as the woman smiled at him and held out a small stone in her hand. She pushed the stone toward him.

Runes. He knew immediately what it was, though he'd never seen them. He turned the stone over to look for the markings. It was blank.

Chance's head dipped, he was curious. Why had this woman just gifted him with a blank stone, a Rune, something that was meant to tell of intuitive powers? But this one was blank. He felt his lips parting, and turned toward Sabu.

"There is nothing here."

"There is if you know where to look," Sabu answered. "That is the Rune of blankness."

Not knowing what else to do Chance stared first at Sabu, then the woman before fixing his gaze on the stone and turning it over and over in his palm.

"Blank is the end, blank is the beginning. This is the Rune of total trust and should be taken as evidence of your direct contact with the divine."

This was not real. He wanted to disbelieve Sabu, but as he watched the man's face, he also watched the woman. Something in him told him Sabu would not lie about something with so much meaning.

"Is that all it means?" Chance asked at last subdued, the child was holding his hand beaming at him. He'd done nothing, certainly nothing to warrant the look of trust in the child's eyes

Damn, why had he thought of that word? He shook his head; it had to be Sabu and what he was saying about the stone. Yes, that must be it. At last he allowed his fingers to take the stone from his palm and placed it in his pocket. Reaching out he clasped the woman's outstretched hands. He glanced quickly at Sabu. "Thank you," he said to Sabu wanting him to repeat his words to the woman.

"You're welcome," the woman answered and again she smiled at Chance.

"Do you want to know more of the meaning of the stone?" Sabu asked.

"Yes." Chance brought the stone from his pocket and stared intently at it. Once again he turned the stone over in his palm. "What else does it mean?"

Better to find out now and get it over with, still he felt as if he was being set up. Only this time it was the powers of heaven that was setting him up.

"This stone also bring to the surface your greatest fears. Will I fail? Will I be abandoned? And will she love me?"

Sabu stopped and Chance could feel his throat closing. He felt a tightening in the very pit of his gut. He wanted Sabu to finish, hurry and get the words out, enough with taking his time.

Hell, it was obvious they'd all conspired. Since the moment he'd first arrived in India everyone wanted to know why he was there. They all assumed it was unrequited love. Now here was this woman offering him a gift that told him of his own pain. They must have bribed the woman.

Chance almost ignored the tugging on his hand when it became more insistent. He looked down into the radiant brown eyes and returned the smile the child was giving him. He gave the girl's hand a gentle squeeze. He would stand for another moment and listen to Sabu. It was the polite thing to do. He kept his eyes riveted on the child, if he didn't he was afraid he would bolt from the room.

"Dr. Morgan, do you wish to hear more?"

"You've got to be kidding me," Chance answered. "Isn't what

you've told me enough?"

"There is more."

Chance marveled at the man so loved by his people, by all the staff, yet he didn't appear to have the least bit of a sense of humor. "Tell me," Chance offered at last thinking it was better to get it over with.

"Very well," Sabu began again. "As I said, this Rune brings to the surface your greatest fears. Will it all be taken away? And yet it does something else. Our highest good, our truest possibilities, and all our fertile dreams are held within the blankness of that one Rune."

Sabu stared long and hard at Chance and Chance felt his stare clear to his bones. He waited, holding tighter to the little girl's hand. "There's more isn't there, Sabu? Go ahead tell me all of it."

Sabu's face was void of emotion, as blank as the Rune the woman had given him, but his eyes glowed with an internal knowledge. For the first time since Chance had met the man, he seemed less annoyed at having to deal with foreigners, and awed that the woman had given such a gift to Chance, a man who lacked much in Sabu's eyes.

"Sabu," Chance called softly and watched as slowly the man's lips parted and what he supposed to be a smile came on his face. He wasn't sure if it was a smile as he'd never seen Sabu give one, but still he thought this just might be the first time.

"The blank Rune calls for an act of courage, an empty- handed leap into the void. Drawing it is an act of faith. Willingness and permitting are what this Rune requires."

"But I didn't draw it," Chance objected holding his hand out. "It was given to me." He waited while Sabu spoke to the woman in their native tongue.

"She drew it for you."

"Does that count? She didn't ask my permission and I didn't give it."

He'd not intended to raise his voice and only noticed he had when he felt a loosening of the little girl's hand in his own and looked down at her. Damn would he ever learn to stop offending these people? Immediately he reprimanded himself for his thoughts, 'these people' were of itself an offensive word.

"Do you object to her pulling the Rune for you?" Sabu pointed at the woman and waited.

Chance gazed in the woman's direction, the peaceful smile she'd worn was now tainted with worry about the appropriateness of her gift. That wasn't what he'd meant at all and he was damn sure Sabu knew it.

"Sabu, all I was asking was, is the meaning the same without my permission? That's all. I'm extremely grateful for the Rune and I want to know everything it says, so please tell her that, and then tell me the rest."

This time there was a genuine smile on Sabu's face. He practically grinned at Chance then smiled at the woman, talking in rapid speech. At last he turned his attention back to Chance.

"Dr. Morgan, you should be honored, besides being a direct test of faith, this Rune is related to your karma, everything you've ever done in your past lives. The sum total of your actions and their consequences. These are the lessons for you in this lifetime. Live this life well, for the Rune teaches that the old debt of karma shift and change."

"Are you saying that I can change my karma by how I live this life?"

Without a doubt he saw the spark in Sabu's eyes, the man probably thought he was going to have to debate Chance on the possibility of reincarnations. Little did he know, he was well past that.

"Sabu, can I change my karmic debt?"

"Nothing is set in stone, Dr. Morgan, nothing is predestined. The debt of old karma shift and evolve as you shift and evolve. What beckons is the creative powers of the unknown."

Sabu laughed aloud, truly a miracle if Chance had ever seen one. He spoke to the little girl's mother who laughed also and before long all the children were laughing running toward Chance, covering his face with kisses when he bent down toward them. He didn't know what had just happened, but he liked it. Hell, it was the best he'd felt since coming to India.

"Dr. Morgan, take heart," Sabu continued, "whenever you draw this Rune or it's drawn for you, know that the work of self change is progressing in your life."

Chance smiled at Sabu, the children and the woman. Self- change. Huh? Until a few hours ago he was arguing with George Trammel about breaking his commitment and high tailing it back home. If the universe thought he needed change he just might have to think about listening.

CHAPTER EIGHT

He wasn't sure if he were asleep or awake. In some ways it felt like a dream. He could hear movement outside his room and knew the rest of the crew had returned. He should get up and get started on the morning chores, but soft hands were caressing him. A shudder of desire coursed through his body and he grabbed the hand that caressed him. "Michelle, he whispered into her ear, "Why did you stop loving me?"

"Chance, I love you, I do. You have to believe me. I always have and I always will. That will never change, but you must go on with your life. I want you to be happy. We will be together again, I promise."

He wanted nothing more than to touch Michelle, kiss her, hold her, but she was crying, her arms flung out in front of her in a protective manner indicating she didn't want to be touched. He was confused. Her actions didn't match her words.

"If you truly love me, let me hold you."

"That's not going to do either of us any good, Chance. I don't want to risk never having you in my life again. Our being together is not the path we're on right now. We have to find out why in order to erase it and safe guard our future."

He was tired of listening to her, tired of not being able to hold her, of thinking of her in Larry's arms. "You should have waited. You should have known I would find you. Didn't I always?"

He watched the tears slid down her cheeks and moved toward her, he heard her soft, "No don't," and he ignored it and her. Enough. He was going to hold her. Her body soft and pliant in his arms melted into the flesh of his body. Shivers of delight danced up and down his spine.

His hand wound around her hair, lifting long cinnamon colored strands to his nostril to breathe in the fragrance of flowers. He trailed kisses along the side of her neck saving the true nectar until last. He held her tightly in his arms knowing soon she would be gone. He kissed the salt from her tears, from her cheeks, then her eyes. His lips rested softly over hers and he felt the tremble that went through her body, the jolt of electricity that ripped through him, heard her mummer, "Chance, this is wrong." A moment later she was gone from his arms as he'd known she would be.

Chance sat up, not a dream, not a vision. He inhaled deeply and the essence of his own sweet Dimi was still in the room with him. Only now she was Michelle and she belonged to Larry.

Damn. Thousands of miles away from home and still she haunted his thoughts. *Get over her, start over.* How he wished someone had the answer to just how the hell he was supposed to do that.

As he ran his hands across his face, the feeling of loss, became acute. There was little that he could do to stop it so he allowed the hurt to seep into him, wash over him and envelope him in total despair. George Trammel was right; a woman had brought him so far from home. Hearing a knock at his door he groaned in annoyance.

"Chance, may I come in?"

The soft voice was preceded by another light tapping on his door, one Chance had chosen to ignore. Now hearing Karen's voice he smiled to himself. *It's not going to be that easy, Dimi, she's not the one I want. You are.*

"Chance?"

Chance inhaled and exhaled quickly wanting to take the scent of the woman he loved inside his lungs and store it in his body. He was aware the moment Karen entered the room he would lose the smell of herbs and flowers.

"Sure, Karen, but give me a few moments too get dressed." He needed time to let go of Dimi's scent. Once he was dressed, he yelled out, "Come on in." Sitting on the bed he studied Karen for a moment. "How was the cleansing?" He looked at her wishing his words had not come out sounding sarcastic, but there was no pulling them back.

"It was beautiful, but of course the ceremonies always are."

Chance looked her over for a long moment. "Have anyone told her children that she's never coming back?"

"No, of course not. That would be a lie."

He shook his head. "They need a mother now, Karen, not in the next life. What the hell good will her new incarnation do them? What if she has an entirely new family? Do you think she's still going to have them in her life? Do you think she will even know them?"

"I don't know about any of that. And it's not what the family is concerned with. They know she's no longer in pain, that she no longer has hunger. And for that they're truly grateful. Besides, they now have someone in the afterlife who will look out for them."

"That's a bit of a contradiction isn't it? How is she going to be reincarnated, yet remain in limbo somewhere in the afterlife to take care of her family?"

"I can't be sure, but I think she'll linger around her family until they no longer need her. Then when the time is right she'll choose to be reborn."

"Do you believe in destiny, Karen?"

"I don't know exactly. I believe in karma, that we amass karmic debts, that when we're reborn we have to repay those debts. But as for destiny, I think we can change that. What we do in each lifetime and how quickly we learn the lessons we come back for are up to us, I believe."

He watched Karen's face as she smiled. She looked nothing like his Dimi, didn't smell like her. Chance couldn't love her like he loved Dimi. Yet he knew with a certainty born of loving the same soul for lifetime after lifetime that Dimi had somehow engineered Karen's being in his room. Damn it, Blaine was right. He'd have to remember to think of his Dimi as she was now called. Michelle.

He imagined Michelle wanted him to look at the woman and see below the surface, to suddenly fall in love with Karen and free Michelle of her guilt for not being with him. If that were the case, it wasn't going to work out like that. He wasn't attracted to Karen, and he wasn't going to force an attraction he didn't feel.

"Why are you looking at me like that?" Karen asked with a bit of a puzzled look on her pretty face.

"I'm sorry if I was staring. I was just wondering do you believe that in the entire universe we all have a soul mate, just one soul that's meant to be united with us?"

"I don't know. Do you?"

"Yes."

"What happens if you never find your soul mate?"

"Your soul can never be happy."

"Do you think a person should spend this life alone if they don't find that one person?"

"Yes, I do," Chance answered without hesitation.

Karen was smiling sadly at him, a look of pity in her eyes and it was annoying the hell out of him.

"Now it's my turn to ask you a question, Karen. Why are you looking as if you suddenly feel sorry for me?"

"I would hate to think of you squandering the precious gift of life, wasting away not loving someone because you didn't find your soul mate."

"What would be the use, if I know that my soul mate is not available? Why should I settle?"

"I didn't say you should settle, Chance. Each life is meant to learn from and grow. If you shut yourself off from love, from living, you're not growing, you're doing the exact opposite, you're merely existing, a living death. The Runes teach us to embrace each life, to learn."

Ahh. It was as he thought. They had conspired and manipulated against him. He picked up the stone the woman had given him. "You mean these stones?"

He watched Karen's face closely, frowning at her look of surprise. He'd have to say one thing for her, she was a damn fine actress. He could almost believe she didn't know about the woman giving him the stone.

"So you're familiar with the Runes?" Karen asked.

"Not really, a former patient's mother gave it to me a few hours ago."

"That's a powerful stone you have there, it's the rune of blankness."

"So I've been told."

Chance walked closer to Karen. Using his height to his advantage he peered down at her. "Don't you think it rather odd that just a few hours after this woman gave me this stone you come knocking at my door, telling me, I need to learn some life lessons and talking about the Runes?"

"What are you trying to say?"

Hmm. He must have gotten to her because he noticed the friendly tone of her voice slipped just a bit. This to, he thought, must be part of the act.

"Well, you tell me, what you would think? It sounds to me as if the rest of you have decided to fix me."

"Fix you...fix you?" Karen laughed. She laughed until fat droplets of water ran down both cheeks. And still she continued.

"Chance, you are the most arrogant man I've ever met," she said at last shaking her head in amusement at him. "We can't fix you.

Besides, I didn't know you were broken. You can only fix yourself, and that my friend I think is a job none of us would want to tackle, even if we could. You need a lot of work."

"Then why did you mention the stone?"

Inhaling for a moment, Chance stepped away from Karen. A breeze had blown through the small room and he'd suddenly become aware of a spicy odor clinging to her.

Stop, I don't want to notice anything about her, he muttered inside his head. *This isn't going to work.* Still he moved even farther away. "You have to admit this smells like a setup." He walked as far from Karen as he could possibly get in the little room.

"You find it strange that you're in India and more than one person speaks to you of spiritual matters? Duhhh, wake up, Chance. The entire country is on a spiritual quest."

With that she stomped from the room, letting him know exactly what she thought of him. He seemed to have developed a penchant as of late for offending people.

Chance held the stone tightly in his hand. He needed to talk to Blaine. He felt a twisting in his gut. He wanted to talk to Michelle, really talk to her, not the Michelle he'd become adept at creating out of the empty void to fill his arms, but the flesh and blood woman. He needed to hear her voice. He was going crazy with wanting her. India wasn't working. If anything it was bringing all his pain to the surface.

Pausing in his thoughts something slowly clicked into place. He looked down at the stone still resting in his hand. Damn, what was that Sabu said about the Runes bringing all his fears to the surface? Now he was repeating it.

For one horrible instant he wondered if they were spiking his food with something. He couldn't remember thinking these thoughts when he was only eating from his own stash of supplies.

Yes, that would have to be another thing he asked Blaine to get him. He had to get back to eating food he knew for sure wasn't tainted. He didn't come to India to become a damn guru, nor was he on a spiritual journey. He only came to this God forsaken place to forget.

Twenty two hours, two minutes and eighteen seconds. That was how long it had taken for Chance to have his call put through to Blaine. Knowing the futility of even trying his cell phone the annoyance of waiting for calls to be put through the land line was getting to him.

As he listened to Blaine lecture him, he wondered why he'd gone to all the trouble. There were enough people in India to lecture him on opening himself up to receive the gift of knowledge.

"You're regretting your call to me, that's okay."

Blaine laughed easily the sound snapping Chance out of his self imposed funk. "You're psychic, that's not fair for you to do that."

"Why Chance? You're psychic yourself. Didn't we prove that?"

Chance rubbed the bracelet he was wearing, feeling the heat from the stone burn his flesh slightly with the knowledge that what Blaine said was true.

"It's hard for me to think that all that stuff happened. You, Michelle and I being a psychic trinity, battling evil and winning." He couldn't help smiling to himself remembering his relief when Blaine's plan had worked. It could have gone much differently.

Suddenly the tone of Blaine's questions changed from playful to serious. Chance didn't want that. He just wanted to forget, sink into oblivion.

"Chance, don't shut me out. I lost you once. I don't want to lose you again."

"Now you're using my guilt against me, that's also not fair. I told you, I'm not going to do anything stupid."

"But you are. Don't you think shutting yourself off like this is hurting me? I want you to be happy."

"There's only one thing that can ever make me happy."

"The last time you spoke those words to me you willed yourself to die. It wasn't fair for you to leave me alone."

"Again with the paternal guilt. I've apologized for that. Blaine, you were an adult, you were fine. Besides, we found each other again in this life."

"And you think that makes it fine? You weren't there with me, Chance, you were dead. And so was my mother. Did you ever stop to think how alone I was, how unhappy?"

"I couldn't live without her."

"I know. How do you think knowing of your desire to rejoin her made me feel every day of that lifetime? To see in your eyes that you blamed my living on taking away the life of the woman you loved, that no matter how much I loved you, it wasn't enough. Being my father wasn't enough to stop you from taking your own life."

"You make it sound like…" Chance winced

"Like what it was." Blaine interrupted. "No, you didn't put a gun to your head, or take poisons, but you stopped living and willed yourself to die. How was I supposed to live with that?"

For sure now Chance wished he had not made the call. He wanted Blaine to understand. Who knew that he would find his son again in this life, and that his son would remember the life before and that he would be hurting from it still? In past incarnations he'd only had to worry about finding his wife. He regretted he'd not thought of finding his son.

Chance was silent, Blaine's pain becoming his own, this son whom he'd found again. He didn't want to hurt him, not again.

"You said you'd forgiven me," Chance whispered at last.

"Yes, and you said you would never put me through what you did the last lifetime."

"I'm not."

"Chance, you are, by refusing to be happy, your soul is withering up and dying."

"I'm trying." Chance shut his eyes tightly to keep Michelle's face from forming.

"I know it's hard," Blaine answered him at last, "but you have to keep trying. I don't want to lose my father for a second time. Your wasting away is not your destiny."

"What is my destiny, Blaine?"

"I don't know."

A long wistful sigh escaped Chance's lung. "I see her here all the time. I hold her in my arms. I can smell her scent on my clothes now, lingering."

"Did she astral travel to you?"

"No."

"Then how?"

"I don't know. I just touch her picture and think of her and she's here. It's so real."

"Chance, this isn't healthy."

"And you think bilocating is, or you going inside someone's head to chase out demons? Do you think any of the stuff we've done in the past two years is healthy?"

There was silence on the other end. *Good,* thought Chance, Blaine needed to not feel so smug.

"I don't feel smug."

"Stop that," Chance scolded, knowing full well Blaine could not stop reading his thoughts if he'd wanted to. He secretly thought that was Blaine's way of making sure he stayed safe.

"Let's see, for twenty years you searched for this woman, your soul mate from another life, and miracle of miracles you found her. Then wait...oh oh— another miracle. You find the son you left behind, the son you left to fend for himself. Now there's a wrinkle in your plans. Your soul mate has a husband, she's married. Sure, she remembers you. She even loves you, but she can't leave her husband. How am I doing?" Blaine asked of Chance.

"Great, continue," Chance answered.

"Okay, let's see where the story picks up from there. We get attacked by psychic vampires, take on evil body snatching entities, almost get killed in the process and still your soul mate remains with her husband and begs you to be happy. And you my dear father take off for India, the land of true learning and what do you do?"

"I don't know, Blaine. You seem to have all the answers, you tell me."

"You close yourself off, that's what you do. You put down everything that's happening to you."

"Blaine, you have no idea of what I'm going through here. They're all nuts. Everyday someone's clamoring for me to tell them why I'm here. They think I need to change, grow. This whole place is crazy and I can't wait until my time is up and I come home."

Chance closed his eyes. He could see Blaine's face, a look of sadness and pain straining his features. "Don't worry about me, Blaine."

"I have to, you're my father and I love you."

"I can take care of myself, don't worry."

"Chance, answer me this. Is there any doubt in your mind about anything that's happened to you in the last two years? Are you positive Michelle is your wife, your Dimi, and that I am your son?"

"Yes, of course I'm sure," Chance answered without hesitation.

"Then why is it so hard for you to believe the things that are being put to you in India? How many people in America do you think believe us? If we were to write our story down someone would think it was bad science fiction."

"What do you want me to do?"

"What you promised you would do before you left. I want you to live again."

"I am living."

"No, you're simply existing. I want you to open yourself up to the possibility of loving someone. I want you to be happy."

Silence.

"Michelle wants you to be happy, Chance."

There was really not too much left for them to say, they'd been over this road so many times there were ruts in it. They both knew the script by heart.

"I'll try, Blaine."

"Try hard."

They both laughed as much to break the tension as anything. "Don't forget the supplies." Chance pushed the button on the phone to sever the connection but didn't hang it up. He stood for a time with it in his hand. Everywhere he looked people were saying the same thing to him, the conspiracy was becoming much larger than he would have imagined. He sighed loudly. Replacing the beeping phone at last he started to walk away.

"Anything I can do to help, Doctor Morgan?"

Chance turned back. George Trammel was smiling at him. "I don't think so," he answered George, "Not unless you have some magical powers I don't know about."

"Well, we all have a bit of magic inside us."

His lips were smiling and Chance knew the man was teasing, yet there was something more, something a bit mysterious about his colleague.

"George, what's your deal? Why are you here in India?"

"It's my home."

"No, I don't mean now. I mean what brought you from America? Everyone here seems so interested in why I came, tell me why you did?"

"I gave you my answer. It's my home. One day I woke up and I knew finally where I belonged. So, I made plans to return home."

Here we go again, Chance thought as he pulled up a chair to listen.

CHAPTER NINE

Chance's head was reeling. He glanced at the watch on his wrist, not out of boredom but out of a sense of disbelief. He'd sat stunned listening to George Trammel talk about his life. Hell it was almost a mirror image of his own life with one exception. George had gone searching after his country, and Chance had gone in search of the woman he'd loved for centuries.

"You're looking at me strangely."

George had a smile on his face. The man's upturned lips made Chance attempt to smile in return, but he found he couldn't, a frigid cold had invaded his body while George spoke. It had robbed him of his ability to move the slightest muscle.

"Are you all right, Chance?" George inquired looking more closely at him.

"I will be," Chance replied. He looked sharply at the man seated in front of him. "George, are you telling me the truth?"

"Of course I am. I have no reason to lie to you. Your belief is not my concern."

Chance couldn't help but note the tone. Once again he'd offend someone without really trying. "I'm sorry," he offered, "I didn't mean to imply that you were lying, it's just...well not what one hears every day."

This time George smiled and Chance relaxed, pleased that the man had a thicker skin than most of the people he'd shared living quarters with for the past month. Two months to go, he thought before shaking the rest of the unformed thoughts from his brain.

"Can I ask you something?"

"Of course, although I'm sure I know what it is. But by all means, Chance, ask away."

"Well, you said before you came here you had an unusual aversion to the people of this region that lived in the States. When you got here did those feelings go away?"

Laughter bubbled out of George Trammel. He got up from his seat and walked across the room. Chance watched as George rubbed tears of laughter from his eyes with the worn sleeve of his shirt.

"Hell no." George bellowed. "I brought my preconceived

prejudices with me."

He began laughing again. Chance glanced away partly because he was feeling a bit apprehensive, partly because he hoped the man was not some madman with a weird story.

Chance stood and walked along the length of the room also. "You said you couldn't stand even the smell of the people when you treated them in the States. You said that you would turn your nose up whenever you had to treat them."

"Yeah can you imagine that as a doctor trained to heal, touching them was the very last thing I wanted to do?"

"Then how?"

"How indeed?" George said softly causing Chance to have to strain to hear his words.

"I guess my soul convicted me. No one else did. My entire staff had taken on my own demeanor and dislike. One night I dreamt of lying amidst squalor, sick, starving and at the mercy of a doctor that didn't want to touch me."

For an instant George was lost. Chance saw the strange look come into the man's eyes, the stillness with which he stood and knew in that moment George was reliving his past.

He watched as the subtle changes occurred in George, loosening the past's hold on him. His arms loosed and once again the man was smiling.

"It's a little amazing to believe you went to bed one night and woke the next morning feeling differently."

"Amazing? Try, that didn't happen. No, I had that same dream more than three dozen times before I decided to examine it."

"And because of that dream you came here?"

George was smiling broadly his head shaking form side to side. "I guess I'll have to tell you all of it won't I? I didn't think you'd be interested." He glanced once at the clock on the wall. "I expected you to high tail it long before now."

"Why?"

"Why?" George laughed again. "Chance, you've wanted to leave here since the moment you arrived. We all know that you think we cooked up this conspiracy to make your life miserable, or to convert you."

"You spoke to Karen?"

"Yes, she told me, but it wasn't something new. We were already aware of your feelings."

"You would have to admit if you were in my shoes that it does look a bit suspicious."

"Chance, we don't have enough hours in the day to take care of patients, you know that. When would we find the time to plot a plan to change your mind?"

Chance's head dipped sheepishly. George was right, they were all working very hard night and day, and emergencies arose at any hour.

"Everyone keeps asking me what brought me here."

"I apologize for that, it's probably my fault. I'm always talking about the reason we're here, not just in India, but on the planet. I can become rather zealous at times."

"Rather," Chance laughed, "try you're like a bull-dog after a bone."

George's look turned thoughtful leaving Chance to wonder if he'd once again offended the man.

"I never thought of myself like that." He smiled. "I guess it's because of all the bad karma I've built up in this lifetime. I'm trying hard to show others a different way, to tell them that they don't have to make life so hard for themselves, that there..."

He stopped abruptly snapping his head forward and began grinning.

"What's wrong?"

"I just realized you're right. I am a bit of the bull dog." He laughed and Chance joined in. "I was telling you my story wasn't I? I promise no more lectures, at least for today," he added with a twinkle. "Now are you tired, or do you want to hear the real reason for my transformation?"

A yawn chose that moment to rise to Chance's mouth. He stifled it with the back of his hand. "No way am I ready to end this discussion." The yawn he'd been holding back managed to escape. "Finish the story, George. I'm awake."

"I haven't told anyone this, but one morning I woke speaking perfect Hindi. In fact I could speak about twenty different Indian dialects. I thought for a time I was dreaming. I couldn't speak or understand English. I went to work anyway and didn't speak a word that day. That was until a patient came in and I finally had someone to talk to. It was obvious to me the patient was from India."

George smiled. "It was the first time the smell of spices did something other than make me want to puke. I asked the man what was troubling him and he was surprised that I spoke in his dialect. I understood him perfectly.

"Within a few days I could once again understand English, but my newfound knowledge of Hindi was still there. That first patient had spread the word, my office was now overrun with natives of India. They were amazed and in awe of my ability to understand them.

"I didn't know what the hell was going on, but one day a couple came in and smiled at me, said I was a true brother and the woman kissed my hand when she left the room clutching as many samples as she could carry in her arms.

"Things went on like that for about a month. I noticed that my staff began to change as my own ways changed. One day a patient came in. When I asked what he was there for he smiled at me, held out a small gray bag and instructed me to put my hand in, but to focus on what my needs were before doing it. I smiled, closed my hand wondering if there would be something in the bag that might take a nip at my hand."

"Suspicious, hmmm?" asked Chance.

"Much like someone else I know," George answered, "but I decided to go for it. I put my hand in pulled out this strange looking stone and pulled it from the bag. The patient smiled at me said this stone was called the Runes and I had drawn the rune of self, the very first rune.

"I'm not sure if you're being serious now or if you're pulling my leg."

"Chance, I believe you've had a little experience with the Runes yourself haven't you?"

"Tell me something, George, do you have eyes in the back of your head, or do you read minds?" But he smiled after the words hoping George would know for once that he was only kidding.

"You'll find that nothing much is kept secret here. No one thinks anything of privacy." George shrugged, "I guess that's because we're all so concerned about the patients first and foremost and if we have a little time left over, we're all striving toward completeness."

"Did you know that you were striving for…this completeness before you were given the Rune?"

"Nope." George grinned. "Hell man I was a doctor, in America. I'd made it to the top of the pinnacle. I was rich, successful, well respected, sought after, I thought I was complete."

"A little stone changed all of that?"

"What, you don't believe me?"

"Lets just say I find it doubtful."

"Do you even know what the rune of self teaches?"

"Not really, I was only given one and Sabu told me its meaning." He looked at George hesitating in his speech. "Sabu told me what the stone means, but then again you know he doesn't like me very much."

"I don't think Sabu dislikes you, I think he's losing patience with teaching. Maybe I should give him some time off, let him get away."

Chance cocked his head toward George. "What do you mean, Sabu's teaching?" He was afraid he knew the answer. "I thought Sabu was just your assistant here."

"He is my assistant. He's here to teach us all that in the grander scheme of things we're all here to assist. That is our function, to teach and assist."

Chance watched the look on George's face change from one of amusement to one of wonder.

"Dr. Morgan, would you like to know what the first stone I ever received told me?"

"I think I already know," Chance answered, "it told you to come to India."

"Not quite," George laughed. "It told me to be modest, to strive to live an ordinary life in an ordinary way."

"That's it?" Chance was growing impatient. All this stuff sounded well and good but nothing that he couldn't get out of a book of mediation or daily affirmations.

"Isn't that enough?" George asked.

"No."

"No? Of course from you my skeptic friend the answer would be no. Well, if that had been all I probably would have still been in America, but the Rune had more to say. It said now is not the time to seek credit for accomplishments, that the self must know stillness before it can learn its true purpose."

This time Chance wasn't sneering, the look in George's eyes would have prevented it. "George?"

"I know what you're thinking, Chance, and no I don't have to be a mind reader to know. Everything the stone said was what I thought of myself. I was filled with self importance, I counted my accomplishments. I thought I was better than my patients, hell, I thought I was better than my colleagues."

"Better than your colleagues?"

"I was also a surgeon, Chance. I dare say at one point I may have thought I was better than God. I know I joked enough about it. Whenever a patient would tell me they were praying for the outcome I'd answer, 'no need, I'm here. And as long as I'm here you have no need to worry. Once I had the audacity to tell a patient who had told me how God had pulled her through when she was unable to be treated by me. I answered her flippantly, 'Yes, God does make a good assistant.'"

Chance's mouth fell open.

"What?" George asked, "do you think what I did was any worse than your thinking you held the power of life and death over that poor woman?"

"But I never said."

"You may not have said the words, but you sure as hell thought them."

"I didn't," Chance attempted to protest.

"Ahh but you did, you kept going on and on about how you could have saved her. We all attempted to tell you the truth; to point out your words to you, but you wouldn't listen."

Chance thought for a moment about what he'd actually said and done and what George Trammel had told him.

"George, did you just feed me a load of bull about what happened to you? Did a patient really give you the Rune of self, and all the nonsense about your thinking God to be your assistant?"

George smiled slowly before answering. "I wish I could say that everything I told you was a lie. It would make me appear so much nobler, but alas I'm sorry to say its true, every word of it."

"Tell me something," Chance was once again walking toward George until he stood toe to toe with the man eyeing him with a straight forward stare. "Am I now supposed to stay here having received a stone?" He shook both hands in the air making a derisive noise.

"That's your decision."

"You're right it is. Thanks for the bedtime story." Chance grinned at George as he walked away ticking off the two months remaining on his contract. He would be happy to leave before he went bonkers. For a moment there he'd almost bought into George Trammel's story.

Almost.

It wasn't that Chance didn't believe in the possibility of the things he'd told him being true. After all the things that had happened to him, he was aware anything was possible. If only he didn't feel as though some plan was in motion to guide him to a certain path. If he could dispel the doubts about that, he'd believe George without reservation.

CHAPTER TEN

Something was wrong. There was a stillness, a hush Chance had not experienced since he left the states. It was so damn quiet that the very nothingness of it woke him from a sound sleep.

For a moment he thought he was dreaming, the place was never quiet. An unease slithered over his body jangling his nerves. For the first time in months he allowed himself to go within. Concentrating on the rest of the staff Chance began breathing deeply, his eyes closed as he focused only on the staff.

It worked, he saw them all gathered somewhere sitting in a huge circle. He couldn't tell if they were happy or sad, merely focused, as he was now.

Before he had a chance to contemplate his decisions he had dressed and was heading out the door. He looked around in all directions, but saw nothing and no one. He panicked. He was in a hostile place, what if something had happened and he slept through it?

"Don't be afraid." The words popped into his head suddenly and with great force. The voice wasn't his own. How he wanted it to at least be the voice of his son, but it wasn't.

"Concentrate." There it was again. Ice skittered up and down his spine, for a moment he thought he was going to fall ill, maybe he already had, he'd half way expected it.

Then the sound of laughter echoed though his head. "You're not sick, Chance, you're afraid. If you want to know where they are you have the ability inside yourself, tune in and follow what you are given.

He closed his eyes again, ignoring his sweaty palms. The image of the entire camp came to him again and he set off in the direction he saw in his vision, wondering why he cared where they were? Wasn't this just what he'd been after, some peace and quiet? Hadn't he gone to bed wishing they would all just disappear? And the patients, why weren't they storming the place demanding to be treated?

Chance kicked at a stone in his path angry and confused. Two more months, he thought, then his life would return to normal.

A nanosecond before he gave up thinking he must have been walking in the wrong direction, he heard the sound of laughter being carried on the wind. He listened intently wanting to hear it again. Nothing.

But at least it gave him hope that he was walking in the right direction. For another five minutes he walked until he spotted a mound and he found himself smiling. Somehow he knew over the mound he would find his colleagues.

Karen turned toward him, a welcoming smile of surprise on her face. Chance watched as she moved to the left to make room for him. Taking a glance around he made a quick decision to not sit near Karen. He didn't want her or anyone else getting any ideas. He moved toward Aaron, a male doctor was a safer alternative.

"Welcome, Dr. Morgan, glad that you joined us," Sabu said.

Chance felt the heat of embarrassment rise to cover his face, he mumbled, but didn't answer. He stared fixedly at Sabu wondering what the hell was going on. Sabu was wearing a robe that shimmered with iridescent colors, it was clear that he was the one in charge, the teacher.

"I should have known," he whispered bending his long legs to fold into the spot next to Dr. Sanders. "I should have known," he repeated as he sat down, his legs vying for more room.

"Shush."

Several people turned toward him their fingers to their lips. He hadn't talked loud enough to disturb anyone, their shushing him annoyed the hell out of him and made him wonder on his decision to find his missing colleagues.

"Don't," he heard Sabu say, "Questions and comments are welcome. Please everyone, let's welcome Dr. Chance Morgan into our midst and give him the respect due any seeker."

But I'm not a seeker. Chance thought the words, but had the good sense not to speak out loud again.

"Dr. Morgan did you have a comment?"

"No," Chance muttered back at Sabu, wishing the man hadn't singled him out, wishing the people staring at him would just mind their damn business. Hell, he wasn't a stranger to any of this stuff and he hated being treated as an imbecile.

Sabu was smiling at Chance. "I'm surprised that you came looking for us. We're talking about the stones, the Runes," he amended. "And all seekers are welcome."

"But I'm not a seeker."

This time Chance didn't care that people turned to stare at him. "I'm only here because...because I was wondering where everyone was, and I just started walking."

"That may be true to you at this moment, but you've always wished for peace and quiet, for privacy, yet you sought out our presence. That makes you a seeker."

The man was beaming at him. Chance couldn't stand it, he glanced sideways, his eyes landing on Karen's face. She too was beaming at him. He scanned the area quickly. The same expression resided on the entire staff and on the faces of total strangers.

Yep, he was right. The people were definitely brainwashed. Come on, it was fine to study Eastern philosophy, but to sit there beaming at him because he got bored and came looking for them, well that was another story. He thought of Michelle and the look of terror on her face when he first met her, the disbelief when he informed her she was his wife from a past life. She'd thought he was crazy.

Chance shook his head; maybe he did have something to learn. He closed his eyes, an immediate picture of Michelle coming to his mind to be joined seconds later by Blaine. Yes they would want this. They would want him to listen to Sabu.

"Dr. Morgan, I understand you've had little dealing with the Runes and I ask you this next question not to embarrass you, but in order to teach, to make sure you have a full knowledge of the ancient Runes."

"So ask me your question." Chance spoke more harshly than he intended. Hell they both knew the man was purposely bringing attention to him, more than likely angry that he burst in on his little teaching session. Well next time he woke to find the place deserted he sure as hell wouldn't go looking for them.

"I think I'll save the question for later. But if you think of something you'd like to ask, don't hesitate to join in. With that Sabu moved his attention away and Chance heaved a huge sigh of relief. He caught Karen smiling from his peripheral vision. She was standing and then moving to sit next to him. Hadn't she gotten the message that he didn't want to sit next to her. She touched his hand the contact startling him.

He sat in stunned silence as she twined her fingers in his. They had never had such intimate physical contact before, why now? Why was she holding his hand? He didn't want this, didn't want a relationship with another woman, he was already in love: With his wife:

He looked down at his own hand joined with Karen's. He had every intention of pushing her away until Michelle's face became vivid behind the veil of his eyes. Only this time their son wasn't with her. It was her husband, Larry and she was holding him, telling him she loved him.

Chance shuddered, he felt the sorrow more deeply each time. He clutched Karen's hand tightly. He was unaware of just how tightly he was holding on to her until a small moan of pain brought him out of himself. He turned to her, her face was ashen and tears stood in her eyes. He released his death grip. He wanted to tell her how sorry he was, but the words wouldn't come. Standing to leave, he heard Sabu answering one question after the other. As he made his way toward the opening, pausing as Aaron Sanders the doctor he'd chose to sit next to asked a question.

"I don't understand why we can only do the lifetime reading only once with the Rune. What will happen if we do it a second or a third time?"

Chance heard the question, but he was too embarrassed to remain for the answer. He left knowing his leaving would cause more talk than his arrival. It couldn't be helped, he had to get away.

Hours passed, still Chance had come up with no explanation to give to Karen other than an apology for hurting her hand. He was grateful they were all still away, yet curious. What could Sabu possibly be teaching that would take all night? Finally a knock on his door and a small voice: Karen. He dreaded having to face her. Why couldn't she have gone to her own room and saved this talk for later? Of course he could pretend, to be asleep, but he wasn't a coward. Making his way to the door he pulled it open and stared at her not speaking, just waiting for her to say what she'd come to say and be on her way. When she refused to speak he moved away from the door and began to aimlessly pace about the small space. Her hand on his shoulder forced him to shake the past life memories away.

"Chance, are you all right?"

He stopped in his pacing; he had not even heard Karen enter the room. He'd thought she was still standing at the door.

"Yeah I'm fine. Listen, I'm sorry about squeezing your hand back there."

He watched as she massaged her hand. He continued watching as a grin broke out on her face.

"That's some grip you've got."

"Why did you do that?" Chance asked moving closer.

"Do what?"

"Hold my hand. Why did you hold my hand?"

"You looked so lost and lonely. I just wanted to make you feel less alone. Instead I think I invoked memories."

She hesitated and Chance knew what was coming. Everyone had asked him the same question dozens of time including Karen. So her asking wasn't surprising. It was him. For the first time he thought he would be able to answer her.

"Chance, I know you don't like talking about it, but maybe it would help if you did. You know…if you brought it out into the open. What made you come to India?"

"My wife."

"You're married?"

"Yeah I am," he answered, not turning away from the mild shock he knew would be registered on her face.

"Are you having problems in your marriage? Is that why you came?"

"You could say that. My wife's husband is the problem." He laughed at her look of confusion.

"How long have you been married, Chance?"

He heard the wariness in her voice, the high pitched sound on the last words telling him she wished she had not brought up the subject.

"I've been married forever."

"What does forever mean? Twenty years… thirty? What are you saying? Do you feel as though you're in a prison? Is that why it feels likes forever?"

He laughed before turning away from her. "No, that's not it. I say forever because it has been that long, several lifetimes in fact," he finished turning back.

"Lifetimes?"

"Yes, lifetimes. So many that we've lost count."

"Chance, I don't…"

"Don't what? What don't you understand? Or is it that you don't believe me? Aren't you the one that's been trying to get me to open my mind, expand my thinking, telling me I'm here to learn? Well, Karen, I suggest you do the same. Open your mind."

She flinched, he saw her as he turned back to face her. He saw the tears that formed in the corners of her eyes and knew she was trying desperately to hold them back.

"I'm sorry for being so gruff," he whispered. "It's just..."

"It's hard to talk about."

"Very."

"Would you like me to leave? I'm sorry I butted my nose in, I won't do it again."

Chance thought over the offer. Part of him wanted nothing more than for Karen to leave him along with his memories, but somewhere deep inside of him an ache to talk about Michelle was gnawing at him.

"No, stay," he answered at last. I think I want to talk about her."

"Were you really reunited time after time?" Karen asked timidly.

"Yes we were." Anticipating the next question he walked toward her. "You want to know how, right?"

"Yes. How did you find each other? How did you know? How...?"

"One question at a time," he answered her, smiling at her inability to speak clearly. For once he'd caught her off guard. He rather liked the feeling.

"In each life we were born knowing the other existed, that we would be together to live another lifetime filled with joy."

"Was it always like that, the joy I mean?" Karen's voiced quivered.

"Mostly." He turned away again. "Our last life together Dimi died shortly after giving birth to our son."

"I thought you said her name is Michelle."

"In this life it is, but to me she'll always be my Dimi."

"Chance, I don't understand."

"What is it you don't understand?" Chance peered at her, noticing for the first time that the woman was very beautiful in her own right. He shook his head. He had no need of her beauty.

"Surely if what you say is true, you had to have experienced death before in order to be reborn."

"I didn't say that we didn't."

"Yes, but you said it was the only lifetime you felt pain."

"Did I say that?" Chance paused thinking over his words, then smiled in Karen's direction. "Excuse me, it was the first time we had died young. Dimi had so much more living to do. She was too young to die. I wasn't ready to live without her."

He felt his throat closing up, the pain of that memory recapturing him, searing him as it had done then. "She was too young," he repeated.

"You found her again in this life, so why aren't you happy. Why aren't you together?"

Now Chance was annoyed. "Weren't you listening to me? I told you that she already had a husband."

"Oh, I'm sorry. I thought you were talking about yourself...that you're her husband."

Karen's voice had become small and she seemed to be disappearing into the wall in her attempt to get away from him. Chance saw it in her eyes, she thought he was becoming unhinged.

"Karen, I'm not crazy. You have no reason to be afraid."

He noticed she paused before she said, "I'm not." Still he didn't miss the backward glance she gave at the door, planning her means of escape no doubt.

"Why is she married to someone else if the two of you were always born knowing the other existed?"

"Something happened this time, something went terribly wrong. We were both searching, but we didn't know for what. I kept hearing her voice for years. It was only after I myself married, that I remembered fully who I was, and I went in search of her."

"This is all so unbelievable."

"Tell me about it."

"How long did it take you to find her?"

"Over twenty years."

"Did she know you?"

"I think she did, even at first, but she didn't want to believe it."

"What did you do to convince a married woman that you were her husband?"

Chance smiled at that, the first real smile since they'd begun the conversation. "I didn't. Our son convinced her, the son she'd never gotten to mother. Together we found him and he made us a family... only..."

"Only her real husband didn't like that."

"I'm her real husband," Chance snarled. "I'm her only husband."

"But you said... you said..."

"Larry is only temporary, until I can think of a way to convince her to leave, that is."

"If what you say is true, have you thought that this time it just might not be your destiny to be with her? Chance, think of the bad karma you'll have for trying to break up a marriage. Do they have children?"

He didn't answer, only glared at her.

"Chance, you want to tear a family apart. What if you're wrong?"

"I'm not wrong." He laughed harshly. "I thought you were the big believer in reincarnation."

"I am. I mean I do believe there's a chance, a real possibility."

She was stuttering. Chance seized her uncertainty and pounced. "It appears you're not as convinced as you claim. Well, Karen, I am convinced, and it doesn't matter what anyone says. Dimi is my wife. I don't give a damn what name she calls herself in this life.

"You once asked me about soul-mates. Well, she's mine, Karen. And to answer your next question, I'm not worried about bad karma, or the next life. I want her, here and now, in this life."

Karen was frowning at him, a look of disgust erasing the curiosity he'd sensed in her moments before. He didn't care. He'd not asked for her pity. She'd been bothering him about his reason for being in India, now that he'd told her, she couldn't take it.

"One of the greatest places on the face of the earth for spiritual cleansing, for awakening, and all you can think to do is plot on destroying the marriage of someone you care about. Is that why you came to India, Chance?"

He glared right back at her. "I came to try and forget how much it hurts to live without her. It isn't working. So, I'm going to find a way to convince her that regardless of the pain to Larry, we belong together. We always have. I'm not worried about some karmic debt. If anything this country has to be hiding a secret way to get around that. When I find it, I'll return and tell her. She'll be more than happy to leave."

"Is she unhappy, Chance?"

"She's not as happy as she would be with me."

"Maybe you're right. Still there are consequences to your actions. You may find what you're looking for, but maybe you should be trying to remember what you've done, what happened in your last life that was different, why wasn't she waiting for you? Have you ever stopped to think, Chance, that maybe you're not with your soul mate because of a karmic debt?"

"Hell yes." He'd thought that a thousand times, only he couldn't figure out what could have been the crime that would exact such a heavy toll.

"Karen, why don't you leave? I'm done."

"You're dismissing me?"

"Karen, just leave, I'm doing my best to be polite to you, but you're making it hard."

She looked at him, anger finally having gotten the better of her. Chance witnessed the crack in her demeanor as she spat the words out at him.

"If this is polite, I sure don't want to be around when you decide to be rude."

He watched as she strode from the room slamming the door behind her in anger. And in anger he went to the treasured photograph of Michelle, Blaine and himself. Slamming the picture to the floor, he shouted. "Damn you, Dimi. And damn karma."

CHAPTER ELEVEN

Shards of glass pierced his finger. Chance looked in horror at what's he'd done. His heart felt as though it had been pierced with the shards of glass. The pain was as real as the pain to his flesh.

"What have I done?" he moaned, bending to retrieve the cherished photo from the ruins. He cleaned away all the broken glass with the sting of tears falling from his lashes. With a sigh, he cleansed and bandaged the cut.

He should be over the tremendous hurt. It had been a year and a half since he'd held Dimi in his arms, since he'd tasted her, known her love. But his memories were more alive than ever and that he couldn't control. He couldn't stop the knowledge that she was his wife.

Chance held the metal frame to his chest, admitting it was the betrayal he felt that hurt him the most. *No that's not it.* The thought flicked across his tortured brain, he tried to push it way but it refused to retreat.

It was jealousy pure and simple. He was jealous that his Dimi was Larry's Michelle, that she could love another man, make a new life for herself, hurt him beyond words. That she was happy was at the crux of the matter, because he knew without a doubt that she was happy.

For twenty years he'd sensed her unhappiness. Now for the past year nothing. She didn't come to him in his dreams anymore to ask him to find him. Not once since she'd gone back to her husband had she called him. He looked at the bracelet on his wrist. Blaine told them that it would bring them all together in the next life. How could it, he thought, when his wife was not yearning for him in this one? What if she just forgot about him completely? What if she changed her mind, decided it was Larry after-all who was her soul mate? What if she spent the next life in his arms also?"

What if, what if? He squeezed his eyes tight against the tears, ashamed for a moment for the thoughts he'd been having. He prided himself on his spiritual maturity. His behavior as of late was a source of contention within his own spirit. Everything he thought he knew, or believed had been turned topsy turvey.

Chance poured a small amount of disinfectant into his own basin, not bothering to look around. He knew from the snickers that he was being watched. He didn't care. When he heard footsteps moving closer to him he had no doubt it was George. Another glance at his bottle and he knew what George was about to say.

"Chance, you're about out of disinfectant aren't you?"

Before answering George he looked a third time at the bottle noting it was only about a quarter full before answering George. "Yeah, I guess I am."

"You're welcome to use what we have." George pointed at the basin that all the other staff was using willingly.

"No, I don't think so," Chance answered. "My son will be sending me supplies, that should hold me until the clinic gets its next shipment."

"As you wish." George smiled at him before looking over his head. Chance turned in the direction that George was looking and saw Sabu staring at him.

"Am I being judged again?"

"Chance, I thought we covered this…oh well." George waved his hand in the air. "No matter. I can assure you you're not being judged. One of the things the Runes teach us is that in order to release the ties that bind us to our pain and unhappiness and stop us from completing our journey, we must release judging."

Right. No judging. He glanced over his shoulder in the direction of Sabu. "You want me to believe you've all given up judging. I don't believe you. I see it in everyone's eyes all the time. Whatever I do someone's there watching with a look of disapproval."

"Perhaps you're right. In that case let's say to not judge is what we're all striving for. If any of us wants to be truly free we must give up judging, comparing and asking why."

Chance lowered his eyes, squinting purposefully around the room. "Then I'm not the only person that needs to work on their spirituality. When I entered your little group yesterday I was an unwanted plague and when I left, again I felt the judging."

"Maybe it was you who was judging us."

"That could be true." Chance smiled warmly. "But it could also be that you were judging me as you're doing now."

"How am I doing that, Chance?"

"Why did you come over here to needle me about the disinfectant?"

"I came to offer you to share in ours."

"I don't think so."

"Why's that?"

"The smirk on your face when you came over."

"I thought I was smiling."

"I thought you were smirking."

Chance dried his hands on his last clean towel. He stood observing George Trammel, looking for a chink in the man's armor. Surely there was not one single person who remained calm all the time. Maybe he had not been in India as long as George, but he was no stranger to the idea of growth. He was tired of being treated as though he was some escaped heathen.

"Do you think we can call a truce here, Chance? Otherwise this could go on all day and I do believe we have enough work to take both our minds off of our hmm... debate."

Chance watched as George turned from him and walked away. Again he'd gotten away with being the bigger man. It irked him that George Trammel was always so smug in his superiority. *Well, if you want him to know you're not ignorant, you'll have stop behaving as though you are. You're going to have to open up.*

The voice startled him for a moment then he looked around the room before realizing the voice came from inside himself. It was Blaine's voice. George was laughing at him before turning toward Sabu.

"Sabu, did you come here to judge Dr. Morgan or did you want something else.?"

"I came to deliver a message. Dr. Morgan there's a package for you in the common room."

Chance was annoyed as he looked over at Sabu, knowing within his heart that if a package had arrived for George Trammel, Sabu would have hustled it over to his room straight away.

"So why didn't you bring it in with you?" Chance asked, not even masking his irritation.

"It was too heavy for me to carry, so I thought it best if you collect it yourself."

With that Sabu went off in a different direction. If the damn package was that heavy then Chance would need help carrying it. The least Sabu could have done was offer to help him bring it back to his room. It wasn't as though the things that were sent to him by his friends and colleagues in the States weren't used for the good of everyone. Sure there might be one or two items he still hoarded, like bottled water, but most of the things he divvied up with the rest of them.

He walked quickly toward the common room thinking it would serve them right if he kept each and every item in the box for himself.

He walked in the room looking around in surprise. There were a few boxes sitting beside the computer with his name on them, but none required the strength of Samson to lift them. That did it. That was his proof Sabu disliked him.

"Hello, Chance."

Chance stood still a moment. He knew the voice was Blaine's. Hell, he heard him talking enough in his head to know his voice when he heard it, but this voice didn't come from inside himself. This voice came from across the room. An excitement began to build. It couldn't be. He turned slowing, praying with all his might that for once his wishes would be granted.

"Blaine."

"Yeah, it's me in the flesh," Blaine teased smiling broadly."

With only two steps Chance bridged the distance and had his arms wrapped around his son. He held him tightly.

"You're going to break my ribs."

"I'm sorry. I'm just so damn glad to see you."

"Yeah, but when you were hugging me, it wasn't me you were thinking about was it?"

"Blaine, don't you ever get tired of being a psychic?" Chance backed away in disgust. "Can't I be happy to see my son?"

"Sure you can. And I didn't mean to imply you weren't happy to see me. I just felt your loneliness. You're still missing her, aren't you?"

Chance refused to answer. As far as he was concerned that was a dumb ass question that didn't deserve an answer.

"Okay, how about if we try something easier? Do I ever tire of being a psychic? I don't know. It's who and what I am. It's not something I can turn on and off at will, but I'll try to refrain from voicing it. Is that acceptable?"

Shaking his head at the smile on Blaine's face, the teasing sound in his voice, he gave into the temptation to hug his son again, only this time not so tightly.

"What the hell are you doing here?"

"Isn't it obvious? I came to visit my father."

Chance stared at his son for a moment, concentrating. "There's something else isn't there? You're worried about me?"

"You might say that, but I wanted to bring you a present and I wanted to deliver it in person."

Blaine held out a medium sized gaily wrapped box to Chance and stood back to watch the expression on his face as he unwrapped the package.

An eight by ten acrylic frame twinkled up at Chance.

"It's unbreakable," Blaine laughed.

"Thanks." Holding the frame to his chest his eyes closed. With every fiber of his being he was calling on his inner strength. He didn't want to cry in front of Blaine, not right now. "Why did you come?" he asked.

"You needed me, didn't you?"

"Yeah, I did," Chance answered opening his eyes ignoring the tears that were slowing seeping from his eyes. "I did need you."

"It's okay," Blaine spoke softly as he walked toward Chance taking the package from his hand. "You didn't finish looking at what I have in here."

Chance watched as Blaine's hands dipped into the box and pulled out a new frame, this one a bit smaller. He felt a small lurch of his heart.

"Here."

He took the picture from Blaine his eyes falling on Blaine with Cassandra and their new baby. He took a long moment hoping his disappointment at not having another picture of Michelle had not shone through.

"You guys look really happy," he managed at last.

"We are."

Chance saw the huge grin that was splitting Blaine's face in two. "So how does it feel?"

"I don't have words to tell you."

"So the baby, is he...?"

"Only time will tell. But for now, I can say, he's a very smart and beautiful baby.

"A little biased, I see."

"Well, I'm not the only one, Cassandra thinks so."

"She would, she's the mother. Let's go to my room."

With their arms around the other's shoulder, Chance and Blaine walked to his room and closed the door. The mood had lightened considerably. It almost seemed part of a dream that he had participated in fighting against powerful psychics seeking to impregnate Cassandra in order for her to produce a super baby, a super psychic.

He glanced sideways at Blaine, remembering how he'd thought his son was insane to have fallen in love with Cassandra Boozer. An ancient prophesy stated that a baby would be born of two twenty-first generation psychics and would be the most powerful psychic the world had ever known. It had been determined that Cassandra was the female psychic the prophesy spoke of. For generations the psychic community had been on high alert, each waiting the prophesy to be fulfilled, each wanting the baby to be born into their family. When Blaine and Cassandra met she was running away form the prophesy and from the male psychics determined to mate with her by any means necessary. The very idea that a powerful group of male psychics, all with twenty-one generations pedigrees were vying for the attentions of one woman was too much to believe. That people were dying in the attempt even more so. Initially Blaine was thought of as the baby psychic no one worried about him because they didn't believe he had the lineage necessary to produce the super gifted baby. There was just one catch. The understanding of the prophesy was wrong. Because of his and Michelle abilities in their previous lives, Blaine was a twenty first generation psychic. It not only put their son in the running to fulfill the prophesy, it put him in danger.

Chance shivered still caught in his memories of the sight he'd walked in on. The fear still remained with him that in one moment he could have lost Michelle and Blaine. Together the three of them had combined their powers. Blaine said they were a psychic trinity, a triad. Whatever they were, they'd combined their powers and had defeated evil. Now all was well in their world.

Well almost. Everyone it seemed, was better off after the battle, but Chance. He'd been left alone.

Again.

He'd received the sharpest of cuts. Michelle thanked him for coming to save their lives from inside the protective enclosure of her husband's arms.

"Chance, don't."

At the sound of Blaine's reprimand Chance glanced up. "I'm trying. I'm doing nothing but trying. Night and day I try to erase her face from my mind. I can't."

"Then stop trying, just be grateful that you found her. You will find her again. You know it's true."

"You didn't come all this way to tell me to do the impossible."

"You're right. I didn't."

"Then besides knowing I needed you, why did you come?"

"I wanted to see the people you were working with, see what was making you so unhappy."

Chance rubbed at his eyes, wondering if he'd given his son the idea that his colleagues were to blame for his depressed state.

"You're fighting so hard not to know."

"Not to know what? What are you talking about? I've done everything you suggested. I've given her space, I haven't tried to contact her, not once."

"I know, but this isn't you, Chance. Your behavior." Sucking in a breathe Blaine paused. "You're bitter and angry. That's not you. You're a loving and forgiving man. Don't allow your hurt to take that away. This isn't who you are and we both know it."

"I have no idea who I am anymore. I thought for most of my life I knew. I wish I could have behaved as Michelle did, just gone on thinking it was a dream— that I didn't know it was all true. I wish I had never remembered her."

"You're lying."

"I'm not so sure. Sometimes when I'm hurting so badly that I want to die, in those moments I wish I'd never known she existed." A shudder went through Chance and he saw the tension in Blaine. "No, Blaine, I'll never will myself to die again. I made you a promise. I was just telling you that there are moments in my life that I wish I hadn't found her."

"And what about me? Do you wish you had never found me?"

"Not once." Chance smiled at his son. "Not one moment have I ever wished that."

"You're wasting a perfect opportunity to find out why you two aren't two together. There must be a reason."

He couldn't help it, Chance laughed at Blaine. "Seems like when you first found us you wanted us to be together. You didn't care about her leaving Larry."

"I was selfish. It wasn't the right thing for any of us."

"You can say that because you get to see her, you're in her life, Blaine. I'm not." Chance roared so loudly that Blaine stunned, took a step away from him.

Chance was glaring at Blaine, not wanting to admit he was jealous of the time Blaine was allowed to spend with Michelle.

"I didn't make things the way they are. But I'm not going to stop seeing her. What is it you want, for my life to be as miserable as yours? I lived one life with one parent. In this life, I have an opportunity to be with both of you. Do you want me to give that up? Tell me Father, what do you want? Are you going to sulk and threaten to not be in my life if I see my mother? Would you take my father away from me again?"

Wincing as though from a physical blow, Chance brought his gaze to rest on Blaine. "That was low."

"And what you're doing to me isn't?"

"I told you how sorry I am that I did it." He'd struck a nerve in his generally calm son. Even now he could see him trying to control his temper. When his deep breathing ceased, Chance was aware he'd lost the battle. Blaine was angry and rightfully so. He was glaring back at him and he didn't blame him.

"You talk about what happened as if it was nothing more than forgetting to send a birthday card. My mother had no choice in her death. You did."

"Blaine. I'm...."

"No, Father, you had a choice. You chose to die, to leave me alone."

As suddenly as he had started, he stopped. "I'm sorry, Chance. I shouldn't have done that. I didn't—"

"Don't," Chance interrupted him. "Don't say you didn't mean it. It's not your fault that you can't forgive me."

The two men stared at each other for a long moment not knowing how to breech the sudden divide. How could they continue going over the problems and hurts from a previous life? If only they didn't remember the hurt and the pain.

"How about showing me around the place?" Blaine smiled limply at Chance.

"Good idea." Once again he'd accept the olive branch from his son. Chance attempted to smile, grateful that Blaine had given him an out once again. There was nothing either of them could do to change what had been done before. With a ton of luck perhaps they would secure their future happiness.

The tour was short and sweet. Chance had introduced Blaine to every colleague they'd come upon. When he saw Karen approaching, for a moment he thought to turn and walk in the opposite direction. He'd been trying to put distance between them, knowing that in spite of her denial she was attracted to him. Shrugging his shoulder because of the inevitable, he kept walking forward. She'd already seen them. To his other colleagues he'd simply introduced Blaine as the world renowned psychic. He'd felt disappointment emanating from Blaine and knew he wondered why he didn't introduce him as his son. Heck, he would have been proud to do so. He just hadn't been sure if Blaine would want that.

"Karen, this is my son. Blaine—" He'd not intended to tell her but the truth tumbled out as so much of the truth about his life seemed to do when he was talking to her.

"Blaine MaDia. This is your son?

"Long story," Blaine said smiling sincerely for the first time since leaving with Chance on the tour of the place.

"So nice to meet you, Karen. I've heard nice things about you—"

"Don't lie. I'm sure you've never heard of me."

"Considering who I am, you shouldn't be so sure of that."

Chance marveled at the speed of Blaine's recovery, surprised he'd been able to forget their disagreement so soon. He noted the look of awe on Karen's face as she talked with Blaine.

"I take it you've heard of Blaine."

"Of course. Who hasn't heard of him? I've followed his career for a number of years." A puzzled look crossed her face. "I thought your bio said you were an orphan, that you were raised in an orphanage. What happened? I mean how?"

Chance and Blaine looked toward each other, Blaine frowning

slightly, looked away. "Another time, Karen," Chance said. "I want to introduce Blaine to a few other people." The color quickly flooded Karen's cheeks forcing Chance to look away. He knew he was being rude, but there was no way he could get into the complicated details of Blaine being his son. He didn't want to explain.

"That wasn't necessary."

He ignored Blaine. It was necessary. Karen was not one to let go of a puzzle and for certain she would find their connection a puzzle. Right then the last thing he needed in his life was to hear one more person tell him what a horrible thing he'd done. The look in Blaine's eyes was more than enough.

"There's George Trammel." Chance headed in his direction, checking to make sure Blaine was following him instead of lingering with Karen. He was.

"George, I want you to meet—"

"Blaine MaDia, Yes, yes... I've seen him on television."

What was he thinking? Of course George Trammel and everyone else would know who Blaine was. Chance looked toward the rear corner of the room and saw Sabu looking in their direction.

Oh no, he thought he's coming this way. And before the thought was completely formed, Sabu was indeed walking toward them a puzzled look creasing his brow.

It was too late. He had no choice but to introduce Sabu. Sabu's smiling face was deep in concentration. He looked first at Chance then at Blaine as Chance made the introductions.

For the next hour every single person in the room came up to Blaine. Chance had stopped attempting to introduce him as it was obvious Blaine needed no introduction.

After the last person strolled away with promises and assurances that Blaine would be around for a while Chance looked the group over coolly before his gaze caught the look that Blaine was wearing. Another reprimand, he could feel it coming. "What's wrong?"

"Why do you automatically assume something is wrong every time I look at you?"

The reprimand was there, but Blaine was smiling, teasing, making Chance smile back at him in return. "You've got that look on your face that tells me I'm in for a lecture."

"I'm just curious about the people you're working with. I find them so fascinating. They're all open to learning. I would have thought this would have been the perfect group for you to be with."

"They're too damn nosy," Chance replied, staring after the departed group.

"Have you ever thought that maybe they're interested in you and your journey?"

"Well my journey is my journey. If I want to share don't you think I would volunteer the information?"

"Some do, some don't. They wouldn't know if they didn't ask. Chance, you're not giving them a clue. Take Sabu, I'd love to spend some time with him. I find him the most interesting of all."

"Him? He hates me. You must be kidding. I told you how he is."

"Since I'm a thinking adult, I don't choose to make my opinions of others based on biased information. I don't understand the problems you're having with him, but he invited me to come to one of his sessions. It sounds like fun."

Chance could only stand in front of Blaine and stare, amazement sinking in. His son, there for little over an hour had won over the one person above all others who hated his being in India.

"What? Weren't you invited to go?"

"No, I wasn't. It doesn't matter. I'm not interested."

Blaine blinked quickly. Chance couldn't fail to miss it. He rushed to explain before Blaine could make the offer. "Don't worry, you go ahead. They know I'm not into that."

"Chance come on. What do you mean you're not into that? You of all people. You've probably experienced more than most of these people ever will. You're rare, don't you know that? There are not many people who can remember their past lives in vivid detail. Truly, you're a rarity."

"I do feel rare."

"I meant that in a good way. Think of the things we've been through in the past year. Our entire family has been reunited. We have been given a second chance."

"Do you truly believe that?"

"Chance, you found Michelle and you found me. Things may not be the way you want them but, they're the way they are for a reason. Maybe you should try harder to find a way to understand what happened, why you're not with her now."

"Don't you think I'm doing that? I've done nothing since she left but try and make it right."

"No, that's not true. You've done nothing but try and see what you can do in this life to make her yours again. It's not going to happen. She's married to Larry, she's going to remain married to him. Chance, please don't make me say it. She loves him."

Feeling the darkness rolling in, clouding his vision, rendering him cold, Chance took a deep breath then another hoping to cleanse his soul by breathing in. He turned away not wanting Blaine to read his thoughts as easily as seeing the light go out of his eyes.

"Chance."

"Blaine, do me a favor, whatever you do, don't read my mind, not now."

"I wasn't going to."

The tiny seeds of an idea came to him. "Blaine, did you really come because I needed you?"

"Of course."

"Then maybe you could help me find the cause, the reason, perhaps if I did I wouldn't be so...." He couldn't finish the thought. There was nothing that was going to take away his pain. Rubbing at the bracelet on his wrist before glancing at the identical one Blaine wore he couldn't stop the grimace of pain that creased his face.. "I'm so afraid this isn't going to work." He looked down at the silver band

"We have to believe it will but we have to start doing something to make sure."

"That's what I'm trying to do. Tell me how."

"I can't."

"Do you know what I need to do?"

Blaine didn't answer.

"Are you saying you know what I did wrong, what I have to change in order to ensure my life with my wife, so the next time she doesn't come back looking for Larry or someone else?"

"I have a guess." Blaine answered Chance awkwardly, his eyes averted, he was doing everything in his power to avoid direct contact.

"Do you plan on making me beg you for the answer?" Chance's voice was cold, harsh. There was an edge of steel to it that had never been there when he was talking to Blaine. Now it was. "You're saying you know what I can do and you don't plan on telling me?"

"I could tell you, but I don't think it's meant to go that way. I think you're meant to learn it for yourself. It's like you said before, it's a journey, your journey, and there are just certain things you're meant to accomplish alone. If you asked something that wouldn't hurt your growth I would be more than happy to tell you. But this, I think if I tell you the effect will not be the same. You will not have grown. You will only have learned."

"What's the difference? Either way I have to learn."

"But first you must grow."

Chance's eyes closed and he rubbed his head. Shaking his head in astonishment he debated if behaving as though he were a three year old throwing a tantrum would have any effect on his son.

"Isn't there any way we can have a good visit without Michelle? I really value our time together and I don't want to lose that."

The underlining sound of loneliness in Blaine's voice hit Chance. He swung his head back around to face his son. "You're right." Then he forced a smile to his lips. "A few hours ago I would have given anything to have you here with me, now look at me. You must think I'm ungrateful."

There were tiny lines, new ones he'd not noticed before etched around the corners of Blaine's lips, worry lines and there was no doubt in his mind that his son's preoccupation with him had put the lines on his face.

"I bet anything your new bride could have killed you when you told her you were coming here."

Blaine smiled.

"Of course she could. I don't blame her. Tell me everything, I want to know what you've been doing. Tell me every new detail of the baby's life. Bring out that wallet you've being dying to show off."

He laid an arm casually across Blaine's shoulder, noticing as he did so that his son's smile became genuine and his hand reached into a pouch around his waist. He pulled out a miniature album bulging with pictures of his wife and son.

"Just a couple of pictures," Blaine grinned.

"I can see that." Chance reached for them, knowing this was what he should have done in the first place. It was definitely going to be hard to do the right thing for the next life when he kept screwing up so badly the things he was doing in this one.

CHAPTER TWELVE

Three days. Three days of having his son in the same country as he, yet he'd spent only a few hours talking to Blaine. The entire compound enthralled had cornered Blaine lassoing his time.

Chance was a bit miffed, at his colleagues for taking so much of Blaine's time. He was annoyed with Blaine for being so accommodating. And lastly, he was annoyed at himself for being jealous of Blaine's time. As badly as he hated to admit it those were exactly the feelings he was having. That knowledge irritated the hell out of him, destroyed the last vestige of his own self-image. For over a quarter of a century he'd thought himself enlightened, proud, knowing everyone had their own destiny and he would not dare to change it. Now his behavior sickened him. He was something he'd never been: rude, disrespectful and mean. His dignity lay in shreds.

Sitting on his hard straw mattress, he sighed in disgust. Shaking his head and slowly glancing around the room at his surroundings he rested his gaze on the cherished photo of the woman who'd haunted his dreams all those years. Even with her he'd attempted to retain his dignity. It wasn't until the very end when he'd known she was not going to spend the rest of this life with him that he'd been reduced to begging. Still, he'd acquiesced in the end, letting her go, allowing her to live her life with Larry, to fulfill her destiny. She'd convinced him along with immense help from Blaine that it was what was meant to be in order for them to be reunited in the next life.

Chance fingered the bracelet he wore. Blaine's idea of what would link the three of them throughout eternity. Supposedly powerful, it would allow them to proceed into the next life with their memories intact. Only no one had told him how the bracelets were to survive. Were they supposed to come out of the womb wearing jewelry?

He almost laughed, knowing how obstinate he was being. The jewelry was used as a soul conductor, encoding his life into his DNA, his memories and his love. And then when the time was right somehow they would recover not only the bracelets but each other.

If it worked.

So how had he gotten from such a state of enlightenment to where he was now? An almost bitter man, surely unhappy and now childishly jealousy because this son he'd known only a short time was not spending enough time with him. He couldn't blame Michelle for not wanting to be with him.

Almost.

The familiar stab of pain to his heart stopped him abruptly from continuing those thoughts. He stood for several seconds not sure what to do. Today was his day off and the rarity of the situation was that there was no overload of patients. He couldn't volunteer to help, there was nothing for him to do.

Without thinking he headed out the door and down a worn path, thinking perhaps a walk would clear his head, help him put things in perspective. He could feel his lips pulling and wondered why the thought of walking was making him smile.

It took no longer than a millisecond for that smile to turn into a half frown. Straight in front of him was Blaine talking animatedly with Sabu. Every instinct in him told him to turn and run, but he couldn't make his feet obey. Too late. Blaine turned slightly, acknowledging his father with a smile and a wave of his hand. Chance had no choice but to continue forward.

"Hello, Doctor Morgan," Sabu greeted.

"Hey," was all Blaine said smiling broadly.

"Hello yourself," Chance answered Blaine pretending not to have heard Sabu. He wanted to say, 'hello stranger,' but restrained himself. There was no need in everyone knowing he was behaving as a child.

"Dr. Morgan, I have something for you. Your son thought you might like it." Sabu smiled warmly at Blaine but his smile dropped a tiny bit when he turned toward Chance.

"I'm sorry I've been so hard on you. It's just that I could see the wasted potential in you from the moment I picked you up at the airport. I'm human also. I reacted. I saw you didn't really want to be in my country and I should have understood that your not wanting to be here is part of your destiny."

He held out his hand toward Chance, who was frowning slightly in Blaine's direction. What was this about? His son going to the class bully and asking him to play nicely with him. Disgust filled Chance at the thought. The hatred he could take. But pity? No way, no thanks.

He stared into Sabu's weathered brown hand. Another stone. What was this? He was going to have an entire set of Runes before he left India.

He took the stone from Sabu observing the markings. What looked like two boomerangs facing each other had no meaning to him. He looked toward Blaine whose bright smile told him that these simple markings would no doubt have some profound meaning.

"Thanks," he finally muttered, the words sounding forced, as if he'd choked them out.

Sabu and Blaine stared at him for a moment identical quizzical looks on their faces before they both erupted into laughter.

"Chance, there is hope for you yet." Blaine laughed as Sabu walked away. "I saw that look by the way."

"What look?"

"Oh, you rolling your eyes in disgust. But you did take it. And you did say thank you. That's the first step."

"Has Sabu converted you?"

"Why are you asking me that?"

"Well, you have been spending an awfully lot of time with him, it seems. Hell, to be honest it seems as if you came all the way to India to visit Sabu"

Blaine smiled, throwing an arm around Chance's shoulder. "I'm sorry. I guess I have been neglectful."

"No, don't worry about it. Hey, if you find the guy fascinating by all means you should spend time with him. Besides, you didn't come all this way to hold my hand." Damn why had he allowed his feelings to rise and tumble out? They were always so close to the surface, but never had he lost control. Now he truly was disgusted. He twisted away from Blaine, causing his son's arm to fall away from his shoulder.

"Chance, I wasn't spending time with Sabu because I didn't want to be with you. I want to help you as much as I can, as much as I'm allowed." He hesitated, "It's your journey, but I can't help wanting to make it easier for you. Sabu has been teaching me how to read the Runes."

Chance held the stone out toward Blaine. "This is supposed to help me?"

"It can, yes. Besides I think you'll like this meaning."

"How did you learn all about this so quickly?"

"Sabu's a good teacher."

"Good for Sabu."

"He doesn't hate you," Blaine laughed. "In fact it's quite the opposite. He likes you, likes your spirit, feels sorry about your pain."

A flash of annoyance claimed Chance's features, not quite anger, but stronger than being just plain miffed. "You didn't tell him did you?"

"About Michelle? Of course not. But did you think it was some big secret that you're hurting? Your pain is so obvious. The brusque manner in which you treat your colleagues, the standoffishness. Those are not your character traits and it shows. It's like a coat you put on that's many sizes too large. It doesn't fit."

Here we go, Chance thought and he was right.

"Chance you're probably right that the people here have pushed a little too hard prying into things that you don't wish them to know. That often happens with new converts to spiritual teachings. They find something and they want to share. In your case they believe they've found the answers they believe may help you. They've found peace and they want you to have it."

Chance looked over Blaine's head. There was no one here in India that could give him peace. But would that stop Blaine from trying? Of course not.

"They want to help you. Chance. None of them hate you. They all like you very much."

"What have you been doing, Blaine, trying to garner support for me? Don't bother. I won't be here long enough for any of it to matter."

"Even a day of unwarranted pain is a day too long. I told you I came to help and I couldn't very well help if I don't see what kind of people you're working with."

"So, they're all on the right path and I'm not?"

"I'd say you're much farther along on your journey than any of them. You've just allowed yourself to become derailed. Loss does that sometimes, but you have to go through this and come out on the other side."

Chance ran his hands through his hair repeatedly, tangling it in the process. "I don't get it. I am going through this. I've been going through it for over a year now."

"Chance, you're existing, not learning from the experience, you're bitter and hurting and you refuse to heal yourself. You can do it if you focus."

For the first time something Blaine said made sense. Chance

thought about it. He really didn't want to feel better. What was the point? The rest of his life he would be alone. Why pretend there was joy in that prospect?

"Father, you don't have to be alone. That too is your choice."

What kind of answer was he supposed to give? He glanced at his son knowing Blaine was only trying to be helpful. Hell, he'd gone way out of his way to be helpful. Coming to India was definitely out of the way.

"Blaine, is that what this is about? You've decided I need a woman in my life and came to help find me one?"

"Not really. But from the look on your face it was very easy to figure out what you were thinking."

"I'll bet," Chance muttered under his breath. "Sure that's how you knew."

"I promised I wouldn't invade your thoughts and I haven't, but I can't help it if information comes to me can I?"

That one didn't require an answer. Chance shook his head slowly, feeling his face wrinkling against his will. He held his hands slightly above his head in mock surrender. "I give. Tell me, what does the Rune say?"

For a moment father faced son and neither of them spoke. Chance had learned in the short time he'd been reunited with Blaine some of his characteristics. It was obvious he was miffed that Chance wasn't showing the Runes the proper respect, perhaps a bit disappointed that things weren't going as he'd hoped.

"Blaine, you're a psychic, tell me, did you really see this as being easy when you decided to come here?"

Chance watched as his question sunk in, then the crinkle began around the corners of Blaine's eyes and a smile broke out on his face. Chance smiled too. It would be okay.

"No, I didn't. Still I had to hope, I'm only human remember."

For a brief moment Chance saw Blaine not as the man he was but as the little boy he'd been, the son he'd loved and protected from before. He'd not done enough, he'd not given his son the one thing that would have made his life easier: A father. If only in his last incarnation he had not willed himself to die. If only he had not left his son alone, to fend for himself. If only Blaine had not carried that past life memory, here with him to this life.

"I thought you would be alright, you were there, on the brink. A fine young man. I knew you would marry and have children. I believed you would have a good life. I didn't think you needed me anymore. I thought it would be safe to allow you to fly unattended."

"I know," Blaine answered him.

Chance looked directly at Blaine now. He was going to ask the question he'd not had the courage to ask before. He ran his tongue across his lips pulling his upper lip into his mouth. Still the asking came hard.

"Why did you think I did it?"

He watched as Blaine's eyes clouded over becoming moist and he wished he hadn't asked. "Did you think I did it because I didn't love you?"

"Partly. I knew you loved me, just not enough, never enough. It didn't matter what I would have done, there was no way for me to replace her, no way for me to take over that part of your heart that belonged to her."

"I wish you didn't remember the whole thing so clearly."

"Ironic isn't it?" Blaine asked, "That I should remember everyday of that life yet not remember a thing about the woman who gave birth to me in this life."

"It wasn't that I didn't love you, Blaine, it was just..."

"Chance maybe you should start by admitting the truth to yourself. No one can ever take her place. That's not a bad thing."

"If it isn't bad why are you forever after me to forget her?"

"I've never told you to forget her. That would be impossible. I've only ask you to let her go."

"I did."

"Not psychically Chance, let her go from your heart. Acknowledge the pain you're in. I'm not asking you to deny it. Acknowledge it and learn from it, then release her, free yourself to live again."

Chance swallowed, closing his eyes. He breathed in as his fingers tightened around the Rune.

"What is this?" he asked changing the subject. "What does it mean?"

"That's the rune of harvest."

"I get it, now I'm going to reap what I sowed. I left you and now I'll be left alone." Chance laughed sharply and without mirth. Blaine wasn't joining in. He could tell from the stubborn set of his son's jaw that he saw nothing amusing in the situation.

"Chance, whenever this rune is drawn it's a sign of hope. That's a good thing. It shows beneficial outcomes to whatever endeavors you've committed yourself to."

"Good. Then if I chose to stay on my course, I'll be successful."

"Are you serious?"

"I'm just asking."

"The Runes are purely intuition. It was pulled for you. You alone know the answer it means for you. Should you continue on your chosen path, to destroy Michelle and Larry's marriage, it's possible that you will be successful.

"Michelle loves you as much as you love her. I'm sure if she had any idea how miserable you're making yourself she would not hesitate on throwing away what she knows would be a wrong decision for both of you. But I do believe she'd ignore the truth the damage would do and come to you in order to end your pain."

"In spite of her turning me away, her making a new start with Larry, her loving him, you still believe there's a chance she'd come to me if I needed her?"

"Yes. Even now I believe if you asked, she would come to you, but at what cost? That's what you have to ask yourself, Father. What is the price? Are you willing to gamble on a few stolen years and possibly destroy what could be centuries together? Are you that immature and that selfish that you would deny all of us a chance at a full life together?"

"We don't know for sure."

"We do. How many lives can you remember spending with her, eleven, twelve?"

"More," Chance answered softly.

"Then you know you'll find her again."

Chance breathed deeply. So deeply in fact, it felt as if he'd pulled the air that lingers between the very bursa sacs hidden in between his toes, even that minuscule amount of air had been inhaled.

He could feel the wavy motion moving through his limbs warming in his belly, detouring there, then splitting off and continuing up his arms only to dip and meet up again in his lungs. He expelled the air out in one long sigh. "Don't think I haven't noticed that you play the 'Father' card to your advantage."

"I do what I have to do in order to make sure you hear me. And

I've noticed when I call you Father you are more attentive, a bit more patient. Perhaps I should stop calling you Chance altogether.

"Is that all the Rune has to say, that I will be successful?"

"No, there's more."

Blaine's voice was cracking. Chance had seen him blinking furiously trying to keep the tears away. Immediate love for his son overwhelmed him. Tears were catching at the back of his throat. He pulled in a hard breath and waited for Blaine to continue.

"This isn't going to be an easy task, nor will it be quick. The Rune also stands for one year, a full cycle, a span of time before you can reap of the harvest."

"Are you saying I have to go through this pain for another year? In a year I'll be able to let her go?"

"That's just symbolic. I don't know how long it will take. I only know that you have to try."

"What if I can't find the key to doing this?"

"That's the beauty of it, Chance. You've already laid down the ground work from your many years of studies. Just remember the things you already know and draw from that."

"What I already know?" Chance spoke softly his thoughts going inward, his eyes focused on his son. "Isn't there anything else you can give me, some little hint?"

"Just this, the stone also offers encouragement. Know that the outcome is in the keeping of providence and continue to persevere."

"That's the hard part isn't it?" Chance smiled slightly, his eyes unmoving from Blaine's face. "I want to be the master of my fate, but you tell me it's in the hands of providence. That's a hell of a thing to know. That's a very shredded rope you just threw to a drowning man."

"But never-the-less, it is a rope." Blaine smiled back. "It is a rope."

CHAPTER THIRTEEN

One week of serenity. It was a gift and Chance accepted it as such. Since Blaine's arrival the entire tone of the place had changed. George Trammel, Karen and Sabu were forever seen engaging Blaine in conversation.

Chance smiled at the way people would gravitate toward Blaine and the easy way Blaine handled it. No longer did he mind the time his son spent with the others because some unspoken boundaries had been established. The nights belonged to father and son alone.

Those nights were what made the week serene for Chance. They would talk long into the wee hours of the mornings, Blaine mindful that Chance would have to work hard the next day. Chance not caring, only wanting this time with his son.

"You're looking awfully happy these days."

Looking down into Karen's smiling face, he didn't deny it. He was happy. "Yeah, I suppose I am."

"You love him a lot don't you?"

"Blaine? Of course I do." Chance puzzled over her statement for a moment. "Oh, I see, you don't believe the past life son part?"

"No, that's not true. I do believe it. You searched for your son, didn't you?"

Chance licked at his lips. "I wasn't searching for the son I left behind. I didn't remember him." He lifted his eyes to Karen. "It's hard to forgive myself for not searching for him. He was searching for us."

"But you remember him now."

"Yes."

"I never met anyone before you who remembered their past life, let alone found people they'd known. I think you're being too hard on yourself. You remember him now. That's all that matters. Forgive yourself."

Karen was watching him, something strange in her gaze. For a moment, just a moment, Chance wanted to accept the comfort she was offering. It had been so long and he was so damn tired of being lonely, for he knew Blaine would leave soon. He had to. He had a son and a wife waiting for him.

"It must be really hard to not be able to forgive yourself for something you did in a previous life." She smiled at him. "I'm glad I can't remember any other incarnations. It would be impossible. Be happy you remembered your wife and searched for her."

"I think that's the part that hurts Blaine the most, he's never admitted it, we've never even talked about it, but still it's there. I was only looking for my wife. I love him, but I don't know if my love now will ever make up to him for all the hurt. He can't forgive me, not really, so I can't forgive myself. He says he has, he even thinks he has. But he hasn't"

"What about his mother? Your wife? Did she? I mean was she searching for a lost son?"

"No."

"Was she searching for you?"

"Only in her dreams." Something he'd almost forgotten came to him. Michelle's dreams had not been just of him, she'd dreamt of her son, crying out for him. He remembered now. It was what caused the friction in her marriage. It was what made Larry threaten to have her committed if she didn't stop talking about her lost son and reprimanding her that the only son she had was theirs. How could he possibly have forgotten all of that? He didn't have time to sort it all out now, but he'd have to sort it out. It was important, the reason why Blaine had completely forgiven his mother and not him lay in that memory. Shaking his head slightly to clear away the memory, he refocused on Karen. "She didn't do a physical search for me."

"Does Blaine feel less loved by her because she was only looking for you?"

A sound half way between a grunt and a laugh erupted uninvited from between Chance's lips. "No, because when he first touched her he relived the experience of his mother's death with her. He heard her pleading with me to love the baby, he felt her love. And he knew that he was wanted that he was the most special gift to her."

"And you, Chance, what did he feel from you?"

"Anger and sorrow that he was here, and my wife was leaving."

Chance stopped speaking. He was looking directly at Karen, but not seeing her. Instead he saw the scene as it had been before, his Dimi, their infant son, the blood. And as always he felt the torrent of hurt rushing in.

"Do you wish you'd never met him again in this life?"

"Never met him? Are you crazy? Of course I'm glad to have found him. It's a miracle. Why would you ask me such a thing?"

"Because it would be so much easier for you if you'd never known. You wouldn't be constantly bogged down with guilt."

"I'm thrilled to have found my son again in this life, to have the opportunity to make it up to him for the things I didn't do before. Yes, I suppose there is some guilt with our relationship. There would have to be. Do you know of anyway for me to release it?"

"Yeah, but there's no way that you'll go for it."

Chance thought for a moment, frowning in concentration. Then he remembered The Ganges. "That polluted water! Hell no. You're right. I'll just have to learn to live with the guilt." Without so much as a nod, he walked away from Karen in search of his son.

Basking in the pleasure of having Blaine to himself for once, Chance was content to answer the guarded questions his son was throwing at him in the guise of innocent query.

"I see you're getting along better with your colleagues."

"That's because you're here. Somehow you've managed to cast a spell over them. Believe me it's not usually this peaceful around here."

Blaine smiled, his look mischievous. Chance knew without him uttering a word what was coming.

"You talked to Karen for quite a while today. She told me earlier that you talk to her as little as possible. Why is that, do you think?"

His eyes were twinkling and his voice was playful but underneath Chance knew Blaine was asking him a serious question and he was well aware of what the question was. "Before you start fantasizing, I'm not falling for her. I don't want her."

"It would be okay if you did. Chance, you need someone in your life. You need a woman in your heart and in your bed."

"I already have a woman in my heart. Just so you know, it's not Karen."

"You need a woman you can touch."

"Blaine, cut it out. She's not interested. She told me herself. She has no desire to become involved."

"That's what she may have told you, but I see the way she looks at you when she thinks no one is watching."

"She loves puzzles, that's all I am to her. Either that or she feels sorry for me and wants to be the one to save me."

"That wasn't a look of pity I saw in her eyes." Blaine grinned at his father. "I know that look. With just a hint of encouragement you could turn a smoldering ember into a roaring flame."

"She's not my type. I have zero interest in her."

"She's single."

For a long moment Chance was quiet, perplexed about the conversation he was having with his son.

"I was sure Karen would be right for you."

"Stop."

"Okay, but there aren't any other unattached women here at the clinic."

"Blaine, I swear you're tenacious. Are you a psychic or a pimp? Stop trying to set me up. It's not going to happen."

"Maybe not Karen, maybe it's too weird. Perhaps when you return home you can go out with one of the nurses from the hospital, or one of the doctors. It doesn't have to be emotional if you're both in agreement. It can be purely physical."

"Now, you really do sound like a pimp."

For nearly a minute the men laughed easily together before Chance stopped, his voice and face once again serious. He shook his head slowly. "I can't."

"Why, Chance?"

"It would feel like I'm cheating on Michelle."

"Michelle is married. Besides, she told you she wanted you to be happy, to find someone else."

Chance watched as Blaine got up from the extra cot that had been brought into the small room for his use. His pace was quick. He was agitated and Chance could feel the lecture coming on. He braced himself for it.

"Damn it, Chance, don't you ever get horny?"

Horny. That was the last word he'd expected out of Blaine's mouth. He started laughing. "I don't believe you just asked me that."

"Well, do you?"

"I don't think I've thought of it in those terms, but let's just say I'm not dead."

"Good."

Blaine was looking pleased with himself, strutting about like a peacock, making Chance laugh even harder. "That's what you've been waiting to hear, that I get horny?"

"No, that you're not dead. Hallelujah. Now it's time you started acting like it."

With a groan Chance offered a compromise. "I am ready to live again in some areas. Since you're learning to read the Runes, would you mind teaching me?" Pride shone from Blaine's eyes before he rushed to hug him. A smile broke out on Chance's face as he returned the embrace. He was enjoying having done something his son approved of.

After his conversation with Blaine, things begin to slowly shift inside Chance's soul. As he worked during the day there was an underlying peace. There were even moments of unexplained joy. He wasn't exactly sure what it was, but things felt lighter. To his amazement he realized for the first time in a long while he was truly interested in learning something new. He wasn't just running in place. And since wanting to learn the Runes had brought a smile to Blaine's face, he knew he'd made the right choice.

Later that evening when it was his time with his son he found himself on edge wondering what stone he'd pull and what it would mean. The moment Blaine joined him in his room he nearly pounced on him.

"Did you tell Sabu why you wanted to borrow the Runes?"

"No, but I think he could figure it out if he wanted to. I don't think he cares who want to use them, only that they offer some help."

"So what do we do?"

Blaine sat on one end of Chance's straw mattress ignoring the discomfort. The Runes in a gray, felt bag lay between them. A book containing their meanings lay close to Blaine's thigh.

"It depends on what you want to know, what kind of reading you're after. What do you think?"

"I don't know. Both times I've been given stones others have pulled without my permission. I'm just wondering what I would get if I pulled it myself."

"Then let's do it."

Chance stared at the bag. Sure, he'd studied many different philosophies. Those were to him a matter of science. That his son was a psychic and he himself possessed such gifts—those facts he could understand. But this putting his hand into a bag and learning something about himself...He took in a deep breath and sighed. He doubted, so he just sat, not moving toward the bag.

"Chance, they're not going to bite you. And you're not going to hell for doing this. It's not fortune telling. It merely puts you in touch with your unconscious self. It's your own intuition that makes this such a valuable tool. Try it. If you don't think it makes sense, you don't ever have to do it again."

Slowly Chance reached toward the bag, thinking nothing good could come of this. Every time he'd come in contact with the Runes, it seemed that others thought he was lacking in something. He could only imagine what would happen.

"Chance, what's wrong?"

"I'm not sure."

"Is it that you don't want to do it? You don't even have to tell me your question. I should have thought of that. If you want privacy you can read the meaning in the book. You don't need me."

Chance swallowed. "I do need you. I want you here for this."

"Then what's the problem?"

Chance smiled. "You didn't tell me what to do."

"Sorry. Just think of an issue, something, like, 'what is it I need now at this moment in my life?' And see what Rune you pull."

Simple enough. Chance again approached the bag as if it might bite. He put his hand into it, first feeling the side of the warm fabric before letting it slide down into the bottom. Once there, he allowed the coolness of the stones to brush against his hand. He played with them, his eyes closed, concentrating on what he needed to learn. When he was ready he pulled a stone from the bag and laid it in front of Blaine.

"So give me the bad news."

Blaine smiled in earnest. "There is no bad news. The Runes are strictly to help, not to accuse."

"Harrumph."

"What was that?"

"Never mind," Chance muttered. "Tell me what this means."

He looked at the markings that were making no sense to him. It looked like a very badly drawn X by a preschooler.

"This is Nauthiz. It represent constraint, necessity and pain."

"It figures," Chance groaned.

"Yours is reversed."

"How can you tell?" He noticed the raised brow which of his son which indicated he wasn't going to answer the question.

"Nauthiz is the great teacher disguised as the bringer of pain and limitation. It has been said that when we reach the darkest point in our live only then can we recognize the light."

"Then that should describe where I'm at right now. I don't think things could ever be darker than they are right now: At this moment."

Blaine smiled. "I hope you're right."

"I have to be." Chance looked away. "So what exactly do I have to do to go to the light? Does the stone tell you that?"

"Well, it doesn't tell me, but it tells you."

"Don't get technical. What does the rest of it mean?"

"It means that a cleansing is required. In doing so, the will, will be strengthened."

"Any suggestions?"

"Yeah start with the hardest thing and proceed to those that aren't as hard. Either way you're advised by the Rune to remember that suffering really means undergoing. You're not really suffering in a very real sense. You're just going through something or undergoing a change that you, your spirit self need."

"And?" Chance knew there was an and, or a but coming. He could tell from the way he pursed his lips that Blaine was thinking how to put the rest of the meaning to him.

"Well."

"Well what? I'm a big boy I can take it."

"Well, you have to learn to control your anger, restrain your impulses."

"How important is all of this?" Chance teased.

"Extremely. I would say that doing these things is essential when you're facing challenges."

"Of course, why wouldn't it be? Like I said, Blaine, you're not giving me a lot to hang on to. That rope you threw me is getting thinner and even more frayed."

"And like I said, Chance, at least it's a rope."

"I want to pull another stone." Chance teased Blaine half expecting him to say no. Instead what he heard was, "Go ahead."

He stared at Blaine, curiosity pulling at him. "Are you sure that's permitted? I mean you've only been studying these Runes for a few days."

"I'm sure. Why? Are you afraid of what you might pull next?"

That was a challenge Chance heard in his son's smiling voice. And if he had any doubt at all the sly smirk was enough to give it away. Blaine thought he wouldn't do it. With great flourish, Chance reached for the bag only to have Blaine pull it away.

"I thought you said it was okay for me to choose another stone."

"It is, but you can't just do it without any thought or preparation. At least frame a question in your mind."

"What if I don't have any questions?" Chance countered.

"That's a great place to start. Ask the Rune what it is that you need."

"Fine." Chance mock growled, reaching his hand again toward the bag. "I know what it is that I need and so do you." Blaine stared back at him unblinking.

"Let's see the stone," Blaine demanded and Chance lifted the dusty -colored stone from the bag and laid it in the palm of his left hand.

A smile covered Blaine's face from ear to ear turning into a full-fledged grin in a matter of seconds. "I'd say you have your answer, Chance."

Glancing at Blaine, then at the stone, not knowing what the marking meant, Chance waited for an explanation, something more than the laughter he was getting. When none was forthcoming, he was forced to ask. "What is it? What stone did I draw this time?" he asked with a slight nervous twang.

"It's the stone of wholeness. You need to be whole."

CHAPTER FOURTEEN

"Chance, stop fighting so hard to deny what you know to be true. I need you to be happy. I need you to live." Michelle smiled at him, her lips mere inches away. *"I need you to be whole."*

"Dimi," Chance called out to Michelle, moving to touch her. And just like that she was gone. Another dream. *What the hell is happening?* Chance thought, rubbing his hands roughly over the faint beginning of a beard. Glancing toward Blaine's cot he was relieved to see no movement from that side of the room. He hadn't disturbed his son. Now he could examine his dream without Blaine's input.

First the Rune, now Michelle and they both talked of the need for him to be made whole. Chance glanced at the luminous dial of the alarm clock. It was three A.M. .His eyes continued their journey across the room until they rested on Blaine's cot again. Adjusting his eyes to the darkness, he noticed something he'd not seen before. He'd not woken Blaine because his son was not in the room.

Where the hell could he be? They'd talked until well after one, when Chance had finally fallen asleep. Blaine was undoubtedly with Sabu.

The thought made him at once angry and proud. Angry that the man so fascinated his son, proud that his son was able to grasp all the knowledge that he himself had come here for.

So many thoughts were running through his head, thoughts he wanted to deny but no longer could. He felt as though a stranger was inside his own body. Someone who was stretching the skin to fit and finding it confining.

He thought of Salvatore, one of the world's most powerful psychics, and a rival after the woman who'd become Blaine's wife.

Out of pride, Salvatore had allowed a demented entity to inhabit his body and had not been able to wrest it from the fiend's control without help. He wondered if Salvatore felt the same as he was feeling now. Doing things foreign to him, behaving in a manner not his own.

A tremor stole through him. It was time to right things within his body. It was time he began to accept things as they were.

Chance sat up on the cot, no longer thinking but reacting. He reached out a hand to retrieve the picture of his family from the small container that served as a dresser. It was so dark in the room there was no way for him to clearly make out the faces. But it didn't matter. He saw them through the eyes of love, and he traced their images with the tips of his fingers, imprinting them on his very soul.

"I'll always love you Dimi. But I think you're right. I've got to stop this period of mourning, or I'm going to lose my son and myself as well." His fingers lingered on the far left corner of the picture where he knew Blaine was standing, smiling out at him.

His son needed to know that in this lifetime he was important to his father. Chance would not wither away and die. He would live, for his son, for Michelle and for himself. Blaine was a highly evolved psychic, but he hadn't become that without help. He and Michelle were his parents. Their gifts were what Blaine had inherited. He took in a breath. He would be happy that Blaine was getting things from his trip that his soul required. He would stop behaving in a possessive, jealous manner. Turning back toward the wall, he replaced the picture to its original spot and went back to sleep, this time filled with peace.

It wasn't until the next night that he got more than a few minutes to spend with Blaine. He'd reached a decision. He would make every moment of the visit count. He would return to the world of the living and he would search for the things his soul needed in order to heal. With determination he began "I think I'll go to Sabu's next lesson' with you." Chance couldn't help but notice the surprised look on Blaine's face.

He almost laughed at the way he was being observed. Why shouldn't Blaine be suspicious of his motives? When they went to bed the night before there had been no indication in Chance's words that his feelings about Sabu had changed.

During the long days' work he'd not seen his son. Blaine couldn't possibly know of his decision to come into himself, to reenter his own skin.

"Chance, are you still feeling...well... a. little jealous of Sabu? You don't have to be. Really."

He smiled at his son. He was trying so hard to protect his feelings .A tiny stab of guilt pierced him, guilt that he'd thrust Blaine into the role of parent caring for the child. That wasn't what he wanted. It was not the relationship he craved from his son this second time around.

"I'm not jealous, Blaine. I just thought I'd like to come along. I did come to India to learn, didn't I?"

"I thought you came to serve."

"Both. For by serving we learn."

Blaine was thrown off guard, it was obvious. The wide eyed stare lasted a brief millisecond before he burst into laughter followed by Chance's deep voice laughing with him.

"Are you serious?" Blaine asked, "Do you really want to listen to Sabu?"

"Yeah, I'm serious. You don't have to wait until I fall asleep and sneak away to talk with him. It's okay." Blaine blushed easily at Chance's words, but the smile remained.

"Sabu's been telling me about the ceremony in February, the cleansing away of all the sins of the past. I was thinking about coming back to do it."

Chance eyebrow's arched and his mouth quickly turned downward in disgust. "Did Sabu tell you that you will be doing this among the remains of cremated bodies?"

"He did."

"And you still want to try this?"

"The concept sounds appealing. Maybe I'll bring Cassandra back with me and both of us will do it." He smiled then, "I just might bring the baby, give him a head start."

Chance couldn't tell if his son was teasing him or not. What right thinking person would bring an infant and dump him in that murky water?

"If that's what you want to do, then, Blaine, by all means go for it."

"What do you think? Do you want to join us?"

"I'll join you for Rune lessons, not for a swim in cremated remains. No thank you."

"Would you like to try an experiment?" Blaine asked, the hesitancy carrying through in his voice to Chance.

"What sort of experiment?"

"I wanted to see if the two of us can link."

"Like you do with Michelle?" Chance was aware how much Blaine wanted to feel the same things with him that he felt with his mother.

So far they'd not had much luck.

"If you'd rather not," Blaine began.

"No, it's okay. Let's try." Standing, he stretched and walked over to the cot where his thirty-three year old son sat waiting expectantly like a small child. Chance only hoped something would happen, anything.

Together they held hands, father and son linked together psychically, their eyes closed in contemplation. Without warning it was happening. Being awed was putting it mildly. They'd tried countless times to make a link and always before nothing had happened. Now he could clearly see scenes from their past life. He was holding his son who had to be about nine or ten. A look of pride and love shone from his eyes. He was tickling his son.

"I love you Demetri. You are everything in life I've ever wanted or will ever want. I'm so proud of you."

The son not answering, but blushing madly, basking in his father's love, his praise. His head was tucked beneath his father's arm for protection against the tickling attacks. A fresh wave of giggles erupted from the boy's mouth and a feeling of untold love washed over Chance then and now.

The connection broken, Chance held on to his son's hand. "It's still true you know. I love you and I'm awfully damn proud of you."

And just like the little boy in the vision, Blaine was again unable to speak. Chance realized he was holding his words inside allowing himself to be held by his father. Chance felt the love for his son in the present overlapping with his love for him in the past.

It was what both of them had needed. The final knowing. Despite his actions in his last incarnation, Chance had indeed loved his son.

"It's funny that I never knew my past life name. You named me after my mother."

"Yes."

"Thank you."

"You didn't have a mother. I wanted you to have some part of her with you."

"Did you just recently remember my name?"

"No, I've always known it."

"Did you tell, Michelle?"

"No."

"Why didn't you ever tell me?"

"I'm not sure." Chance hunched his shoulder. "I've been so unsure of the things I did to you. I wasn't sure if you'd understand why I'd given you your mother's name. I didn't know if you'd think it meant I loved you less."

"I know exactly what it meant. You loved me. That's all I need to know. Would you like to draw another stone?" Blaine smiled and returned them to safer ground.

CHAPTER FIFTEEN

One day left to go. For three weeks Chance had an ally, a friend, family. For three weeks he had a son. He would hate to see Blaine leave, but knew it would be something he could bear.

Blaine's trip had worked. Chance was aware of the reason his son came, to make his relationship with his colleagues more tolerable, and he'd done that not by coercing them, but by gently opening Chance's eyes to his own faults.

Chance still wasn't sure if he liked or hated the Runes. Sometimes it seemed to be too much enlightenment, too much looking into his soul and saying the very things that were in his thoughts. It was sort of eerie in a way, but oh so true.

Whatever had happened, Chance no longer felt alone. Even when Blaine boarded the plane he would not be alone. For the past week he'd battled to get in touch with himself and he'd done it. He'd also begun to drop most of his resentment of Sabu after going to several of his late night or early morning teachings. He had to admit that in spite of himself he was impressed not only with the Runes but the entire culture.

After having coffee and breakfast he headed out to begin his day knowing beforehand it would be no different than any other day. Patients and sickness would not wait while he had one last day alone with his son.

"Good morning," Chance said brightly to the crew working the early morning shift. Several heads turned toward him in greeting and surprise.

"Chance, what are you doing here?"

Chance frowned at George Trammel, scrunching his nose up before glancing around at the other people assembled in the huge room.

"It's my shift."

"Today is also Blaine's last day." George surprised him by putting his arm around Chance's shoulder and walking him toward the door.

"What about the patients? They have to come first." Chance's mouth was feeling like cotton, his head was spinning. He was aware of the gift George might be offering him but couldn't believe it.

George moved closer to him and whispered in his ear.

"Patients, we'll have with us always. But your son will be here for only a few more hours. Take the day and be with him."

"But, but, who's?" Chance closed his mouth embarrassed by the stammering.

"Don't worry," George laughed patting him on the back heartily. "Dr. Danton is going to cover your shift."

Chance stood in the doorway, glancing first at one of his colleague then the other until his gaze came to rest on Doctor Danton.

"Mike, thanks for covering for me. I owe you one."

"You're welcome," Mike replied, "glad to help."

"George thanks? How did you know…I mean about Blaine. That he's my son? I didn't tell you." He peered across the room spotting Karen, the only person he'd shared the true link of his relationship with Blaine.

"Did Karen tell you?"

"No."

"Then who? Blaine?"

"No."

"George, how did you know if no one told you?"

"The look of pride when you look at him and the look of love when he looks at you."

"Still, that's not enough."

"Enough for what?" George laughed as he teased him. "Enough to know that this is not your first incarnation, that Blaine is your son from a past life."

This was a little too spooky, even after everything he'd gone through in the past two years. This information did not compute as the saying went. He looked up at the sound of George's laughing.

"Chance, do you really think no one heard of the psychic battle that took place in the States? Rumors spread like wildfire about how the psychic trinity had been used to stop the invasion of evil."

"But how? No one knew."

"Everyone knew. Everyone's been waiting for many years to see the fulfillment of the prophesy, to see this baby born of the world's two greatest psychics."

"Then why didn't you tell me?"

"You seemed so set on no one knowing anything about you. We respected your wishes and didn't mention it."

"So why now, why are you telling me now?"

"You're different now, Chance. I didn't know you before any of this began, so I'm only guessing. You seem more like the real you that I believe you were before all of this happened."

Chance stared in amazement. "Are you telling me everyone here knows about this, that it isn't a secret?"

"Yes, we all know who you are."

"If that's true, why were you all forever asking me about myself, asking me to tell why I came to India?"

"Because what we heard were mere rumors, we're nosy. We wanted to hear the whole story from you. Heck, Chance, we're human, we're curious. So, execute us, why don't you?"

This time Chance laughed, surprised that after all these weeks his well guarded secret was out in the open. "I will agree with one thing you said, George. You guys really are nosy."

He grinned at his colleague and turned to walk away, intent on spending the day with his son. Chance felt giddy as a school child overflowing with happiness

"Hey, Chance."

With a smile, he turned back. George had such an open joyful face, he was practically glowing.

"Will you ever tell us what happened?"

"Yeah, I'll tell you. When my son leaves," he amended. "Remember I didn't come into the battle until the very end. Blaine is the one that was there the entire time. Maybe you should be asking him."

He saw the look of hunger, of innate curiosity cross George's face. The look was replaced by one of resolve.

"Thanks Chance, but no. Father and son need this time alone to talk, but thanks for the offer. We'll be more than pleased to hear about it from you."

This time it was George who turned away and began working on a patient. Chance smiled at the man's back before walking away. *Well I'll be, damned*, he thought, I'll just be damned. They already knew.

He was doing something he hadn't done since he'd been a child: Whistling. What a difference less than a month made. He owed it all to his son. Opening up the door he bellowed.

"Blaine are you going to sleep all day?"

He was surprised his shout didn't immediately wake Blaine.
Shaking his head, he moved farther into the room and stood over
Blaine's cot. He couldn't resist waking him. They had been given a
gift of time; they couldn't afford to squander a moment of it.
"Blaine," he called again more loudly, ignoring that Blaine had only
just gone to bed a couple of hours before.

"What's up?" Blaine asked, squinting at him. "Why aren't you
working yet?"

"I have the day off. George told me to come be with my son .Can
you believe it?"

"Yeah, I can."

"Well, I can't," Chance countered. "Usually he's a real slave driver,
but today he's like, 'patients we'll have with us always', sounded like
something I've heard before."

"Don't you know who?"

"Not exactly," Chance answered.

"That's what Jesus said about the poor. He said the poor we'd
have with us always but that he would be around just a little while."

Chance allowed the words to roll around inside his head. "Yes,
you're right, Jesus did say that." He squinted at Blaine. "Isn't it
amazing that most people think if you have a gift they can't
understand that you've taken up with the dark side, that you can't
possibly believe in Jesus."

"Yeah, I know, but I don't let that bother me. There is of course,
lots of hate mail, telling me I'm going to burn in hell, but then there
are so many others telling me how much I've helped them. Besides, I
know God will be my ultimate judge anyway."

This was something Chance hadn't known. Of course if he
thought about it, Blaine would undoubtedly get some hate mail. But
people thinking he was going to hell that was a different matter.

"Why do they think you're going to hell?" Chance asked sincerely.
"Because you're a psychic?"

"Because I commune with the dead, that's in the bible you know.
You're not supposed to do it."

Chance only admitted to having read bits and pieces of the bible,
when in actuality he'd read the entire book but never considered
himself a bible scholar. "You were born with the ability."

"I know." He smiled. "Don't let it bother you. I don't. I believe
it's a gift from God through my parents and until God says

otherwise, that is what I will always consider it to be."

He gave a shrug, then a sad smile claimed his features, making the tiny lines around his eyes more evident. Chance observed his son. There was nothing he could do to take away other's preconceived notions. He waited for some clue from Blaine.

"Anyway," Blaine continued, "since we don't have much time I want to teach you something."

"What, no threats?" Now that they were out of religious territory, he felt more comfortable, but as the hairs rose on the back of his neck, his suspicions mounted.

"I just want to teach you how to reach me. It won't hurt. I promise." Blaine laughed, and at last Chance joined in, knowing his son more than likely wanted more.

"You know, Blaine, I can always pick up the phone and call you or send you an email."

"They're not always reliable."

"And thoughts are," Chance teased.

"If you do them right."

This son of his had a mouth on him. Chance cocked his head to the side to peer at him. He loved thinking of Blaine as his son, even more he was glad to see Blaine was more at peace. He'd been that way ever since they linked. He smiled, grateful that the one memory that came through for them was a happy time filled with love and pride. He shuddered to think that the long-buried memories that could have surfaced may have been one of father scolding son. Because surely that too would have happened.

"Ready?" Blaine called out.

"I'm ready." Chance answered.

"Then close your eyes and meditate. Feel your entire body filling with white light. Let the light envelope you."

The time was right. Chance was also at peace and open to learning. Being able to connect to Blaine in his mind was something he should have been able to do without training. Perhaps he was already learning from the Runes. "I'm ready," he said and made himself comfortable. After several successful attempts at reading Blaine's thoughts, Chance sat back and observed Blaine. "Were you aware they already knew you were my son?'

"Of course."

Grinning, Chance had to admit to himself there wasn't much

Blaine MaDia wasn't aware of.

A day later Chance was inwardly wishing for more time with
Blaine. It seemed his time with him had gone by in the blinking of an
eye. He'd known eventually Blaine would have to return home. Still
he wished for more time. Together they sat father and son, waiting
for Blaine's plane to be called. Sabu waited outside in the truck
having driven them to the airport and said his good-byes outside.

"Are you going to be okay now?" Blaine asked Chance.

"I am. Thanks for coming."

"What about Michelle? Are you going to be able to let her go?"

"About that I'm not sure," Chance answered truthfully. "But at
least I think I can stop plotting Larry's death."

At first Blaine didn't smile as he'd expected him to do. He was
breaking a promise and scanning Chance. Instead of anger, Chance
felt amusement.

"Did you find what you were looking for?"

"You really meant it."   Blaine's voice held a touch of
astonishment.

"Of course I do. Michelle was right. Hell, you both were. You
know this all seems like some sort of dream state I'm emerging from.
You know, like none of this stuff really happened." He shook his
head in frustration. "I really do think I'm finding my way back. But
as for Michelle, I can only tell you that you love who you love. I've
loved her too long to stop."

"Chance, do you remember the last Rune you drew?"

"Yeah, I remember. It was the Rune of wholeness."

"Do you still want to know what it means?"

"You told me it means I need to be whole."

There was noise in the background. They both strained their ears
to hear. It was Blaine's plane being called. Blaine barely glanced at the
boarding pass in his hand before staring instead into Chance's face.

"Do you want to know what it else it means?"

"Do you have time to tell me?"

"I'll always have time for you. If the plane leaves there will be
another one."

Chance grinned. "Miss this one and Cassandra will kill you."

Blaine smiled in return. "Then we'd better hurry because I think
you may be right. Do you want to know?"

"Yes." Chance answered observing the way Blaine was twitching in his seat a little anxious to get the words out.

"Actually," he began, "the Rune is Sowela meaning wholeness, that which our soul requires. It embodies the impulse toward self discovery and indicates the path we must follow if we pull that stone. Seeking after wholeness is what you strive for. But in actuality it is what you already are."

"So you're saying all this time I was already whole?" Chance asked in astonishment.

"Of course you were." Blaine cocked his head to the side. "You've been unhappy for so long you've just forgotten it. But—"

"I should have known."

"Yes, you should have known, Father. You're an intelligent man. Though there is something broken inside of you, you are still whole because you once were. You will have to find a way to heal the pieces that are in need of wholeness."

Blaine was eyeing him sharply. There was no sign of recrimination from him. Chance watched as slowly a half smile formed around the corners of his son's lips a moment before he spoke.

"Why don't we start with healing your heart? I forgive you, Father. I never should have blamed you for something you did in the past, but I want you to know, I forgive you. Michelle forgives you also. I know she does." He hesitated but a moment. "The only thing left for you to do is forgive yourself."

"I thought I had," Chance mumbled softly, trying to figure out what more he could have done, what, if anything he could do now.

"Not yet," Blaine answered his questioning look. "But I believe you're coming to terms with it. Once you face the darkness, it's not as dark anymore."

The sound of the person calling the seat numbers changed and took on a more hurried tone. As it was they'd had trouble making out the announcement over the sound of the faulty equipment. Both of their ears were tuned to the numbers announced, both of their gazes were drawn to the card in Blaine's hand.

"I guess I have to go now." A lazy, sad smile crept across Blaine's face as he walked the few inches toward his father to embrace him.

"I'm going to miss you," Chance whispered.

"But I'm only a thought away," Blaine answered a moment before he walked toward the door that would take him back home.

CHAPTER SIXTEEN

The drive from the airport had been spent in quiet contemplation. Every moment of Blaine's visit appeared to be on automatic replay. Reincarnation, Chance thought was a real bitch. Life was given and taken away and the cycle repeated itself bringing hurt and pain each and every time. How was one supposed to learn from the lessons of the past when faced with hurts in the present? It was a mystery he'd yet to unravel. Looking up, he was surprised to see they'd already returned to the compound. The sound of Sabu clearing his throat meant one thing: His moment of contemplation had come to an end.

"Dr. Morgan your son asked me to teach you the Runes. Would you like to continue your studies with me?"

Chance stared for a moment at Sabu. Since the ride back had been so quiet it surprised him that Sabu was talking.

A glance around the compound had Chance wondering where everyone was. The place was generally bustling with people. Now there was not a single soul outside. *That's strange,* he thought, someone's always around.

"Dr. Morgan, are you looking for an escape?"

"What are you talking about?"

"Instead of answering me, you're looking around. I was just wondering."

Chance shook his head, his eyes closing. This felt too much like a dream to be real. "Sabu, does anything appear out of order to you? I mean it's too quiet. Where is everyone?"

The moment he asked the question, he remembered Blaine's warning before coming to India. It was indeed a troubled time for an American to be outside the country. With a picture in his mind of all his colleagues dead, Chance jumped from the truck and began running, praying hard that he would be wrong.

"George, Karen, anybody," he shouted, bursting through the doors of the clinic, he ran toward the common room.

A swarm of voices rose in confusion as the entire compound turned toward Chance.

"Dr. Morgan, is something wrong?" George asked.

Relief spread through him at seeing George and the others alive.

Chance was trying hard to explain to George what he'd imagined had happened to them, but he couldn't get the words out. His eyes searched the room for Karen and in relief he saw her rushing forward to join them

"Chance, are you alright? Did something happen to Blaine?"

He shook his head in the negative, still unable to speak. He looked at Karen, clasped her hand in his and pulled her against his chest, glad that she was alive. For a moment longer he held her, ignoring the stares of the shifting bodies around them or George Trammel looking at him as though he were now possessed.

"He saw the place deserted and thought something had happened to everyone."

Chance turned toward Sabu, grateful to him for being able to put some sense to his craziness, to give voice to the words he had been unable to say.

George Trammel was smiling now. "You thought that rebels perhaps had been here and you ran in here not knowing what you would find, if they were still here or not?"

"I didn't have time to think about any of that," Chance answered rather sheepishly. "I was just worried and I needed to see you, all of you." His glance slid to Karen then again to George before circling around the room. "I needed to make sure all of you were safe."

He moved away from Karen, feeling embarrassed about the way he'd cradled her to him. There had been nothing sexual in his embrace, but still he didn't want to give her the wrong idea.

"I'm sorry about that, Karen." With those words he moved even farther away as though being near her were wrong. He blinked then shook his head to clear it. There was still something strange happening.

"Where are all the patients, George? What are you all doing in here?"

"I'm sorry if I forgot to mention it to you. I thought for sure someone would have told you. Today no one works. The sick, no matter how ill, remain at home. We don't even cook, nothing is done. This is a day of.... How should I say it: Atonement? A time to cleanse your soul of what troubles it. That's all."

How should I put it? Was that really what George had said? As if he had to find words simple enough that he would understand. Chance didn't know whether to be insulted that the man found him stupid, or grateful that he'd found them all alive.

He thought of Blaine and of Michelle. He knew what they would want him to do. He smiled at his colleagues who were rapidly becoming his friends. He would forgive George's insult—.He was grateful they were alive.

"But Sabu drove me to the airport. And the people at the airport are working." George shrugged his shoulders

"Doctor Morgan, now that you know everyone's unharmed would you care to answer the question? Do you want me to teach you the Runes?" Sabu asked."

He should have known Sabu would be relentless in his pursuit. And Blaine, he could picture him this very moment, on the plane laughing over what he knew was happening to him.

There was no longer any escape. He would do what everyone thought he would. Hell, what harm could it do? He would learn the study of the Rune.

"Okay, Sabu, you've got yourself another student. Teach me."

"Good. But we will begin later. For now we will join the others in the atoning.

Chance found a spot next to George, ignoring the empty seat beside Karen. Another relationship was still something he was not ready for. Neither Michelle, Blaine or the Runes could ever make him forget his wife.

Chance sat alone with Sabu in his quarters. As much as he had gotten used to the group sessions Sabu taught, it was the private lessons he appreciated. He actually looked forward to spending time with the man he'd once thought of as his nemesis.

"Sabu, can you tell me something? I thought February was the time you...well, your country cleansed its soul. That gathering after the patient died last month, what was that all about?"

Chance watched as Sabu spread a silken square on the table between them to give him his lesson in reading the Runes.

"We have many such holy days. That one was more of a preparation really. There are lots of people who have no means to makes it to Mother Ganges. The gathering ceremony is for them mostly. It's more symbolic, more of an acknowledgment that we have done things in the past that might have an effect on our present or possibly our future."

The words that were coming out of Sabu's mouth sounded like things Blaine would say, and for a moment. Chance found himself smiling at the thought of his son. Blaine was right, he was only a thought away.

"You're thinking of your son now?"

For once Chance didn't try and hide his thoughts. He looked back at Sabu, peering at him in all honesty. "Yes, I'm thinking about my son."

Chance found himself rubbing on the lobe of his left ear, pulling the fleshy part between his thumb and fourth digit. .If Sabu made a crack about Blaine he would kick him out on his skinny little ass and the hell with the Runes.

"I like him."

"What?" The statement startled Chance. He was expecting something different, something more like, 'Dr. Morgan if you're going to learn you must focus all your attentions on the stones, not on your son.' Instead the man had told him he liked Blaine and was smiling. Hell, what did he say to that?

"I'm glad," Chance answered at last. "He likes you too. Now let's study or I'm never going to get all of this before my time here is done."

Was that a smirk he saw on Sabu's face? It probably was, and Chance got the feeling that he'd said the exact words that the other man had wanted to hear from him.

"Dr. Morgan, do you have any questions before we begin?"

"Yeah, why do any of you believe some primitive marking on stones mean anything?"

"Because it's true."

"How do you know it's true?"

"Because I've used the Runes for many years and they've never been wrong, not once."

"But how do you know that?" Chance challenged. "Blaine told me it's all your own intuition. Couldn't you possibly give the markings any meaning you want them to have?"

He watched as Sabu looked puzzled, his eyes almost twirling in their sockets. Ah ha! He'd finally stumped the man.

"You possess psychic powers do you not?"

Umm, so that was it. That was more than likely what Sabu wanted from the beginning. He wanted to learn what had happened.

Chance wouldn't play that game. He'd tell the story when he was ready. And at the moment he was not ready.

"What does my having psychic abilities have to do with anything?"

He watched as Sabu smiled and lifted a stone from the bag of Runes. Sabu's expression never changed as he examined the stone then returned it to the bag to rest there with the other ones.

"Okay, I suppose you got an answer just then from the Runes whether or not I will answer that question."

"No, but I did receive an answer that I asked the right question. Dr. Morgan, it's a simple question. I know the answer and so do you. Why is it so hard for you to say it?"

"It's not hard for me to say."

Silence.

"Then I ask you again, do you have psychic powers?"

"Everyone is psychic to some degree."

"That was not my question. I did not ask about every soul on the planet. Only yours. For the last time, I hope. Are you psychic?"

Sabu had spoken with sarcasm coating his words, Chance thought. He rubbed the bracelet on his arms remembering the last two years, remembering his part in helping his son and the woman he loved defeat evil.

"Yes, Sabu, I suppose I do have psychic gifts."

"Then you've answered your own question."

"What the hell was my question? You've gotten me so off track. I don't even know what I asked." Chance fumed for a few seconds trying hard to remember his original question. With a shake of his head he stared at Sabu.

"How the hell does my being minimally psychic have any connection with the Runes?"

"Because being psychic is no more no less than using your intuition, some are just more finely tuned than others. Your intuition will tell you if the stones are correct. Your psychic abilities."

Chance laughed. "You couldn't just say that in the first place."

"You are a challenge doctor, and you are not willing to be a submissive pupil. So I must come the long way around as you say, to make my point."

"Harrumph."

Sabu's eyes sparkled and his coffee brown skin appeared to gleam as he smiled at Chance. This was definitely a moment Chance would record in his journal.

"Dr. Morgan, would you like to try something?"

"Sabu, would you like to drop the Dr. Morgan and just call me Chance?"

It seemed that Sabu was giving the matter serious thought. Chance couldn't believe it, such a simple thing, no big deal really. Still.

"No thank you. I believe I will continue to use Dr. Morgan for now."

"But you call Dr. Trammel, George on occasion. I've heard you."

"Yes, but I've known him many years. Beside, he's more George on most occasions than he is Dr. Trammel."

"And me? What am I?"

Sabu smiled. "You're Doctor Chance Morgan."

Chance found himself pulling on his ear again, wondering what it meant that Sabu preferred to call him doctor instead of his given name. He forced a smile on his lips. He refused to behave as though it bothered him. Instead he refocused on Sabu's request.

"What did you want to try?"

"I want to begin our lesson with you pulling a Rune to tell us in what area you need to study, then you contemplate that and tell me if the words of the Runes have any meaning in your life."

"What if I still don't want to follow the path the Rune suggests?"

"Then you won't. This is your life, controlled by you, not by a bag of stones."

Somehow Chance no longer believed that. It seemed since he'd received the first stone, his life was no longer his own, as if some unseen force was pushing him in a certain direction. A direction he wasn't sure he wanted to go in, but found himself being dragged there never the less. A willing victim in his own changing.

He ignored the inquisitive smile on Sabu's face remembering Blaine's comment to him when he'd last pulled a stone. *"Come on Chance it's not going to bite."*

Now, as he put his hand into the bag, he couldn't help the thought that came. Perhaps he wouldn't be bitten, not literally, but he could bet it wouldn't be something he was going to like.

The Rune lay in front of him. Chance looked first at the markings then at Sabu, wishing he knew the meaning, himself. Then he smiled, acknowledging the point in all of this was for Sabu to teach him. *Well here goes nothing,* he thought.

"Okay, Sabu, tell me. What does it mean?" Sabu's head tilted and for a moment Chance thought he wasn't going to answer.

"It's Perth, the Rune of mystery. This stone tells that there is something hidden. There are powerful changes at work here, yet what is achieved is not easily or readily shared. After all, becoming whole---the means of it---is a profound secret."

Chance nearly laughed. Here it was again. Something else pointing to him being made whole. What the hell was this, a conspiracy? And now it was saying something about him hiding.

"You don't believe me, Dr. Morgan?"

"Let's say I have a healthy skepticism. Tell me something, why have all the Runes I've gotten tell me I need to grow, to change, to become whole?"

"Only you can answer those questions. Do you feel there is something missing in your life, in your soul that is keeping you from growing, from being whole?"

Chance could feel the immediate change coming over him the clenching of his teeth, the tightening of his spine. If Sabu thought this was a sneaky way of finding out about his private life he had another thought coming.

The two men looked at each other neither saying one word. "Why the hell did I ever agree to having you teach me the Runes? I should have known it would all come down to my private thoughts."

"Dr. Morgan, you do not have to share the answer. It is simply something I put out there for you to ponder."

Chance chose to ignore Sabu. Sure his words were the correct ones, but he knew what the man was hoping to accomplish. From the moment he met Sabu there had been questions, some unasked, some voiced, but always Chance could read the questions that were so vivid in Sabu's eyes.

"If there is a reason for my stunted growth, that is something that is personal and private to me." There was a sort of smile around the corner of Sabu's mouth that annoyed Chance.

"Would you say your personal and private matters are things you don't wish to share with me?"

"That's what personal means," Chance spoke sarcastically. Where this conversation was heading he didn't have a clue.

"Then that would be a secret matter, yes?"

Now Sabu's grin was there full force. For a nanosecond, Chance stared at him then it dawned on him: Perth, a secret, hidden matter.

"Is something wrong, Dr. Morgan?"

If Chance didn't know better, this time it was Sabu's voice that was tinged with sarcasm, but then again Sabu thought himself to be too evolved to use sarcasm.

"No, Sabu there is nothing wrong." Chance would choke before he voluntarily admitted that he saw the Rune he had chosen mimicked perfectly what was happening in his life. Sabu's left eyebrow arched upwards, his mouth opened a slight fraction of an inch before he evidently changed his mind. Chance sat still waiting to hear what he would say.

"You know, Dr. Morgan, this Rune is perhaps one of my personal favorites when I'm teaching a new student. I love when they pull it for themselves."

"Why?"

"Because those who are skeptical, well, they can appoint it whatever place in their lives they think it belongs. But then there is the whole challenge of the mystery involved with this Rune."

"And you enjoy mysteries?"

"I enjoy when I see something that may even be a mystery to the person who pulls the stone. I enjoy when the meaning is made clear to them and they understand it."

"And that's it, that's all you see?"

Chance didn't want to ask Sabu for more, but his dealings with the Runes said things were never that simple, never an explanation with just a few words. There had to be more to Perth.

"I don't understand, Dr. Morgan, what are you asking me exactly?"

"I'm asking you if Perth has something else to say."

"There is more if you wish to hear it."

If I didn't want to hear it I wouldn't have asked. But this, Chance kept to himself. He only allowed the thought to filter slowly through his brain. Instead he sighed softly and answered, Yes, Sabu, is there more to Perth?"

"Remember you asked, Dr. Morgan. Perth has much knowledge. The person who pulls this stone should feel great joy because they will soon find themselves lifted above the entanglement of the ordinary life to acquire broader vision."

"You see all of that happening with me?" Chance grinned, teasing Sabu.

"Not me, Dr. Morgan. The Rune you have chosen. This stone is concerned with nothing external, only the deepest stratum of our being is involved when we receive this Rune. This is the bedrock on which our destiny is founded."

"And?"

"And?" Sabu repeated.

"And what else? I don't believe that is all."

"You're learning, Dr. Morgan, but it is nearly all of it, I promise. Unless of course your own intuition tells you there's more."

"Sabu, why don't you tell me, then we'll decide what my intuition feels about it."

"Agreed."

A semblance of a smile appeared on Sabu's face before he once again became serious and continued with his teaching.

"Dr. Morgan, Perth also tells of death, but symbolically. It instructs us that it's time to let go of something, let go of everything, no exceptions, no exclusions. It is time. Nothing less than renewal of the sprit is required."

"Did Blaine tell you to say that?" Chance ignored the frown Sabu was wearing. He had to know the truth. "Did Blaine tell you to tell me that, Sabu?"

"I don't take orders from your son however much I might admire him. And especially not about something this important, this life changing. I would never lie about the Rune meanings."

Sabu was affronted and Chance didn't blame him. He was aware what he'd accused the man of doing, still he couldn't help wanting the words Sabu had said to have been dictated by his son. It would make his life a lot easier. Everything and everyone it seemed was conspiring to persuade him to give up loving his wife. She was so deeply embedded into his DNA he didn't believe even if he wanted to that it would be possible to let her go.

Chills began creeping up his body until he was visibly shaking. He attempted to use his will to control it to no avail. His head felt as though it was encased in fog, he couldn't think, could barely breathe. Off in the distance he saw a shadowy figure coming closer toward him. Dimi, his Dimi. *"Chance, don't be afraid,"* she was whispering. *"It's going to be fine. I promise you just as Dimi promised Jeremy. I promise you things will work out.*"

Poof! Just like that she was gone, and Chance was left weak and stunned. He'd never had this happened in front of strangers. Michelle was there. He knew it as surely as he knew she had separated herself from her past life. She was no longer Dimi. He was no longer Jeremy. Still how was he supposed to think of her? As his wife, or Larry's?

A secret matter, something he had to let go of. If Sabu was telling the truth and he had no doubt that he was, then the Rune-Perth was speaking to him.

"Dr. Morgan, are you alright? Should I get Dr. Trammel?"

"No Sabu, I'm fine. Just tell me, if Blaine didn't ask you to tell me to let go..." He didn't want to offend Sabu but he had to ask the question. "Was there anyone who asked you to say that?"

"No, Dr. Morgan. No one asked me to say that. How could they? Who would know what stone you would pull from the bag?"

Chance looked at the bag, his suspicion mounting with every breath. He took the bag between his trembling hands and dumped the stones unceremoniously upon the table. He rifled through them, wanting to believe that every stone in the bag was the same. That somehow he'd been set up.

Just as he'd known it would be, every stone contained a different marking with the exception of the Rune of blankness which was void as it should be. Everything was in order. There was no way anyone could have known what he would draw. Sabu was eyeing him, his brows lifted in curiosity, a worried look clouding his features.

"It's okay, Sabu. I'm sorry that I....well..., that I... I just thought maybe Blaine had put you up to this. I know you wouldn't do anything inappropriate." Chance rushed on to explain. "It was just the things you said. It's kinda similar to what Blaine told me, what he's been telling me."

"I know you think we are prying into your life, but believe me doctor, I would never use spiritual teachings to do so. Perhaps it's better if we end the lesson for the day. Maybe start again tomorrow."

"Yes, that would be better," Chance mumbled softly. "Tomorrow." He watched as Sabu rose to leave. "Sabu," he called out to him, "is there anything we can do that doesn't require me pulling a stone?"

"Of course," Sabu answered. "There are many things. We can

discuss the history of the Runes. That we can do without you having to pull or even touch the stones."

"Then why didn't we start with that? Why did you have me pull a stone?"

"I thought it would be beneficial if your higher self dictated the path we should follow in your training."

"And now?"

"As I told you before, this is your life. We will do as you want. You never have to pull another stone until you're ready to do so."

"That may be never."

"Then that will be fine. We will do this your way."

"Thanks," Chance muttered to Sabu's back because the man had already exited the room.

What the hell is going on? The man surely must think I'm a crackpot or something. At the very least he thinks I'm a coward, too afraid to pull a stone from a bag, afraid of the meaning.

"*Well aren't you Chance?*" A disembodied voice chided him. "I'm not," Chance answered the voice. "I just don't want to do it." He closed his eyes and lay on his bed. Bringing his legs up to his chest he concentrated hard on bringing Michelle's face before him. He felt a stab of pain. He knew the reason he didn't want to pull anymore stones, even if he didn't admit it to anyone. He knew.

Everything and everyone was telling him he had to let go of Michelle, and when he did, he would not even have his dreams of her to comfort him. He was well aware what was happening. It was indeed time to give her up. And he didn't want to.

CHAPTER SEVENTEEN

Chance lingered over his mug of cold coffee. He was the last among the stragglers that remained in the common room. He'd seen so many patients and was so tired he didn't want to move, not even to make the necessary steps to his bed. So he remained where he was, sitting there alone, not thinking.

He sensed her before she called his name. For the past two weeks since Blaine had departed and he'd ran into the compound screaming like a lunatic grabbing her and hugging her out of relief that she was alive, Chance had done his best to avoid Karen.

"Tired?"

He turned toward her. There was a nervousness about her, her hands shook slightly as she placed her own cup on the table in front of her.

"Tired is an understatement." Chance answered her. "I was tired when the day began." He watched as Karen smiled shyly at him. That was different, always before she'd smiled easily and readily. His touching her had changed their comfortable friendship.

He didn't know what to say. To voice it would give credence to the idea that he might have thought of her as someone other than a friend. He sipped at the cold coffee and waited.

"Things have changed haven't they?"

There it was out in the open between them. Chance glanced down. He was stuck, he had to answer.

"Not if we don't want them to change." He stared straight into her eyes not missing the tiny flicker that was there for only a moment in time. She was hurt, but why? She'd told him herself that she was not interested in a relationship.

"I miss talking to you, Chance."

"I've been busy."

"I know, so have I, but this is a small place. We've always managed to find a few minutes to talk before…well… you know, before."

"Before I acted like a damn fool in front of everyone?"

"That's not what I meant."

Chance bristled. He hated that he'd not thought before rushing from the truck yelling out in panic. To have broken in on a sacred ceremony, no less. In disgust, he turned from Karen

"Chance, you didn't make a fool of yourself."

He saw the first real smile appear on her face since she sat down. Automatically he wanted to smile back at her. It was only through considerable will power that he didn't.

"Karen, where are you heading with this?" His voice was rough, much rougher than he'd ever intended. He wasn't trying to be rude, but this all felt like someone was again manipulating his life and he wasn't sure if he liked it.

"I just wanted us to go back to the way we were, friends."

She stammered stopped, then tried again, but her voice faltered, causing Chance's brow to rise as he puckered his lips in concentration. "I thought you weren't looking for love, Karen."

He saw the blush spread across her body. He was being a damn heel. It wasn't Karen's fault that he was having one hell of a time getting over Michelle.

He watched as Karen appeared to draw herself up, straightening her shoulders and glaring at him, not backing down.

"I didn't say I was falling in love with you, Chance Morgan. You're an arrogant bastard, do you know that? The moment I begin to think there might be hope for you, you go and pull something like this. You big jerk," she spat out as she rose from the table.

"Karen, I'm sorry." Chance rose also and stood behind her, his arms flailing out at his side. He wanted to touch her. As she turned back to face him, he found himself wanting to do more, he wanted to kiss her. He stepped back.

"Karen, someone wants us to be together. I'm not ready for that."

Laugher met him. She was bending midway, holding her hands tightly in front of her abdomen attempting to talk, stopping, then laughing louder. She was annoying the hell out of him.

"What's so funny?"

"You are, Chance. You're acting as if you have no choice in the situation. What did you think I was going to do, attack you? Do you really think I want to be saddled with an emotional cripple? My God man, you're mourning a woman you can't have. An ex-wife would be bad enough for a woman to compete with, but a wife from the past? That's not something any woman would want to deal with and definitely not me."

She turned sharply on her heels and walked toward the door. "Forget it, Chance."

"I like your friendship."

The words were out before he could retract them. "I do enjoy talking to you, Karen, it's just that I don't want to lead you on."

He noticed she'd stopped walking toward the door. He waited until she turned half way toward him, an expression of compassion washing her face with an inner radiance, a light. Chance swallowed ,gulping down his feeling of panic. *"Michelle, I can't,"* he whispered in his head. *"Oh but you can,"* he heard her voice whispering back.

"Karen, I value your friendship. Do you think it's possible we can return to that?" She wasn't smiling at him, but at least she wasn't leaving or calling him a jerk.

"Yes, Chance," she answered at last. "I'd like that very much."

He sensed a slight hesitation on her part. She was chewing on her bottom lip, her face contorted in concentration. He couldn't help but wonder what she was thinking.

"This Michelle must be some woman."

"She is." Chance didn't dare blink. He caught Karen's gaze with his own, watching as her face softened and she smiled.

"Michelle is lucky to have a man this much in love with her. To have loved her enough in one lifetime that you remember and love her still. Wow! She's one lucky lady."

For a long moment Chance stared at her before answering. "I think I'm the lucky one for having her love me in return." He turned away from Karen, turning his attention now to his ice cold coffee. He knew the question in her eyes.

If she loves you so much, why isn't she with you? Why did she choose to remain with her husband in this lifetime?

He knew the question because he'd asked it of himself a thousand times. If he had the answer he would gladly share it. Sure Michelle and Blaine both believed this time around it wasn't their destiny, something had gone awry, had changed the course of their lives. Since that time he'd been on a quest to find out what. And right the wrong.

He glanced at Karen, now was not the time to tell her any of this. She would only accuse him of not letting go. He was doing his best. It was just taking longer than everyone else thought it should. If letting go meant he would one day hold his beloved in his arms, he would have to find a way to let go, that was for damn sure.

He looked again at Karen, saw her wetting her lips with her lush pink tongue and wondered would he have to fall in love with her to prove to the universe he'd let go, or could he merely make love to her body?

"Chance."

He felt the tips of her fingers on his arms lightly shaking him. He shook his head, wishing he had better control of his thoughts. He'd better learn to let go quickly, before he walked into the Mother Ganges purely by accident. And all because he wasn't paying attention.

"Dr. Morgan, you're a quick learner."

Sabu was smiling at him, and for a quick moment Chance smiled in return. Then as usual he found himself having qualms with Sabu's wording. He wasn't exactly a novice. When Sabu clapped his hands in glee, his eyes sparkling in surprise, Chance was less than amused.

Chance allowed his lips to furl into what he hoped would pass for a smile. "Sabu, at first that sounded like a compliment. But with you, I'm not always sure. You're aware I've studied many arts right? It's not as though I haven't had to use my brain before now."

"I didn't mean any offense, Dr. Morgan. It's just, you've surprised me with your eagerness and your quick, open understanding."

"I've studied eastern religion before. I've studied many things, Sabu. You would be surprised."

"The Runes are not considered part of the eastern culture, no one can lay claim to them really. And I would not be surprised about the things you know. After-all you're the father of a great psychic."

"Is that your interest in me after all these weeks of my being here, that Blaine is my son?"

Chance watched while Sabu pondered his answer. H was smiling as he sat lotus fashion making him cringe at the angle the man's legs were bent. He would be patient. If nothing else he'd learned from his study of the Runes was to have patience.

"That does interest me. I'm curious like everyone else. I've never met anyone who knew for sure they'd found their family and definitely not people who claim to have reconnected this time around. But then again, Dr. Morgan, I found you of interest long before I met your famous son. He was just a pleasant surprise," Sabu continued.

"Why? Did knowing him help you understand me?"

"It did help me understand why you try so hard to push everyone away. And the ones you don't push away you definitely keep at bay."

Chance was aware of the penetrating look Sabu was giving him as though he could cut straight through to his soul. "Are we talking about anyone in particular?" He felt his lips thinning, he could no longer keep up the pretense of a smile.

Sabu rose. "Dr. Morgan, I think we've worked enough for today. How about we pick up where we left off tomorrow?"

"You didn't answer my question, Sabu."

"Your private life is just that, Dr. Morgan, your private life."

The little man was once again annoying Chance. "Look, Sabu, let's cut the crap. No dancing about, gloves off, what the hell were you talking about?"

Chance watched how Sabu's spine stiffened. He had gone a bit farther than he'd intended. Now it was Sabu who was wearing an annoyed expression. Just the sight of Sabu losing control pleased Chance. He was glad for some strange reason to have ruffled the man's feathers.

"Remember, you asked me for my opinion."

"That I did, Sabu, go ahead give it your best shot." Chance braced himself for the best the man could do. He'd taken many potshots at Sabu. He was glad Sabu was finally going to do the same.

"I see that you have feelings for Karen, yet whenever she comes near you, you walk in the opposite direction. Dr. Trammel, he arouses your curiosity, yet you refuse to ask him questions, afraid that you might have to reveal something about yourself if you have a real conversation. As for myself, you've been trying extremely hard to pick a fight with me since you arrived here."

Chance blanched, he should have known Sabu was aware of what he was doing. Sabu was perceptive. He had to give him that.

"What would make you think that?" Chance asked, wondering how Sabu would answer.

"Because, Dr. Morgan, you may have psychic gifts, but so do I. I was aware of your coming and of your inner turmoil. I also knew there would be strife between us."

"Then why are you working with me?"

"Because I saw in the end we would become great friends for life."

Chance smiled, "Then you're a better psychic than I am. I didn't see any of that."

"Good night, Dr. Morgan."

"Good night, Sabu."

Nearly twenty minutes had passed between Chance's confrontation with Sabu and his seeing Karen. She was walking toward him and as he turned automatically to go in the opposite direction he remembered Sabu's words and stopped to wait for her. She was frowning as she came closer, an indication she'd been aware he had intended to avoid her.

Frowning at him, her hands on her hips she looked at him and spoke. "I thought you wanted us to remain friends."

"I do." Chance took in a deep breath and let it out with a loud noise. "I do," he repeated.

"Then why are you still running from me? I know you asked George to change your shift so that we wouldn't be in contact. Chance, none of this is necessary. I'm not after you."

He saw her face redden and felt his own face flushing as well. She'd hit it on the head. Now what was he supposed to do? Tell her he was still avoiding her? Because she was right— he thought she wanted him.

If he were completely honest with himself he'd admit Blaine had started him to thinking about sex. It had been way over a year since he'd last held Michelle in his arms, had last made love to her and damnit, all of his dreams of her were making him horny as hell.

That was the real reason he was avoiding Karen. He didn't know if he'd give into the temptation of his flesh. He had nothing to offer the woman beyond physical release and despite what Blaine or Michelle told him, he would feel as if he were cheating on his wife to take another woman into his bed.

Did he desire Karen? Hell yes, he desired her. Did he have feelings for her? Possibly, but nothing that he would say even came close to love.

"Karen, it's awkward whenever we're alone. I was trying to not put you in that situation."

"Chance, if you think I'm pursuing you, think again. I've told you this more than once."

He looked at her, at the slant of her shoulders, at the gentle sway of her hips, then he moved his eyes to her face. She was moistening her lips with the tip of her tongue. Her eyes held a faraway look of hunger, and desire that she was trying unsuccessfully to hide.

"Karen, don't take this the wrong way, but I don't believe you." Tears came quickly to her eyes, her face displayed the hurt his words had caused.

"Hear me out," he rushed on. "Karen, I'm not a fool and neither are you. I'm trying to let go of someone I've loved nearly forever."

His throat felt constricted, "That would be so unfair to any woman to think she has a future with me. I can't even offer you a future in the next life. That too belongs to Michelle. I love her. I always have. I always will."

She stood before him blinking away the tears, biting down her hurt, and he admired her strength in not running away. She could have. It would have made it a lot easier for the both of them.

"Chance, you're not fooling me either. I've seen the hunger in your eyes when you look at me. Deny that you want me."

He swallowed she didn't really want the answer to this question.

"Chance."

"I have had thoughts of making love to you. But. I don't want more with you, Karen."

"You run hot and cold. That day you ran in here thinking something had happened to us, to me, you grabbed me and held me. You cared about my safety. You cared about me. There was something there."

"I was worried about you. And I do care about you. But the times you may think I'm running hot then cold, I blame that on two people who love me and think they know what's best for me. They've been trying to force me to want someone, anyone."

"What about the desire. I've sensed your desire for me."

"For that I blame my own hormones. You're a very beautiful and desirable woman. And I will admit I've thought of…taking you to bed. "

"Are you saying what I think you're saying?""

She was getting angry now. Chance could hear it in the rising tenor of her voice, the slight tremble of her hands, the way her body straightened and the fact that her nostrils were flaring, and she was taking in breath after deep breath in an effort to calm herself before she spoke.

"Chance Morgan, are you telling me that you've been merely looking at me as a piece of tail?" A choked sound came out of her mouth. "What gives you the right to look at me like that? What gives any of you the right to think I would just be here to take your mind off a woman you love? I don't hop into bed with men that easily."

"You have no idea how truly powerful my son is. Somehow Blaine and Michelle have attempted to engineer an attraction between us. They only want me to be happy. They didn't mean any harm to either of us."

"And what about my feelings? Do you think they are behind what I feel, that they planted thoughts in my mind as well? Do you think I'm so weak-minded that I wouldn't know that?"

"I'm afraid I've given you the wrong idea. Neither of them would do anything...perhaps a whisper. I'm not sure. It's just that from the moment you and the others returned it seemed as though you had a rather odd fixation on me and it made me wonder if somehow they'd arranged it." She was staring at him her gaze making him uncomfortable. "What is it?" he asked at last.

"I'm sorry my interest in you appeared to you as though I was fixated on you. I had known the treatment you would receive from George and I knew you would be dying for a little friendly companionship. We met and there was an immediate connection. I saw the spark of interest in your eyes. Had I not..."

"Karen come on—"

"You've made yourself very clear, Dr. Morgan. I will leave you alone. But there is one thing I was wondering about. Why don't you call her, this Michelle of yours? Ask her if she's sending psychic waves to either of us. Ask her what you really want to know, Chance. Ask her why she's finding it so much easier to get on with her life than you are."

With that she left. Chance didn't want to call her back. Her statements were legitimate. He deserved every harsh word she'd uttered. Here he'd practically accused the woman of not being able to keep her hand off him. And after his 'we're being manipulated' speech, surely she had to have some fear now that she was being manipulated.

Damn it, why did I tell her that? Chance reprimanded himself. It seemed to him that for the past two and a half months, he'd been in India, he had been plagued with self-recriminations.

Karen was right about one thing. Despite his promise to her, he had to talk Michelle. She was the only person who could make the ache in his heart go away.

Or, you could hurt more than you do already. He heard the voice whispering in his mind but chose to ignore it. It didn't matter. One way, or the other, he had to find out. With this thought in mind he walked toward the common room to use the phone.

As usual his cell was useless. Lack of towers. After nearly two hours waiting for the operator to dial back when a connection was made to the Sates, Chance held the phone tightly in his hand not caring that he was on one side of the world and Michelle was on another. He knew she would be sleeping. It didn't matter, he had to talk to her.

"Hello."

He took in a deep breath trying to bring her essence closer, wanting the scent of her to waft through his nostrils. The ache became stronger as his rehearsed words disappeared from his mind.

"Chance?"

He'd wondered if she would know it was him. She had.

"Chance, is something wrong?"

"Yes, everything."

He heard her muffled voice and a surge of anger overtook him, anger at the man lying next to her. Without hearing her words, he was aware she was informing Larry, her husband, that it was he who was on the phone. He wanted to yell for her to stop. It should be the other way. It should be Chance there with her, holding her. And him she was turning to, to explain a late night caller.

"Michelle," he asked softly. "Are you happy?"

"Yes, I am."

He heard the sound of her moving and knew she was walking from the bedroom. Her words had not been spoken for the benefit of her husband. She'd truly meant them, which meant she was happy.

"How can you be, happy?"

"Would you rather that I was miserable?"

"Yes."

The silence between stretched out as they both took in his truth.

Chance slid the phone from his ear to his chest, closing his eyes, wishing he'd been stronger, had not called her.

"Do you ever think of me?" He clenched the phone so tightly that the veins in his hand became engorged with blood. "Have you forgotten me completely?"

"We agreed. All of us. Chance, you shouldn't be doing this to yourself. What is it that you want me to say?"

"I want you to tell me it's as hard for you to live without me as it is for me to live without you. I want you to tell me why, if you love me as much as I love you, you're not here with me, why you're sleeping in Larry's bed, in Larry's arms."

His voice broke. This wasn't how he'd wanted his conversation with Michelle to go. He was not a weakling. His love for her was making him into something he was not.

"That's not true, Chance, it's not my fault."

"Are you reading my mind?"

"It wasn't deliberate. Your thoughts just came to me. You blame me for the pain you're in. You're wrong. This is not my doing, and I'm not the one who has the power to make things right. It all lies in your hands."

"You're talking later. I'm talking now! I want you now."

"That's part of the problem isn't it?"

He ignored her. She was skirting around the questions he'd asked, throwing up puzzles for him to figure out. He wasn't in the mood for puzzles. He wanted answers.

"You didn't answer my questions. Is it because you don't love me? Or is it that you don't think of me? Is it because you have Larry and I have no place in your heart?"

"Chance, you know the answer to the questions you ask me."

"That's not good enough," he shouted. "I want to hear you tell me that you love me." He heard sounds in the background, Larry's voice, Michelle answering him, telling him she would only be a minute.

"Tell me that you love me."

"You already know that."

"I want to hear you say it."

"Don't make me do that. I've put Larry through a lot. My family is just beginning to heal."

"Tell me that you love me," he interrupted her. "Tell me now. I need to hear you say it."

"That is not what you need, Chance."

"I suppose you know what it is I need."

"Yes, I know."

"Then I wish you'd tell me because I believe I know my needs better than you, and it's you I need."

"Blaine told me you were beginning to understand."

He'd been about to press the issue. Damn Larry listening in the background. He had no intention of hanging up the phone until she declared her love for him. Now she'd completely thrown him off course.

"Have you been discussing me with Blaine?"

"Of course."

Chance held the phone away from his body as if it had suddenly turned into a slithering snake. He'd expected Michelle to deny discussing him, but there wasn't even the slightest hesitation.

"When?"

"All the time. He told me about his visit with you, how well-liked you are by your colleagues. And he told me about this woman Karen. He thinks you may have feelings for her."

If it didn't take hours to get a decent line to the U.S., Chance would have hung up the phone. "And if I do have feelings for her, can you handle that? Can you handle the thought of me making love to another woman the way you want me to handle Larry making love to you?"

There was silence.

He shouted into the phone, "Can you handle me loving another woman, Michelle? Answer me."

"No, I can't."

Thank God. He'd feared for a moment it would go the other way. He'd been afraid she was going to tell him it wouldn't bother her in the least. He didn't know if he would have been able to take hearing that.

"I'll never be able to completely handle it if you fall in love with someone else. But I have to, Chance. It's not what I want, but it's the only way. You have to let me go. And I have to let you go. We have to."

She was crying, her voice filled with sadness was breaking his heart, yet he pressed on. "I have let you go."

"You haven't."

"I'm here in India and you're there, in bed with Larry. How much more proof do you need? I let you go."

"You know what I mean. You have to live your life, Chance. You have to try and be happy."

"And if I can't?"

"Then you doom us all. This may well be the last lifetime you will know of me."

Chance closed his eyes and rubbed his hands roughly across his unshaven face. "Maybe I love you a hell of a lot more than you love me. It's not that easy for me to want someone else, to crave another's touch. Perhaps you never loved me, even in the past. Did you bring resentment of me to this life?"

"What are you talking about? Why would I?"

"Because it was my fault you died!" Chance whispered the last.

"Chance."

He heard her calling to him. His limbs were trembling. He'd never known that thought was there lurking in his subconscious, but now that it was out, he realized it was true.

"Michelle, is that the reason you're not here with me? Do you hate me?"

"Hate you? For what? How could you possibly think my death was your fault?"

"It was my fault that you became pregnant, that you lost all that blood, that I couldn't save you. I didn't know how. We had no money. It was all my fault."

"Chance, listen to me. It was what we wanted, what I wanted. I wanted our baby. I wanted your son. I wanted him, do you hear me? You need to remember all of our past. I begged you to take care of our son and to love him. Do you think I would have done that if I hated you? I loved both of you, and I would do it all over again if I could. It was never your fault, Chance. Listen to me, I loved you then and I love you now."

He cut her off and replaced the phone. Tears were streaming down his face. He could no longer distinguish his life as Chance Morgan from that of Jeremy, the man who'd lost his wife to childbirth. The man who couldn't save his wife.

Dr. Chance Morgan, a man of healing, only he was born a lifetime too late. It was too late to save his Dimi, too late for his entire family.

CHAPTER EIGHTEEN

For two days Chance had holed up in his room not caring for the patients, not eating, and not admitting visitors. George Trammel was worried. Chance could tell from the number of times the older man had come to his door.

There was nothing anyone could do for him. Blaine and Michelle had told him to keep searching for the reason they weren't together, and now he knew. The answer had come to him as plain as day. In their last incarnation he should have never released his seed, should not have yielded to Dimi's pleas for a child.

Even a call from Blaine was not enough to rouse him. When Blaine attempted to use mental telepathy he'd shut down. He didn't want to talk to him. Not now.

"Dr. Morgan."

"Go away, Sabu."

"What is wrong, Dr. Morgan? Perhaps I can help."

Chance didn't answer. If he was quiet maybe the little man would go away.

"Dr. Morgan, it's time for our lesson."

"Not now, Sabu, I'm not in the mood."

"Then that's the time to study the Rune. Perhaps it can help whatever's troubling you."

"Not this time, Sabu."

"How do you know if we don't try?"

"Sabu, get the hell away from the door," Chance yelled. "I don't want to be helped."

Chance waited, he didn't hear the sound of Sabu leaving from the door. Nor did he hear the man attempting to speak again. He could sense Sabu was standing behind the closed door. An hour passed and Chance continued to feel Sabu's presence.

"Sabu, come in," Chance called softly hoping that he was wrong, that Sabu was not waiting outside his room.

The handle of the door turned and Sabu entered, a tray containing, canned fruit, sardines, and two bottles of water in his hands.. Chance looked at the tray.

"Bottled water, and sardines, Sabu? Before you always looked at me in disgust when I drank it, and you made me feel as though I were a criminal when I hoarded the sardines. Why now are you giving me these things? Are you all afraid that for the first time a physician will come here and will die?"

Sabu set the tray down on Chance's bed but continued standing. The entire community is worried about you, Chance."

Chance cocked his head sideways then rose up an inch or two from the pillow. "What happened to your only wanting to call me Doctor Morgan?"

"I'm here as your friend, not your teacher."

"Hmmm."

"Would it help if you talked about what's troubling you? Blaine has called several times and he emails at least every ten minutes. If he doesn't hear from you soon he'll return to India."

His groan was automatic. He should have thought of that himself. "Would you call him for me? Tell him there's no need for him to come."

"I don't think that will be enough. I believe it is your voice he wishes to hear. There was also a woman who called for you. She said her name is Michelle Powers. She's also worried."

Sabu hesitated. Chance could sense the slight pause, the not knowing if he should continue. After an awkward silence, he watched as a light came into Sabu's eyes and he made a movement with his tongue. It struck Chance as funny. It looked as if the man's tongue had been literally stuck to the roof of his mouth.

"She sounds as if she's in great pain. I attempted to help her. She only wants to talk to you."

Sabu's head was bowed. Chance was aware it was from the embarrassment of knowing intimate details Chance himself had not divulged. Glancing over Sabu's head to the framed photograph of himself with Blaine and Michelle. It surprised him that Michelle had called, and more still that she'd given her name. All of them had taken every precaution to keep the news of the trinity out of the limelight. An impossible job keeping something of that magnitude from a group of psychics. Enlightened though he might be, Sabu was curious to know the details from him about the battle. It would have been easier for him to have gotten the information from Blaine. Whatever the reason, everyone wanted to talk to him. To hear his perspective it seemed. In the past weeks he'd attended Sabu's group seminars and he'd participated, even sharing some of his thoughts with the group. But he had yet to tell any of them what happened. He waited, wondering if Sabu would say anything else. When he didn't, Chance sighed.

"You know who she is, don't you?"

"Everyone does. She's your wife, your soul mate."

"Yeah." Chance turned his back to Sabu, burying his face in the pillow. "She's the reason I came to India." He waited but Sabu didn't interrupt.

"I've spent this lifetime looking for her, searching everywhere and I found her." He closed his eyes slowly remembering the moment he'd known it was her.

"Where did you meet?"

Chance turned back. Sabu had taken up a lotus position on the floor, his face open and his curiosity getting the better of him. He didn't blame the man. He'd kept quiet much longer than Chance would have if the situation had been reversed.

"We met in the parking lot of a grocery store. It was raining. I helped her with her groceries."

"But how did you know?"

"I held her in my arms. She was crying in the rain, a stranger and I pulled her to me to comfort her. I knew."

Chance felt his throat closing with the memory. It hurt to think about, but then again he would never wish not to have found her.

"Did she know as well?"

"Yes, but she didn't want to believe it. She was afraid of the feelings she felt for me." Chance stared hard at Sabu. "She was married when I found her, with five adult children. She had a lot to lose."

"You didn't?"

"No, no ties. I was married before, but I got a divorce when I knew my dreams were real. My wife Dimi..." He caught the automatic slip. "She's Michelle in this life. Anyway she kept coming to me in my dreams asking me to find her. I had no choice, I had to."

"What about your wife, how did you explain all of this to her?"

"I told her the truth, that I was from another time and place and that I was married and my wife was searching for me and I had to find her. I told her how sorry I was, but that I couldn't continue in our marriage."

"It was that simple?"

"Even more so," Chance almost laughed. "She thought I had cracked up. She didn't want to be settled with a nut case. She gladly gave me a divorce."

"You never doubted your sanity, Dr. Morgan?"

Chance glanced down at the floor to where Sabu was sitting. "What happened to calling me Chance?" He watched the little man, sure that if he were able to, he would have never called him Chance. That had been done out of desperation.

"I'm sorry," Sabu apologized. "It just seemed more appropriate. I feel as though the story you're telling me should be viewed with reverence. Using your title seemed more respectful."

Chance smiled. "Don't worry about it, Sabu. As for me doubting my sanity, there were plenty of times. I listened to my heart and knew the truth. "I studied. I went through past life regression countless times. Each time I was regressed I recovered more memories of my past lives. I remembered everything about my last incarnation with my wife and our life together. The more I remembered the more that came back, life after life. I don't think I've ever been without her."

"What happened in this lifetime?"

"She didn't wait for me. She got married."

"So did you."

"Yes, but I ended it, she didn't."

"You love her a great deal don't you?"

"More than life itself." Chance spoke softly, remembering what he'd done, remembering that by his act of willingly dying, Blaine had almost not forgiven him.

"Dr. Morgan,--" Sabu stopped at the look on Chance's face. "I'm sorry, Chance. Why didn't you re-connect sooner? Do you have an explanation?"

"Yes, karma."

"Karma?"

"Yes, that's what Blaine and Michelle keep telling me."

"What? Do you think your karmic debt was what kept you apart from your soul mate after finding each other again lifetime after lifetime? What do you think happened that keeps you apart this time?"

"I was the cause of my wife's death." Sabu's eyes lifted and

Chance saw fear creep into them before he asked, "Did you kill her?"

"Yes," Chance answered without hesitation.

"How?"

It was a tiny squeak. He glanced at Sabu and wondered if he was thinking of trying to make him pay for his crimes by informing the authorities. He laughed out loud at the thought.

"I'm sorry. I shouldn't have asked."

For a moment he'd almost forgotten Sabu. "No, don't be sorry. I killed my wife by planting my seed in her, by not having enough money so that I could afford medical care. By not knowing what to do myself, to save her. You see, Sabu, if I had never gotten my wife pregnant she would have never died, not then anyway. She was much too young."

Sabu stood, his small stature towering over Chance as he lay in the bed.

"But if you had not given your wife a child you would have missed having your son. Then and now."

Chance stared hard at Sabu, listening to his words, slowly realizing their meaning.

"Would you rather your son was never born?"

Chance's jaw went slack. A cold chill crept up his spine. He thought of Blaine. "That wasn't what I meant," he whispered more to himself than to Sabu.

"That is what you said."

"I loved my son."

"But you loved his mother more."

"How am I to answer that?" He remembered something Michelle had said to him once. "Sabu, there is no scale on which to measure love."

"Maybe not, but you need to make a choice. It won't change the past, but you need to know in your heart if you could have made a choice if you would have given your son's life so your wife would live."

"I won't answer that question." Chance was angry now. "No more questions." He ignored the sadness conveyed in Sabu's demeanor. He was saturating his entire room with it, permeating his spirit and his soul with the coldness of it.

"I didn't want you to give me the answer. That question is yours alone. I respect your privacy in this matter. However, Chance, it is something you need to answer for yourself."

"What good will it do? We can't erase the past."

"You said you believe you're not with your soul mate because of karma. Maybe you can change your future."

"How?"

"By knowing and allowing the truth to be known in your heart. It's only you who know even if the question I ask is the right question. It may not be. There may be a more important question blocking your future. You must be at peace with yourself. And that includes your past self as well."

Chance moved farther down on the flat straw mattress. He no longer felt like talking. For nearly three months every person he'd spoken to, everything he'd done was pointing fingers at him, telling him it was his fault Michelle was not with him

He didn't bother watching Sabu walk to the door nor did he acknowledge his goodbye. It was only when he poked his head back into the room that Chance responded.

"Please eat," Sabu encouraged. "Your son needs a father."

Chance glanced at the tray of food and again at Sabu. He allowed his hand to move and retrieve a can of fruit. He ate until there was not a morsel left. Next he ate the sardines and drank both bottles of water. Sabu was right. His son needed a father.

CHAPTER NINETEEN

Chance's time of feeling sorry for himself was over. He couldn't help but think he'd undone all the good he'd managed to accomplish. He groaned. It appeared instead of cultivating personal growth, he'd degenerated into a thoughtless invalid. The push and pull of letting go made him realize he'd never truly let go. It didn't matter that he kept saying it. His actions proved otherwise. Hopefully he could atone for past life wrongs by taking care of as many patients as he could in this life. Glancing upward he spotted George watching him as he'd done for the past few days. Before he uttered one word he knew what was coming.

"Chance, you don't have to work so hard. Every one of us has had to take a few days off from time to time."

Chance barely glanced at George before looking down at Aisha, the child he'd treated only moments after he arrived. It appeared the child had developed a fondness for him. Since the day her mother gave him the Rune the little girl had been back several times with numerous complaints. None of them serious.

The child smiled at him her brown eyes glowing. Chance knew what she was waiting for. He stripped away his gloves and plucked a bright red lollipop from his near by stash.

"Here you go, Aisha, this should make it better."

At the questioning frown on the child's face, Chance began to hold up his fingers until he had seven long digits in the air. Then and only then did the child smile while clapping. Chance was her willing servant and she knew it. She had managed to insert herself into his life, twisting off a piece of his heart for her very own.

When he placed the seven suckers into her hands Aisha leaned over and planted a wet, sloppy kiss on his cheek before hiding her face in her hand.

Chance smiled at the mother before lifting Aisha from the examining table. "She's fine," he told the mother, then made gestures with his hand shooing Sabu away from him. He didn't need nor did he want an interpreter. He was being observed . The hope that George would disappear hadn't worked.

"What's going on with you, Chance?"

He had to give it to George. He was persistent. Gritting his teeth, Chance turned to the older man. "Nothing, George. I'm just doing my job, taking care of patients."

"No one has ever complained of you not doing your job, but, Chance, you're over doing it. All of us work ten hours days, but you you're working twenty. You can't keep on like this."

"I have to." Chance looked away trying not to focus on anyone in the room. "I have to do what I can to help. It's why I'm here."

"We all came here to help. But I don't want you to kill yourself in the process."

"No George, I don't mean India. I'm here in this life to help. It's my destiny to heal, to save lives."

"But, Chance, you can't.—"

"I can't what? Save lives? I know what you think about that and you're wrong. That is my purpose, my destiny." He winced inwardly, forcing himself to say the next words. "I've done it before many times. I am a healer."

He couldn't help but travel backwards in time to when his abilities would have meant more, to the one time when he didn't know what to do. If his helping the sick in this life would wipe away his karmic debt and clear a path for him to be with his family then he would work twenty-four hours a day if need be.

Looking into George's worried gaze, he smiled. "Don't worry, George." He really didn't want the man to worry, he didn't feel there was a reason. "This has to be my true purpose for being here," Chance continued. "I have to keep working. What if someone comes in while I'm off doing other things, someone that only I could have helped with my knowledge? How do you think I would feel knowing there was someone I could have saved and I didn't do anything? I have to keep working."

There was no missing the look that passed over his head. George was looking toward Sabu. The rest of the staff had finally called it a night. Only Chance had remained. It had been Sabu who had answered the knock from Aisha and her mother and had sent them away. Chance had seen and had run after them, bringing them back into the clinic.

"But sir, there is nothing wrong with the little girl. She only wants candy," Sabu complained.

Chance had ignored him, his medical knowledge telling him Sabu was right. Still he examined every body part that the child pointed out, determined that if she were really in pain he would be there for her. He would help.

Now Aisha and her mother were gone. He could no longer pretend there was a reason for remaining in the clinic. Still, he stood rooted to the spot not knowing where to go. He didn't want to sleep for he dreamed then. And he could no longer handle his dreams.

"Chance."

It was George poking at him with his bony finger. He turned to face him. "Yes. What is it?"

"The computer is free."

Chance stared blankly. "I wasn't planning on using it."

"Well, Blaine keeps emailing. We've put him off, but he won't stop." George's face grew pensive. "I thought you called him."

"I did."

"He's worried about you, and frankly, so am I."

"There is no reason to be," Chance reassured George. "I just want to do my job. Why is that so difficult? Everyone was willing to help me out, taking over my shift for Blaine's visit and when I... when I was ill." The last he said with an edge. "Now I just want to do my part."

"Okay, Chance." George relented. "What about the computer? Are you going to contact Blaine?"

"Maybe tomorrow," he mumbled then made his way to his room, not bothering to turn on the light or undress. He merely crawled into the bed and threw his hands over his face. He had barely closed his eyes when he heard a low rumble from the corner across from him, the sound of someone clearing their throat. Someone was in his room.

"Damn it, Sabu." He sat up angrily and looked into the eyes of his son.

"Blaine! When did you...?" He stopped, knowing instantly Blaine had not taken a plane to see him. He must have bi-located to him.

"I didn't know your powers were strong enough to send you all the way here."

"Neither did I."

"Why did you come? Is there something wrong with Cassandra, or the baby?" He closed his eyes, he wouldn't ask about Michelle.

"Chance, why won't you tell me what's going on with you? I

know it has something to do with that call you made to Michelle. She's frantic. She thinks you believe she hates you. Where would you get an idea like that?"

Throwing a barrage of mental blocks into place, he stared at Blaine. He couldn't tell his son, he didn't want him to come to the conclusion that Sabu had so quickly come up with.

"Stay out of my mind, Blaine. I'll handle this on my own."

"Yes, you've been saying this for over a year now and you don't seem to be any closer to the truth than you were at the beginning."

"You're wrong. I've figured it out."

"And what exactly have you figured out.

"I'm a healer. I was healer in many of my lifetimes," he paused, shaking away the sadness that had invaded him. With the exception of my last life. Now I'm a doctor is this life, a healer, and that's what I plan to do. I will get rid of my karmic debt by healing."

"Michelle thought your coming here to India was going to set you free. Instead you seem to be in more of a prison than you were before. I knew this wasn't a good idea. You should have never come here."

"Why? I thought you believed it was helping."

"Before you came you at least talked to me, confided in me, now you're shutting me out. Are you angry with me for talking with Michelle, for letting her know how you are?"

A grimace of pain tugged at the corners of Chance's face. "Angry with you? No, Blaine, not with you, with myself."

"Why?"

Chance stared at Blaine the need to put off the telling for just a little while stronger than his knowledge that he would have to admit the truth to his son. "How is Michelle? I mean after my call. Larry was home." He felt the familiar spark of jealousy hit him before he forced himself to continue.

"Did I mess things up for her?" He noticed that Blaine wasn't looking directly at him now.

"Almost," Blaine answered at last. "She had a major fight with Larry. Then she booked a flight to come here. The Mystic, Cassandra and myself, we all had a hell of a time convincing her not to come. I'm afraid her marriage is in jeopardy."

For a nanosecond he couldn't believe his ears. Michelle had wanted to come to him and the people that loved him convinced her not to. He stared open-mouthed at Blaine. "You convinced her not to come to me?"

"I had to. For all of us, I didn't have a choice."

"Of course you had a choice."

"Michelle understands what her coming to you would mean." Blaine paused for a moment. "So do you, Chance. We all do. Still, she was willing to come."

"So why isn't she here?"

"She would have only hurt you by coming."

Chance laughed, walking away from Blaine and shaking his head in astonishment that everyone thought they had a right to tell him what was best for him.

Blaine walked up behind him and laid his hand on his shoulder forcing him to turn toward him.

"Chance, you have to work this out for yourself. You have to find the reason you're not with Michelle in this life."

Now would be the time. Now he should tell his son things that might break his heart. He watched Blaine move back to the chair he'd recently vacated. He thought his son moved as an old man filled with worry and pain. Chance had no choice, he had to tell him and could only pray for the best.

"I found the answer. I know why we're not together." Before he could get another word out, Blaine had leaped out of the chair and was pounding him on the back, his voice filled with praise and joy.

"I knew you could do it. I knew you could," Blaine beamed.

Chance was puzzled. He pulled away just a fraction so he could view the face of his son. "Blaine, why are you so happy? What I did to you, how I felt. I'm so sorry."

"To me?" Blaine's hands fell to the side. "What did you come up with, Chance? What's the karmic debt you're paying off? Why aren't we together this lifetime as a family?"

"I was talking to Sabu. I told him that I was responsible for my wife's death."

"But you weren't."

"Let me finish," Chance pleaded. "That's not all. I remember so well what Dimi pleaded with me for after your birth. She asked me not to hate you. I remember blaming you. You were just a tiny baby and I blamed you."

Tears were streaming down Chance's face. "That's my debt. I

blamed my son for his mother's death." He moved even farther away from his son.

"No, Chance. That wasn't it."

Chance looked at Blaine stunned. "Didn't you hear me?"

"I heard you. First you said you blamed yourself then you said you blamed me. Suppose you tell me what you really think the reason is."

"I just did."

"There has to be more. That's not enough to make you not want to talk to me, to not answer my calls or Michelle, nor to even send an email. There's something more going on here, Chance.

"There is no more."

"Even if I don't read your mind I know there's more. There's a stronger element at work here. The guilt in you is palpable. We've already gotten through most of this. So forgive me if I say I don't believe you."

Chance pulled himself up erect, he didn't want to say the words, but his son had a right to know.

"Sabu asked me if I'd had a choice would I have chosen to have you never born if it meant I could have been with my wife."

"And would you?"

"That's just it, Blaine, I don't know, not even to this day I don't know. I wish I didn't have to admit that to you, but I feel you have a right to know."

"Father, are you worried that you didn't love me? That if it had been possible for you to have traded my life for Dimi, you would have made that choice?"

"I loved you then and I love you now."

"So, what's the problem?"

"What if even for a moment, I had that thought? How am I to know?"

"I do not believe that was the case.'

"What if you're wrong? I'm sorry that you had to hear this from me, but I never want to be less than honest with you."

"Thanks for telling me. But tell me this, why are you so sure this is your karmic debt?"

"Think about it, it's what all the Runes have been saying to me, telling me to search out all the dark places, the secret in my heart, and then to acknowledge it."

"And that's what you're doing?"

Blaine was disappointed. Chance could hear it in his voice, but there was something missing. He'd expected his son to be hurt, but that he didn't hear. Maybe Blaine was blocking it out in order to delay his own pain.

"Blaine, didn't you hear me? I blamed you for Dimi's death. Think about it. As much as I hate knowing that's the debt I'm paying, I can't ignore it. I hate telling you this but that has to be it."

Blaine was being so quiet. Chance wanted to do a little probing of his son's mind but resisted the temptation. Besides there was no way he could without detection. Blaine was too good at his gifts not to feel an intrusion. Only a psychic like the Mystic could get away with that. And now since Blaine had grown much stronger he doubted if even the Mystic could enter his mind at will.

"I know you initially blamed me. Remember I also experienced what happened. But that's not what the debt is."

Chance looked confused for a moment then thought of what Blaine must be wanting him to say. "I know you think it has more to do with what I wanted, a choice I made."

"You're right. Our entire life is about choices. But you didn't choose who lived or died."

"I didn't have the power to choose. How do I know what I would have done? It wasn't in my hands. But surely just the fact that I had those feelings, that would be enough to create all of this, don't you think?" He looked at Blaine almost imploringly.

"Chance, can I ask you something? How long did it take you after my mother died to be able to look at me as your son?"

"What are you saying? You were always my son. I always looked at you as such."

"Yes, but surely if you hated me, and blamed me, you couldn't have looked at me with love."

Chance shook his head. "But I did look on you with love. I gathered your mother in my arms, then I reached for you and I held you close. I can remember crying, telling you that it was just the two of us."

"Is all of that true, Chance? Is that really the way it happened or the way you want to believe?"

"Yes, it's true. I would never lie to you about something so important." Chance looked at Blaine puzzled "Why are you asking me that?"

"Because if that's the way it happened I don't think you would be punished for that. You loved me as a father loves a son. I know that you did."

"Then why were you always so angry with me? It was you who said you couldn't forgive me."

"Yes, but I eventually did. Remember? I never once thought you didn't love me, not really."

Chance was genuinely confused now. As painful as it had been to bring the question to the light, he thought he'd at last found a reason for the pain. The look on Blaine's face was telling him that he would have to continue searching.

"I don't get it," Chance said honestly. You said it was about choices, the Runes said it was some hidden secret, something that needed to be brought to the light."

He watched as Blaine began walking around his sparsely furnished room. Picking up odds and ends lying about, his gaze coming to rest on the one family portrait.

"How's your study of the Runes coming?"

"You're trying to change the subject."

Blaine turned back toward him, a sad smile barely touching his lips. He could sense the uneasiness in his son. The tenseness in his muscles relayed that despite the fact that Blaine was behaving in a perfectly calm manner as if what they were discussing didn't matter in the least, it did. It mattered a lot..

"I'm curious, indulge me," Blaine laughed. "What's the harm?"

"Okay, I'll play along. For now. I haven't been studying with Sabu for awhile now. I just haven't wanted to deal with it anymore. Knowing.," he hesitated. "Knowing what I know has been enough of a burden."

"Why are you working such crazy hours?"

So George Trammel or Sabu had informed Blaine of his actions. Well, no matter, Blaine more than anyone should understand.

"I told you. I know why I'm a doctor in this life."

"Why?"

The simple straightforward question nearly stopped Chance in his tracks. From Blaine he expected so much more. He didn't appear curious at all, merely polite.

"Because of Michelle. I mean Dimi. I think because I couldn't save her then, I'm making up for it now."

"And you plan on doing all of that by killing yourself?"

Chance winced at his son's choice of words

Blaine saw. "Sorry, by working yourself to death how do you think this will help?"

"It may not help, but..." Running his hand roughly through his hair, he tousled it, pulling on the ends until he knew it was standing all over his head. "I'm just trying to put the pieces together. Is there anything wrong with that?"

"No, not a thing." Blaine relented a tiny bit, "Just take it easy okay. I don't want you to overdo it. I like having a father around to talk to, someone who's not locked away. By the way your colleagues have become so worried about you that I thought for sure we would have to put you away."

"We?"

"Well me."

Chance searched Blaine's eyes. "I guess I scared the hell out of Michelle didn't I?"

"You scared all of us."

"I shouldn't have called her."

Chance blinked rapidly trying to forget how he'd badgered Michelle into telling him she loved him, knowing full well her husband was listening. He hadn't expected a response from Blaine and he didn't get one.

"Larry doesn't deserve any of this," Chance mused. "He just got caught in the middle. I wonder if he had a choice to get involved with a bunch of psychics or to fall in love with someone else which he'd take."

Again Blaine didn't answer.

"I know I don't really have a reason for hating him."

"But you do."

Now Blaine could answer. Chance grimaced. "Yeah I do. I guess I haven't grown enough not to."

"You're feeling guilty about hating him?"

This time Chance laughed in earnest. "There isn't much I don't feel guilty about these days." He turned serious. "If I can't have Dimi now I want to make sure this mistake doesn't happen again."

"Michelle."

"Fine. Michelle. Either way I wouldn't want to keep coming back only to be denied loving her all over again."

Chance watched as Blaine fingered the bracelet identical to his own. Out of habit Chance did the same thing. "I can't stop loving her, Blaine." His voice shook but he did not cry.

"You've got it all wrong."

Blaine was looking sadder than Chance could ever remember seeing him. For a moment he wished he'd kept the words inside, then he thought, what difference would it make? Blaine knows I love her.

"No one has asked that you stop loving her, just that you let her go, let her live out the hand she's been dealt. And you do the same."

"I've been trying." A groan escaped Chance's throat a second before he again ran his hand through his tousled hair. "It may not look like it, but I have been trying."

"I know you have, and if this helps, you're on the right path."

Chance's head snapped to attention. Blaine had been giving him little hints. But he'd been so consumed with the dark secret he carried in his heart that he'd not heard. Now he was listening. "Blaine, you know don't you?"

"Yes, Father, I know."

"Michelle? Does she know?"

"Yes."

"Then why the hell don't one of you let me in on the secret?"

He watched while Blaine walked away from him. He saw the shudders raking his son's body, heard the low sounds he couldn't distinguish, then Blaine blowing his nose.

When he turned again toward Chance his eyes were red rimmed. Chance's heart hurt for his son as Blaine's heart was hurting for him. A fresh stab of pain raced through him. If he could stop hurting, Blaine would stop hurting, so would Michelle. His pain was hurting those he loved

"I want more than anything to help you with this, Chance, to just tell you and get it over with."

"Then why don't you?"

"The Mystic warned me not to. He said if either Michelle or I interfered in your natural progression he couldn't guarantee what might happen. He said we can only truly grow by discovering the knowledge for ourselves."

Chance thought of the old man. He'd spent almost as many lifetimes with him as he had with Michelle. If anyone knew the mysteries, it was the Mystic.

"Well, if he said it, it's more than likely true?" Chance conceded.

"You are getting close. Don't lose hope, Father. I know you will figure it out."

Blaine could not offer him more, no matter how it easy it would be to just tell him. Chance knew this and understood.

"How are things with you and Sabu?"

"Better. He actually called me by name a couple of times." He saw the disbelief in Blaine's eyes. "Don't worry, he soon went back to his oh so proper Doctor Morgan."

"Are you going to call Michelle again? Let her know that you're alive and well?"

He'd known they would eventually get around to Michelle. Their conversations always took them there. "You'll let her know that I'm alive. I have no doubt of that." An indescribable look crossed Blaine's face before he answered.

"It might be better if you did it. .Just call her. I think she needs to hear your voice."

Shock didn't begin to describe Chance's reaction to Blaine telling him to call Michelle. "I can't believe this. You're telling me to call her. Why?"

"It's not my voice she wants to hear. Besides, I promised her that if she didn't come here I would see to it that you called her."

"I can't."

"Why?"

"Because I haven't grown enough. If she offers to come to me, I'll buy the ticket."

Blaine chewed on his lips thoughtfully, his feelings moving rapidly. He smiled at Chance before standing and embracing him. "I'll talk to her."

"You do that and tell her one other thing for me. Tell her that until I can truly let go of her, I won't call again. One more thing, ask her not to call me anymore." He dipped his head to the side. "Same reasons."

Chance held on to Blaine until he'd disappeared, leaving his room, Chance knew to reappear in the States. He could say without a doubt that he was glad his son had been born.

Both times.

The next morning he'd reached a decision. He didn't like who he'd

become. He was a selfish bastard to those in his life. At the least he
needed to grow beyond that. Given the way he'd been behaving for
far too long, he was surprised anyone had sympathy for him or even
liked him. Hell, he didn't much like himself. The moment he saw
Sabu come into the dining room he made his way toward him.

"Good morning, Sabu. I would like to restart the Rune lesson."

"Certainly. I've only been waiting until you were ready. Is there
some particular thing you want to know first?"

"Yeah, think you can just tell me without a long lesson how many
Runes there are?"

"Twenty-five."

Chance laughed out loud. "That's it? You're going to give me
answers without telling me of the hidden meaning?"

"For now I am."

"What's the first Rune?"

"The Self, or Mannaz."

"And the last?" Chance noticed the twinkle in Sabu's eyes then
his smile.

"The last Rune is the unknowable, or Odin."

"Can we start with any Rune that we want?"

"Of course, there are no rules. Which would you like to start
with?"

"The last one. The unknowable." Chance shrugged. "I figure it
will only get harder as we study, so we might as well take the hardest
one and work our way backwards."

For an answer Sabu pulled out a stone from his pocket and
handed it to Chance. "This is the Rune of Odin. I thought this might
be the one we'd do today."

"I'm not surprised," Chance answered. "Let's get started. I have a
life to reclaim. By the way, Sabu, I'd like to ask your forgiveness for
my shabby treatment of you. I've been behaving in a mean spirited
and petty manner. Both are beneath me. I'd much appreciate it if we
could start over."

"As I told you, we're destined to become good friends."

There was nothing more to be said, so for once Chance didn't
speak. He merely smiled, believing that he and Sabu would become
great friends.

CHAPTER TWENTY

What he'd come to think of the highlight of his days was now bringing a smile to his face. His time here was coming to a close. Chance took a quick peek in his private stash of lollipops he kept for the children. He would have to replenish soon. Aisha's visits were becoming more frequent. In fact he'd just dispensed a handful of the treats to her only moments before.

"Working late again, Chance?"

Why was it every single time he worked long hours George Trammel happened to stroll in as if to check on him? Chance straightened up from his bent position and turned to greet the older man.

"Not really, George, just one last patient with a very mild case of the sniffles." Chance couldn't stop the smile from spreading across his face. Mild indeed. Fake was more like it.

"I wanted to talk to you about something rather important."

George was hedging. Chance glanced sharply at him wondering what was on his mind. Whatever it was, it had to be bad for Chance. "What's on you mind?" he asked politely.

"Chance you know how the situation is today. No one wants to travel much, and especially not out of the States. I'm almost embarrassed to ask. I know you've been looking forward to going home."

"You want me to extend my stay?"

"Yes, if you could. I'll try and pay you a small stipend, if that would help."

A chuckle was Chance's first response. "I don't need the money, George. But I do have a practice back home. I don't know if I can stay on another three months."

He watched as George's hands flitted nervously, he kept starting to say something then would stop abruptly. Chance was beginning to smell a set up.

"George, what's going on? What's the real reason you want me to stay? Did Blaine have anything to do with this urgent request?"

"Are you accusing me of....of?" George couldn't maintain his indignation, he started laughing. "I'm sorry, Chance. But there is so

much happening in the next few weeks you would hate yourself if
you left."

"I have two more weeks."

"I don't even think you will be finished with your studies with
Sabu in two weeks."

"How did you know I was studying with Sabu?" Chance's
eyebrow quirked upwards. "Never mind, you don't have to answer
that."

"Sabu didn't tell me if that's what you're thinking. Come on, for
almost three months you two are at each others throats. Now you've
become best friends. Of course you're studying the Runes with him.
It's obvious."

"But what would make you think it would be the Runes? It could
have been anything else."

George's eyes twinkled. There was something about the older man
that Chance really liked. On more than one occasion he'd almost
probed into George's private life only restraining himself when he
realized he would have to allow George to probe into his.

"You've studied everything else, Chance. It makes sense that the
Runes would now capture your imagination."

"And you would know that because?" Chance was becoming
intrigued by George's knowledge of his personal life. How the hell
the man was finding out so much about him was making him curious.

"George, I won't give you any guarantees, but I'll see what I can
do about staying on a little longer. First you tell me what's the big
deal, what's coming up, and why is it you want me to stay?"

"To be honest, I was thinking about the karmic cleansing."

"Hell no." Chance cut him off. "Hell no. There is no way I'm
going to do that." He stopped as George held his hands up in mock
surrender.

"I wasn't implying that you would want to join, merely that you
might be curious about seeing it. You really haven't done much sight
seeing since you've been here."

Chance thought back to his trip to One Mile Road the horrid
smell of cow dung, the choking acrid smoke. "To answer your
question about my ever going again onto One Mile Road, it's a
definite no. I've seen everything I need to see there, George. Thanks
for your interest."

Instead of looking insulted, George only laughed at him before shaking his head and walking away.

"Goodnight, Chance," he called over his shoulder.

"Goodnight, George," Chance answered back. "Don't go to bed holding your breath about me going into that polluted water. There is no way on earth I'm going to do it." Louder laughter from George was his response.

It was one of those rare days when everything the Runes had to say clicked for Chance. He didn't have any argument left in him. Sabu was displaying one of his now frequent smiles.

"Why are you grinning like that, Sabu?" Chance was teasing him as they walked back toward the common room.

"No reason, Dr. Morgan. I just don't feel so beat up on as I usually do when we finish with a lesson."

Both men laughed before falling into a companionably silence. Chance should have known it was too good to last.

"Ah, there's Karen," Sabu said softly. "Your last hurdle perhaps, Dr. Morgan."

Chance glanced quickly in Karen's direction before looking down at the rocks in his path, pretending not to take any notice of her.

"She's a woman, Sabu, not some challenge for me. You talk as if she's some accomplishment I have to complete before I'm done with my training."

"I would not have put it in those words but for the last month you've barely spoken to her. I do understand that you don't love her. And I now know why. But you have to find a way to resolve that with the knowledge that you desire her. Your desire made her believe perhaps you were having emotions other than lust. I wouldn't say you've led her on, but I would say your actions have hurt her greatly. She was the first person to befriend you, if you remember."

"I remember."

"Then perhaps there are issues you might feel you need to make clear to her."

"Not really, Sabu. There you're wrong."

"Perhaps."

"There is no perhaps about it. I'm sorry about how things turned out between the two of us, but all I ever wanted was to be friends with her, nothing more."

Sabu was quiet for a moment looking thoughtfully at Chance before he spoke. "Do you know you're the first man she's shown any interest in in the past five years?"

Chance blinked. "Are you blaming me for something, Sabu? I never lied to Karen. I have nothing to feel guilty about."

"No, it's not your fault and I didn't tell you for you to feel guilt."

"Then why are you telling me?"

"I wanted you to know that Karen was never chasing you. At least not in the way you thought. She may have been a little over eager to meet you. We all were, especially after hearing about what happened, but she never meant to make you feel uncomfortable."

"I know you have a reason for telling me about Karen. Go ahead and spill it."

"She lost her husband to cancer about seven years ago. She came here trying to get over his death. I think in you she recognized someone in as much pain as she's been in and she wanted to help."

"Are you sure you're not trying to make me feel guilty? Because it sure is having that effect. I didn't know about Karen's husband." Chance had stopped walking, but his long legged stride had put him ahead of Sabu. He waited for the other man to catch up.

"What's the point of telling me all of this?"

"Because you're leaving soon. Karen isn't. She had healed but now since whatever occurred between the two of you, she's hurting again. I thought maybe since you once thought of her as a friend you could help to heal the reopened scars."

Chance looked directly into Sabu's brown eyes. "I can only offer her friendship, nothing more."

"That's all that I'm asking."

A sigh of resignation filled Chance. "You know, Sabu, it's possible she won't want my friendship. In case you haven't noticed, she's the one who has been avoiding me lately."

"I'm sure you'll think of a way, Chance."

Chance shook his head before laughing. "What is it with you? One minute you refuse to call me anything but Doctor Morgan the next, it's Chance. Why?"

"Because what I ask of you now, I ask as a friend, so for that you are Chance."

Sabu continued walking, leaving Chance to ponder what games the man was playing with him. There was something strange about

Sabu and about George Trammel. Maybe staying a little longer wouldn't be such a bad idea.

Now that he'd made up his mind to do it there was nothing to do except do it quickly like wrenching a bandage off. It would be less painful. He rushed to catch up to Karen.

The air surrounding Karen sizzled with energy. Chance reached out his hand to touch her then pulled back. Any rights to touch her he'd thrown away by practically accusing her of trying to seduce him. He'd have to crawl to get back in her good graces.

"Karen, I haven't seen much of you lately." He braced himself for her cool reception as she turned toward him then turned away.

"We work side by side ten hours a day, Doctor Morgan."

Okay, he thought, it's Doctor Morgan with her too. That was his best indication that she was still angry. "We don't really work side by side, you're usually working with anyone other than me." Chance was challenging her hoping she'd look at him long enough to fight.

Karen was facing him now. Her eyes lifeless, he'd at least expected some fire, some anger. He saw neither and that was scary. The woman had been fighting with him since almost the beginning, now this deadness, it worried him.

"Is there something you want?"

"I just wanted to talk," Chance answered gently.

He watched while she metamorphosed into something different. Her eyes glowed with red flames. He would swear if he'd put out his hand to touch her he would have been burned by the steam. He watched as her eyes darted around. She was making sure no one could hear their conversation and for that he was grateful. He could tell by her stance that he was about to catch hell. Better to have this done in private than public humiliation.

"Now you want to talk," Karen spat out between clenched teeth. "Look, I've been trying to befriend you since you've been here. I admit I completely ignored your hands off sign that you've worn so proudly. Well, now I've got it, do you understand? I hear you; you have no need for friends. You want to be left alone, to be miserable, to live out your life punishing yourself for something that happened a lifetime ago. Grow up, Chance, you're not the first person to lose a loved one. If you're looking for sympathy I suggest you go look for it elsewhere. I've had enough of you running hot and cold whenever you feel like it. I'm tired of trying to get you to live again."

He stood before her and took it. Every word. Chance winced inwardly, thinking how he must have hurt her. It was never intentional. Still a hurt was a hurt, intentional or not.

He swallowed twice trying to find the right words. "I know I've been horrible to you. You've only tried to make things easier. I know that. I was...well. I had some things to work out. I didn't mean to hurt you."

Chance saw her blush and wished he'd used different words. "Listen," he amended quickly, "I don't think I ever properly thanked you for taking me on that tour or, telling me so much about the culture. And I know for a fact I didn't thank you for getting others to work my shift during Blaine's visit."

"How did you know?" Karen's tone was flat.

"Things aren't kept very private around here. Can we start over again, Karen? I'd really like to get to know you as a person."

"What about Michelle?"

Chance felt his guts twisting, the little muscle in his jaw was twitching a mile a minute. He wanted not to overreact, not this time. "What about Michelle?"

"I mean are you capable of being friends with any woman? You're so obsessed with her that I don't know if you can be. I mean if I give you a friendly hug I don't want to send you running, thinking you're cheating on her."

"That wasn't what I did. Look, I admit I may have sent you the wrong signals." He ran his hands through his hair. "I'm sure I did. Look, Karen, I thought that maybe I could fall for you. I allowed myself to think about it."

"Then what happened? Why did you act like that?"

Chance took a deep breath keeping the air in his mouth moving it from cheek to cheek. He wanted to continue to do this right, but people were forever posing questions to him for which he had no diplomatic answer."

"What happened Chance?" Karen repeated.

"The truth?"

"Yes the truth," she answered. "I'm stronger than I look."

Chance smiled. She was strong. She'd lost her husband and yet she'd found a way to go on. He could not be anything less than honest with her. "I care about you, Karen," he paused when he saw her gritting her teeth. He knew this sounded like the typical, 'let's be friend speech', but he had to tell her.

"I've enjoyed being around you, talking to you. You're a beautiful woman. It wasn't hard to imagine that I could one day come to care deeply for you."

"If that's true then I don't understand what happened."

Looking at her for a moment he felt suddenly sad. "I saw the truth in your eyes. You wanted more than I could give. It wouldn't have been fair to you."

For the first time he saw a deep sadness in Karen and wondered how he'd managed to miss it. Had he really been that wrapped up in his own problems? "I would have never been able to give you what you deserve."

"Chance, you silly goose." She was laughing. "There are all kinds of love. Believe it or not, people manage to go on after a loss. It happens all the time, people remarry even after someone they loved very much passes. It doesn't mean that they didn't love that person."

He saw the light shining again in her eyes. This time he didn't say anything, he just listened and watched her face for signals..

"How are you supposed to judge how much you love one person over the other?"

Chance thought about Michelle and what she'd said when he asked how she could possibly go back to Larry, how she could love him when she was meant to be with him. He hadn't understood how she'd professed to love them both. She'd said there wasn't a scale to measure love. He knew now she was right. The same way he couldn't say he loved his wife or child more. He loved them equally he realized at last, just in different ways.

It was the same thing Karen was saying, the same thing he'd told Blaine. He looked at Karen in wonder. For the first time he thought he understood how Michelle could have left him.

He'd never admitted it to Blaine, Michelle or even to himself, but yes he'd been hurt that Michelle had chosen her husband and children over him. Though they would have to be blind, not to have seen it. To them he'd only shown anger. It wasn't the anger that had eaten away at him since it happened. It was the hurt. He'd thought she couldn't love him as much as he loved her.

Closing his eyes, he swallowed the too familiar hurt, knowing with every fiber of his being that Michelle loved him. He also knew she loved Larry. Because she'd stayed with Larry he'd thought she'd chosen between them, that somehow her love for him wasn't as strong. He'd been wrong.

Hell, she'd sent him away because she loved him. To protect their next life together, she was living out this life as she should, happy, loving and being loved. He winced with the knowledge that he hadn't been able to do the same.

"I don't know if I could ever do it," he said at last.

"No one's asking for miracles from you, Chance." Karen smiled at him. "No one's asking you to forget your love for Michelle. I'm just saying you're not dead. It's time for you to stop acting as though you are."

Something Karen said niggled at Chance's brain, something about being dead. He shook his head slightly, trying to retrieve the thought, but it was gone. He glanced instead at Karen. "Let's start slow okay, let's try and be friends."

"That's fine. But don't forget friendship works two ways, Chance. It's not just you taking from me when you need it. I have needs too. Have you ever thought that maybe, just maybe, I have or had someone in my life, I loved as much as you do your Michelle? Maybe I would like to talk about my loss."

Karen was right. He'd never asked her much about herself at all. "I'm sorry," he whispered.

"You don't have to keep apologizing. Just keep it in mind, stop closing everyone out whenever her name is mentioned. Do you think you're ready to do that?"

"What are you asking me exactly?"

"I'm asking you to share your love for Michelle with me. Just talk to me about her. Maybe if you didn't keep your feelings for her bottled up inside, you'd be able to let go."

Chance thought about Blaine and how he was hurting, worrying about him wanting him to discover what happened and Michelle, the woman he loved. He knew she was hurting, worrying about him. He knew his call had more than likely caused conflict in her marriage. He wanted to regret his actions, but he wasn't there yet. And he knew without a doubt he needed to be. Karen was right. He needed to live again. He may as well start now.

"Karen, tell me about your husband."

"Now's not the time. Ask me later and if I feel you're truly interested, I'll tell you."

Smiling at her, he headed for the common room for coffee. He didn't blame Karen for not sharing her life with him.

In his last scheduled days, it appeared he was becoming more comfortable with spending time with the group. Everyone had told of their journey and their growth. He was the only hold out and he could sense George's attention focused on him. So, when he called his name he wasn't surprised.

"So, Chance, are you ever going to tell us what happened when you took on the forces of evil?"

Chance laughed at the way George phrased that. "George, I really came in at the end. I didn't do too much, there were a lot of psychics involved."

"You promised, so how about now?"

They were sitting in the common room. Chance had put them off long enough. For some reason it seemed right to tell them what happened. First he told them how he'd met Michelle, how he'd known she was his wife. He left out only the most intimate details of their time together.

He saw the looks of sadness go through the group when he retold them how Michelle had decided in the end she had to return to her life and live out this lifetime with her husband. They ached for him and amazingly that took some of his own pain away. They wanted him to be reunited with the woman he loved, but they understood she had to live out her destiny.

"Chance, how did the whole psychic war thing get started?"

Chance glanced at George. He would be the one to ask, he thought with a smile.

"Well, most of this is second hand, but it had something to do with a very old prophecy, a thousand years or so I'm told. It said something about a twenty-first generation pure bred psychic would have a baby with a psychic of equal powers.

"That was Blaine the prophecy spoke of?" Karen asked.

"Yes," Chance smiled and continued. "Only no one knew that in the beginning. He wasn't in the running; he wasn't considered a threat. He was thought of as a baby psychic."

"So how did that work? I don't get it."

That was the tricky part. Even after taking part in it, he wasn't sure himself. But he'd do his best to explain it to them. So he began.

"It seems because of our being Blaine's soul parents and the fact that we'd been psychics for many generations our gifts increased from each incarnation, getting stronger and stronger. When Blaine was born he had been given all he needed. His second incarnation was his destiny."

"What exactly are soul parents?" Karen asked a little bashfully, "I mean what about his biological parents, don't they count?"

"Not for the prophecy. You see, soul parents are the ones that first give life to a soul. That is that's soul's first connection, its first awareness. Whatever was there is then imprinted on the soul and is never lost, maybe forgotten, maybe never used, but never lost."

"And the parents Blaine had in this life, what about them?"

"Blaine's different than most," Chance said with pride. "He knew from almost the moment he was born that his parents were someone other than the ones he'd been born to. He always believed he would one day meet his soul parents. He was actually looking for us."

Chance felt a slight electrical charge skitter down his spine. He smiled, remembering the electrical ark of energy that had pulled Blaine to them when they first met.

"What happened?"

It was Karen again, asking for details on his first meeting with Blaine.

"No, Karen, not now." George admonished. "We want to hear about the fight."

Chance smiled at Karen. "I'll tell you later," he promised.

"Now, as for when I came into the fight," he looked directly at George. "It was down to the last two psychics."

"How many had there been and what happened to them?"

This time it was Karen who glared in George's direction and reminded him that Chance could only tell one story at a time.

"Twelve men had been chasing after Cassandra," Chance continued. "That's Blaine's wife," he said proudly to everyone listening.

"We know," they all echoed back.

"The men were trying everything, persuasion, their own psychic powers, entering her dreams. She had an old friend who came back to protect her, or so he said in the beginning."

"Was that Salvatore?" Sabu asked then ducked his head.

It was obvious to Chance that Sabu was embarrassed that he'd interrupted.

"Yes, Salvatore came home and he eliminated a lot of the competition, but there was another major player. Norman Yates."

"Norman was not just a psychic, he's a witch. I met him once." Sabu glanced at Chance. "Sorry," he muttered.

"Don't worry about it," Chance answered.

"But I thought a witch was always female."

The question came from Dr. Sanders. But so many others were nodding their heads in agreement that it made them all laugh as they waited to hear Chance's explanation.

"The only difference between a male witch and a female witch is their gender. To call a male witch, a warlock is highly offensive. A warlock is a witch, male, or female who has been locked out of his or her coven, and the members of the group have turned their backs on the individual labeled as a warlock, because they feel that their traditions or the craft was in some way betrayed."

"In that case which one was Norman using, psychic powers or witchcraft?"

"Both. Norman is a most powerful or should I say *was*, one of the most powerful and evil witches practicing the dark arts. But he is also a psychic. He has a long lineage. The trouble was when it came time for him to be taught by the Mystic, the Mystic saw some defect in Norman and wouldn't take him on as a student. I think that enraged him, made him bitter and probably is what made him turn to the dark arts. He wanted Cassandra and had some sort of hatred for Salvatore for bullying him when they were children. The guy was weird. He did all of this because he was picked on when he was a child by several of the Mystic's students. He thought the others in the psychic community bullied and belittled him.

"That goes on everywhere," Karen offered. "It would be nice if it could change. It would stop a lot of needless pain."

For a long moment no one spoke everyone thinking on Karen's words. Glancing around the room, Chance allowed his gaze to linger for a moment on Karen before he spoke. "Karen, you're so right about the need to stop bullies. Since the news in the States does get to you, I'm sure you've heard of the rise in school shootings in recent years because of bullies. Something has to be done to protect our children. It's time for bullying of all sorts to stop." With a deep sigh, Chance continued. "What happened with Norman was similar, only on a different level. The players were armed with psychic powers and magic."

"Chance, I want to go back to something you said about Norman. It seems he was using dark magic to fight the other psychics. That sounds as though he'd turned before the battle. In that case, if Norman turned evil wouldn't his coven have turned against him? Wouldn't he then be considered a warlock?"

"Not necessarily. If the practicing witch doesn't belong to a group, then that witch is considered to be a solitary practitioner, and therefore must only rectify his or her own karma with the universe. I don't think anyone ever got around to asking Norman if he belonged to a coven. Nor did any of us care." He sighed and it seemed to have been an unexpected signal of sorts. The room remained quiet, no one raised their hand, not one person asked a question. Chance smiled at the group and waited.

It was George who broke the silence. "How did you all stop him? We've heard many rumors that you zapped him with mental telepathy, that you surrounded him and chanted. Someone even said one of you had a gun and shot Norman."

At that Chance laughed. "No, no guns. Although come to think of it, a gun would have made it a lot easier." He looked down at the bracelet he was rubbing absentmindedly. "This is what we used." He lifted his arm high into the air as everyone crowded around to see it.

"A bracelet? What's so special about that?"

Chance looked to see who'd asked. It didn't matter. He knew they all wanted to know the same thing.

"This is what is supposed to bring my family together in our next incarnation."

"How?" Karen asked.

"I don't know," Chance answered truthfully. "It's an amulet that was specially charged by a powerful Mystic. It's encoded with all of our, lets say DNA. Somehow it's supposed to bring us together. But that's a story for another time."

He pressed his lips together to suppress a smile. "Anyway, it turned out that my family held the key. Blaine, Michelle, and I are what's called a Triad, psychic trinity."

He closed his eyes remembering everything clearly. "Both Blaine and I have identical bracelets. Michelle has a necklace. It's the stones the Mystic used. When the three of us were together we formed a triangle. The formation of our bodies somehow charged the stones and emitted this radiant purple healing light. Blaine was able to defeat Norman by healing him, cleansing his aura, taking away the darkness."

"What happened to Salvatore? I heard he was taken over by a demon."

"Not taken over. He willingly allowed an entity,-- a disembodied spirit, not a demon,-- to use his body. Salvatore is so strong psychically that he became bored. That made him cocky and was what gave the entity control over him. If he'd not gotten so cocky, there is no way it would have happened. Then of course the spirit had help, someone who drugged Salvatore in order for the spirit to enter his body without his permission. The spirit got stronger as Salvatore got weaker because the entity continued using the drugs to keep Salvatore sedated. And the rest, as they say, is history."

"Did he fight with Blaine?

"I'm not sure if it was the entity or Salvatore. No one's really sure of that part. Sometimes Salvatore had control and sometimes he didn't."

"We heard Blaine was near death, and you saved him."

"It never happened," Chance said, once again amused by the power of rumors."

"There was no battle to win Cassandra?"

"Cassandra and Salvatore talked and I assume she told him she was in love with Blaine. End of story. Even if it hadn't been, Cassandra said she was pregnant with Blaine's child. It was too late for Salvatore to try and fulfill the prophesy. It turned out that she wasn't really pregnant, but later they married and they now have a son. Besides with everything that happened, the way I see it, destiny was fulfilled. It was meant for Blaine and Cassandra to produce the long—awaited child."

"What happened with you and Michelle?"

Chance glanced over at George. He had thought the question would come from Karen, but one glance in her direction and he knew she would never ask him so private a question in front of everyone.

"Michelle went home with her husband."

"And you were left alone again."

This time it was Karen's voice. Chance looked away over the heads of everyone in the room and blinked rapidly. "Yeah story of my life you might say." It struck Chance how similar his own life was to that of his son.

"That's the reason you came to India?" someone asked, "To mend a broken heart?"

Chance tried his best to stop the grimace. *Mend a broken heart.* That was such a mild way to put it. "I suppose you could say that," he answered, rising at last, tired of answering questions. "Now you know."

He stretched and yawned hoping everyone would take a hint and let it drop for now. "Good night, everyone."

He'd almost made it to the door of the common room when he felt someone beside him.

"Chance, thank you for telling us. How do you feel?"

Chance glanced at Sabu. "Tired."

"I'm not surprised. But you've opened the wound, the poisonous infection can now be treated. You can be healed."

With a laugh, he continued to his room. Sabu definitely had a way with words. Only time would tell if he could be healed. He sure hoped so. He'd not lied about being tired. Moments after he'd returned to his room, he fell onto the bed fully dressed and slept the sleep of the exhausted.

"Chance."

Chance woke startled. At least he thought he was awake.

"Michelle," he asked, "Am I dreaming or are you really here?"

"A little of both," she replied.

"Why are you here? Why haunt my dreams at night, and by day demand I get on with my life?"

Chance sat up in bed, now sure that he was awake. "What did you do? Astral travel here? Where's your husband? Won't he miss you?"

He winced on seeing the pain his words caused her. She was making it damn hard for him to let go. All he wanted to do was comfort her.

"You wouldn't return my calls. I had to see for myself that you were alright."

Chance gazed at the figure in his bedroom, wanting to go to her, to hold her close, but experience had taught him that the moment he did she would disappear into thin air. He wanted to keep her with him as long as possible.

"Tell me something, Michelle, what if you'd appeared in my bedroom and I was with someone else, making love, what then?"

"I would have left."

"Just like that?"

"Chance, what is it you want me to say, that I love you? You already know that I do. If I didn't love you I wouldn't be here now."

Chance lay back on his pillows. "You didn't answer my question."

"It would make me happy to know that you have someone, that you're not alone."

"You're a liar, Michelle. You no more want me with another woman, than I want to see you with another man."

He waited for her to answer, but it seemed that she wasn't going to.

"I can't keep doing this, you're killing me."

"Would you like me to leave?"

"In a minute." He answered getting up and going to her. "In a minute."

He drew her into his arms, and feeling her shudder of pain go into his body, he tilted her chin with the tip of his finger. Her lips were soft and full. Her eyes liquid chocolate.

Tears were sliding down her face. He kissed her slowly, tasting her, pulling her very essence into his soul. For the first time in a long while, she kissed him back.

He'd expected her to vanish as she usually did at this point, but she didn't. He realized what she was doing. It was up to him, she would not leave on her own. He would have to send her away.

Chance continued kissing her knowing what she wanted from him, what he would be required to do. He kissed her hungrily accepting her passion, her love, yet somewhere deep inside he prayed for the strength to release her, to set the both of them free.

He held her tightly in his arms, her tears falling on his face. His heart was breaking in a million pieces just as it always did when he dreamt of her.

Somehow he had to find the courage to end his own pain. It was then he thought of the Rune of Isa. It said to standstill, withdraw.

Tears filled his eyes and scorched his cheeks as the full meaning of the stone returned to him. For some unknown reason he could recite the meaning by heart.

The winter of the spiritual life is upon you. You may find yourself entangled in a situation to whose implications you are in effect blind. You may feel powerless to do anything except submit, surrender. Even sacrifice some long cherished dream. Be patient, for this is a period of gestation that precedes a rebirth.

Could anything be more clear? The words and their meaning were not lost on Chance. He rubbed his stubble roughened cheek against the soft skin of the woman he cherished. She lifted her head a bit, and kissed the tears from his cheeks one by one.

She was willing and he wanted her so badly that the force of his erection was painful, throbbing in its intensity. Thoughts of burying himself in her, nuzzling down between the warmth of her thighs filled him. He knew without a doubt she would not deny him, not tonight. She was leaving the choice to him.

A shiver chilled him to the bone, but did nothing to deflate his erection. No, the chill was draining his will, stealing quietly over his soul, robbing him of the strength to do what he must. He thought of the words of the Rune. He could satisfy his lust for now or be patient and wait for the rebirth.

He thought of this as he held her so tightly that he had to be making it hard for her to breathe. ."God how I love you, Michelle. This has to be the hardest thing I've ever had to do in any of my incarnations."

He kissed her again, slowly. He wanted to remember the taste of her. He ran his hand over her body stopping at her breast. He kissed them burying his face in her silky softness, her flesh yielding and warm.

"It's time my love," Chance said with great difficulty. "Time for you to leave, time for me to let you go."

Her tear—filled gaze lingered on him, moving over his face as though she wanted to imprint his face to her memory. Then she blinked and stared into his eyes. She smiled, kissed him again and whispered, "I love you my darling."

"I know you do," Chance replied.

"I always have and I always will."

"At long last I believe that." With those words, she vanished. Chance closed his eyes tightly. With one breath he exhaled the pain.

He went back to the top of the bed and lay down. He'd done the right thing. It was time to let her go.

He closed his eyes again. It was done, he'd said good-bye to the Michelle in his dreams. He knew one day soon he'd have to do it for real. He prayed his resolve would remain strong when the time came. For it would come. He knew without a doubt one day he would have to say goodbye to Michelle for real and pray the Mystic was right.

Hopefully he would soon learn what his true karmic debt was and erase it. Whatever it took to have his wife again he would do.

Including letting her go.

For now.

CHAPTER TWENTY-ONE

When Chance woke, he felt different. At first he couldn't figure out the reason and that puzzled him. He closed his eyes and inhaled the air in the room.

That was it. *Michelle*. Her scent lingered in the room. Even now he wasn't sure if it had been merely a dream, he thought it was more what Michelle had said, a little of both.

He waited for the onslaught of pain that generally hit him in the mornings after so vivid a dream of her. It didn't come. He remembered. He'd let her go.

Chance glanced at the treasured photograph, he kissed the tips of his fingers before placing them on the image of Michelle. "Thank you, my love."

For the first time since he'd arrived in India Chance joked with the rest of the morning staff as he worked. They were flooded with patients, but he didn't mind. Several of his colleagues had glanced once or twice at him, no doubt wondering if he were going through another crisis. He wanted to shout to them, 'No, this is different. Instead he just continued working, and when his shift ended, he walked over to the communal basin for disinfectant and dipped his gloved hands in laughing aloud when the unflappable George dropped a tray of instruments on seeing him.

Chance helped retrieve the instruments a smile plastered on his face, before he stood and walked toward the door.

"Chance, you're leaving?"

"My shift's over. You told me to stop working so hard, remember?"

"Have you been…. is everything—"

"George, I have everything under control." He laughed again "I really do."

Two steps more and he was stopped again, this time by Karen. He smiled at her. "Are you finished?" he asked.

"Yes."

"Would you like to do something, maybe go to Sabu's open lecture?"

Karen was looking at him strangely. She frowned in concentration then surprised him by putting her hand to his forehead.

"Are you sure you're okay?" She peered closer. "Chance, is this really you?"

For a moment he was stunned before he realized what it was. After the story he'd told them she was wondering if someone had taken over his body. He laughed again. "Don't worry Karen, I'm in here alone. I have not given anyone permission to share my body. Believe me, I'm not that cocky in my abilities."

"Then why? What?"

"What happened is that I've decided I don't like the way I've been behaving. It's definitely not doing me any good and it's not helping my cause." He began walking away, pleased when she followed him. When they reached the door he held it open for her to precede him.

"Your cause is still the same?"

"That hasn't changed. I'm only changing me and how I'm going to go about accomplishing my goal." He knew he was beaming. "Karen, I'm sure I'm close to it. I know it, I can feel it."

There was a strange look in her eyes even as she told him she was happy for him. Now he was more aware of her, of the subtle changing. And he was aware enough now to know he had to take care of another error.

"Karen, I think it's time we talked about you. It's time you told me about your loss."

A quick flash of pain crossed her face. Sabu was right, she had been hurt. Damn. How could he have missed that all these months?

"Chance, you don't want to hear me talk about my husband. But thanks for asking, for being a friend."

He smiled at her. "You're right about one thing. I am your friend. But you're wrong also. I do want to hear, please tell me about your husband. You've heard me talk incessantly about Michelle, it's time I listen to you."

"Are you sure?"

"I'm sure," Chance answered, "What was your husband's name?"

"Jameison."

As they made their way to the common room, he shook his head, remembering the first two weeks he'd been in India. Heading for the coffee, he poured two cups and brought one to Karen. "I'm ready," he declared and lifted his cup. For two hours he listened as Karen told him about her life, how she'd met her husband, their falling in love. She told him they'd never been able to have children. Trembling, she told him that her husband was stricken with testicular cancer and died a horrible death.

When she was done she looked up at him, tears gleaming in her eyes as though it had happened the day before. That he understood. The pain of losing a mate never went away.   Even now if he chose to, he could feel the pain when his own Dimi had died. He could feel it through every cell down to the marrow. But for now he chose not to feel it. He chose to concentrate instead on Karen and her loss.

"I'm sorry for your loss but happy that you found him, that you were happy."

"Thanks. We were happy," she said. "Even in the midst of Jamieson's suffering we knew we were lucky to have each other. Do you think it's silly?" She hesitated, looking at Chance. "I mean the fact that thinking about him still makes me cry?"

He laughed. "You're asking the wrong person about that. Of course you know I find it perfectly normal to mourn forever."

Karen appeared taken aback for a moment then she too laughed.

"Thanks, Chance."

"For what?"

"For listening. It just helps, sometimes it helps me to keep him alive...talking about him, I mean."

Chance smiled as she blushed. He was aware she was embarrassed, her rambling was a dead give away. He sensed she still needed to talk. "What about family, do you have any?"

"Yes, I have two sisters, three brothers and my parents. After a year they tired of my mourning. I knew I needed to make a change. At first I buried myself in loneliness then I decided to give something to someone else."

With his gaze fixed on her he asked, "Is that why you befriended me? You saw the same pain in me that you felt." Again he saw her blush.

"I won't lie. Sabu told me about you before you arrived. Since I arrived here I've only spoken Jameson's name out loud to Sabu. He's the only one that knows about him. I mean *really* knows about him. Everyone is aware that my husband passed away. But I've never discussed him with anyone other than Sabu and now you."

"Not even George?"

"No."

"Then why me?" Chance was puzzled. He watched Karen as she turned her head away, something was wrong. *Blaine.* That was it.

"Karen, it was always Blaine you were interested in meeting wasn't it? You wanted him to contact your husband?"

"I just wanted to make sure it was as I've been told, that he wasn't suffering any longer."

"So why didn't you just ask me?"

"I don't know." She hunched her shoulders. "I was going to, but you were hurting so much, yours was so fresh that I felt like a fraud to ask."

"That's Blaine's job. It's his profession, and you had no reason to feel embarrassed. Did you ask Blaine when he was here? Did he talk to your husband for you?"

Karen's head went down again. She was crying softly. Her hands came upwards and Chance watched as she hurriedly wiped the tears away.

"I didn't ask him to."

"That wasn't my question, Karen. Was Blaine able to help you?" He lifted her head so she was looking into his eyes. "Did Jamieson have a message for you?"

"Yes, he said he loved me, that he was no longer in pain. He told me to stop mourning him that he knew I was, and it pained him to see me wasting my life. He told me to fall in love and have babies. He told me to be happy."

A light went on for Chance. "Did he tell you to be with me?"

"He told me that he knew you were hurting also and that together we might be good for each other."

Karen stopped abruptly. .Chance took immediate notice of it. Apparently her husband had given her another message that she didn't want to share. "Is there anything else, Karen?"

"He was only teasing me, but he quoted a line from a song."

"What was it?" Chance asked, ignoring her reluctance to tell him.

"He said, 'if you can't be with the one you love, then love the one you're with.'"

Chance rubbed his chin lightly, wondering how much of the message came from Jameison and how much from Blaine. His mouth twisted at the thought. Blaine would never do a thing like that.

Blaine is only human, Chance. He loves you, he wants you happy and he wants you to do whatever it takes so the three of you will be together in the next life.

Chance was stunned, those weren't his thoughts. Besides, he trusted his son. He lived by a code of ethics that wouldn't permit him to do such a thing.

He broke that code once, perhaps he did it again.

There it was again that voice that was trying to get him to doubt his son. He wouldn't fall for it.

"Karen, was there ever any doubt in your mind that you were talking to your husband?"

"None."

"Not even about that, 'love the one you're with,' song?"

For the first time since they'd begun talking Karen smiled. "That was what told me for sure it was Jamieson. He sang that song to me all the time. I'd completely forgotten."

"I'm happy that Blaine was able to help you."

"So am I," she beamed. "It seems fate had a hand in bringing you here. If not, I don't see how I would have ever met Blaine."

"Yes, fate is indeed strange," Chance answered her as his mind analyzed the choices he'd made in coming to India. He had a sneaky suspicion that it wasn't just because of the hand of fate that he was there. Neither was his friendship with Karen. As he'd felt from the beginning, someone had orchestrated their meeting and he intended to find out who. The 'why' he already knew.

"Blaine, how are you?" For once an immediate connection was made and Chance thanked providence.

"You're sounding a lot better," Blaine answered, the hesitation clearly there. "What happened?"

Ah, so his son wanted to play games. Well two could do that. "Oh nothing. Karen asked me to join her in the ritual cleansing in February at the Ganges River and I thought, What the heck? Why not go in there and wash away all my sins of the past. Hey, then I know I'll be ready for the next life."

He heard a choking sound on the other end of the line and sniggered. "Blaine, is that you?" He heard the coughing, then the laughter.

"Very funny."

"Cassandra and the baby, they're fine?"

"Yes, they're fine. Anyone else you want to ask about?"

"No."

"No one?"

"No one. Are you having problems with your hearing?" Chance laughed then threw a mental block into place. "Don't you dare try and read my mind. I'm on to you."

"Looks like you're back to studying. How's it coming?"

"You'd be amazed at how latent abilities return once you accept it."

"What exactly have you accepted? Anything new?"

Chance smiled to himself. Blaine was fishing, and he intended to keep him on the hook a little longer.

"Well no and yes," he teased. "I want to see how many of my own powers will come back and how strong they are. Right now I've only been playing around with using my intuition."

"And putting up blocks," Blaine obviously couldn't resist adding.

"I only need blocks when I'm talking to you. As far as I can tell no one else seems to have the slightest interest in probing my mind."

"You never can tell."

Chance thought about it for a moment. What an odd comment for his son to make. "Blaine, is there something else going on, you know more than you're telling me? Come on confess what's up"

"How about a trade?" Blaine was only half joking. "You tell me something and I'll give you the answer to let's see... two questions."

"Why do I have a feeling I'm being set up?" Chance groaned.

"What? I'm giving you two for one."

Chance was laughing, Blaine wasn't giving him two of anything. Whatever he wanted to know must be a doozy. *No, he wants you to tell him about Michelle.* This time the voice in his head was more familiar, but he still didn't recognize it.

"Suppose I go first, Blaine, then you."

"Don't you trust me?" Blaine sniffled hoping to elicit sympathy.

"Nah, and your fake sadness isn't doing it either. Now do we have a deal?"

"We have a deal."

"Did you contact Karen's husband?"

"Yes."

"Was the entire message from him?"

"What do you mean?"

Blaine's voice had become a bit haughty. He was offended, it was too late to back off. Chance wanted to make certain Blaine wasn't in on pulling the strings for his life.

"Calm down," Chance soothed. "I'm not accusing you of anything. I'm only asking. You've been trying to force feed Karen to me even before you met her. I've just been thinking all of this is a little too coincidental."

"What? It was your idea to go to India. I didn't tell you to. In fact if I remember correctly, I attempted to discourage you from going. Remember?"

"I remember that you said the words, but I'm not sure if you meant them. There is something fishy going on here and I have come out of my fog enough to realize that. Before when I told Karen that someone was trying to push us toward each other I thought somehow you and Michelle had gotten together and were manipulating her. Then when she told me you contacted her husband and he said the same thing— that she should let go of him…you can see why I might become a bit suspicious."

"You know I would never do anything like that."

"Not even if it served the greater good? Come off it, Blaine. You did far worse once before."

"I had no choice."

"That's what got me to wondering. Maybe you thought you had no choice this time. Look, I'm not saying I blame you or anything, I'm just saying I know how much you want a family, your mother and me."

"I have a family, Chance. Did you forget I have a wife and a son of my own?"

"Are you telling me that's stopped your craving for having a mother and father?"

"No."

Chance could tell he'd gone a bit far. He no longer had to wonder at the tone of Blaine's voice. It was evident he was angry.

"Chance, I'm not you. I'm not living in the past regretting my decisions. I'm also not waiting breathlessly for the next life, hoping I'll be reborn to you and Michelle. I'm living in the present. I'm loving my wife and son."

Neither father nor son spoke for a long time. Chance was giving Blaine an opportunity to cool down before he spoke again. "Blaine, you're evading the question. Did you try and play matchmaker?"

Silence.

"Blaine?"

"I didn't lie to Karen about talking to her husband or what he said. I didn't add to any of that."

"So are you saying that in some manner you have been trying to get the two of us together?"

"I've already answered two of your questions. Now it's my turn."

Chance shook his head, if his son thought his half assed answers were going to get him to spill his guts he had another thought coming. "Go ahead, Blaine, what's your question?"

"Have you talked to Michelle?"

"No."

"Not at all?"

"Not at all."

"Check," Blaine said.

"And Mate," Chance answered. "Talk to you later, Son. He hung up the phone not waiting for Blaine to say goodbye. So he'd been right. Blaine was in on it and so was someone else. He thought of the voice that kept whispering things to him. Whoever it was, he was sure they had a hand in what was going on. For certain, Blaine was not the only psychic involved in trying to orchestrate, Chance's life. He wondered if Michelle was in on it as he'd thought in the beginning. He thought of her tears and changed his mind. No, as much as she said she wanted him to find someone, he doubted she would be able to hand pick her successor. And who the hell was that whispering in his head? Chance was aware that he was past rusty. It was time to regain his own psychic powers. Just as he'd chided Michelle on regaining her powers in the beginning. As always his mind drifted to her, only now he thought of her without the usual pain. He remembered how he and Blaine had badgered her to remember, to regain her powers. Now it was time for him to take his own advice.

Since Chance had decided to work on his psychic gifts, he'd been focused on the energy that's found in every living thing. He was a big believer in energy healing and had used many crystals from his own personal ills. Some of his beliefs he hadn't shared with the group. After all, he didn't want them to think him a crackpot. He was experimenting and would have loved a larger more open space but was making due with his own quarters. He'd been pretty good at energy work in previous incarnations. But so far in this incarnation, he was having very little luck

He turned toward the door on hearing a sound and groaned, not wanting to be caught doing an experiment without success.

"Chance, what are you doing?"

Damn it. He should have sensed Sabu's presence, but he hadn't. He was too involved in what he was doing. Well never mind, he might as well tell him.

"I'm trying an experiment. I want to see what I can do as one member of a trinity."

"But you were holding your hand over the plant. Why?"

He was wishing Sabu hadn't seen that, but what the hell. "I was testing the energy in plants by using the energy in my bracelet."

"Did it work?"

Sabu was intrigued. Chance could tell by the brightness of his eyes. There was an eagerness. He looked about to jump out of his skin.

"I think so, but it would be nice to have a more controlled study, where I'm sure I'm not manipulating the results. Are you game?"

"Sure, tell me what to do."

"Grab a stick. Let's measure the plant, then when I hold my bracelet against it we can see if there's any change."

"I knew you would regain what you once had." He was talking under his breath but Chance heard him.

"What did you say, Sabu?" Sabu looked stunned that Chance had heard. From the look on his face, it was easy to tell he'd not intended that he hear..

"Sabu, you know more than you're telling me, don't you?" Chance walked toward him, his mind tuned to the other's man's vibrations. He reached out his hand to touch Sabu then closed his eyes, the smell of sulfur filled his nostrils. There was a connection there but he wasn't sure what it meant.

"Do I know you, Sabu?"

"Of course you know me, Dr. Morgan. We've been working together for three months."

"You know that's not what I'm asking. Are we connected in some manner, from before, another life, Sabu?"

"Did you sense something?"

Sabu was behaving strangely. Not the non-committal answers. Those he gave all the time. No, it was the way his body was moving, nearly twitching, as if he could hardly stand still.

"Only a smell, but I sense something deeper. Listen, if there's something you know why don't you just tell me?"

"Would you really like to learn by having it given to you? What good would that be to you? Fruit is so much sweeter if you pick it yourself."

"But we're not talking about fruit. We're talking about connections."

"Chance, don't you think you've met enough people from your past?"

"You think?"

Sabu blinked, at Chance's sarcasm. "Look, I don't find it strange in the least that you would think there was more. You've been busy studying the Runes and at the same time you've been trying to solve the greater issue for you of your karmic debt, something that appears to elude you. So naturally you might start to see that everything is connected, even if it isn't."

"I might," Chance answered. "Or it might be that the things I believe to be connected might actually in fact be connected."

Sabu was staring at him, a shocked expression on his face. "What's the matter Sabu? Did you not expect for me to ever come out of my fog? Well, guess what, I have. I can see clearly."

"I never doubted that. I always saw great promise in you."

"Did you now?"

"It is true, you always showed great promise. And you're as great a student as you are a teacher."

Chance tilted his head to the side. There was a double meaning in that, he was sure of it.

"Are you going to tell me?"

"Not just yet. I think you'll appreciate it more when you put the pieces together for yourself. So do you want to study or continue what you're doing?"

Chance thought a moment. What he was trying with the plants he could really do alone. Besides, he wanted to remain in contact with Sabu for a while longer, something was beginning to break. "I think I'd rather study with you. I think it might help me in piecing the puzzle together."

Hour upon hour they'd gone over the meanings of the Runes. Finally Chance could take sitting no longer, so he had no choice but to stand and stretch his muscles which were tired from the long hours he'd spent on the floor with Sabu as they continually laid out different Rune readings.   He was getting comfortable and familiar with the stones. He knew the names for over half of the stone by sight. And their meanings were known either in part or fully.   He would definitely finish the seven stones he had left before he returned home. His time was officially over and he'd not yet answered George's request to stay an extra three months. He just hadn't left. He still hadn't decided if he was staying until February, but there was a distinct possibility that he would.

"Perhaps, we should stop for now."

"My thoughts exactly. Thank you, Sabu, you're a great teacher." With a smile Sabu took his leave.

Alone, Chance took in a breath and decided to do a few more minutes of study. The sound of someone clearing their throat caused him to glance up. Karen paused at the door to his room her hand raised in midair to knock. He smiled at her. "Come on in."

"Thanks. You're really taking the Runes seriously aren't you?"

"You're supposed to. They're very helpful once you get to know exactly what the whole thing means. Why?" he frowned slightly in her direction. "You don't like the Runes?"

"No, it's just, well for weeks you couldn't stand Sabu. It was obvious. Now the two of you are forever huddled together. Sabu has even canceled several lectures to give you private tutoring."

"I didn't know that. You're right, he's one of the most dedicated people I've met. I'm surprised he'd cancel anything. Why did he do it for me?"

"I wouldn't have a clue. I'm more surprised than you that he's so interested in you. No offense, but I've known him since I arrived five years ago. He takes his commitments seriously, so it must be a very good reason why he's spending extra time with you."

Chance smiled. "Sounds as if you've been missing Sabu's company."

"I have," she answered honestly. "I've also been missing yours."

For the first time Chance did not feel like running on hearing Karen's words of friendship. They had set the boundaries. As hard as it had seemed to him a few weeks before, he'd decided they could have a successful friendship. He would not give voice to the lingering doubts.

"I haven't studied the Runes myself," Karen said, grabbing for Chance's book and holding it away from him. "Suppose I quiz you, see how much you've learned."

She was smiling, permitting him to see something more than the friendship she kept hidden in her eyes. He would ignore it because he enjoyed being with her. He would not question his feelings or hers. They were friends. Period.

"What do you want to ask me?" He smiled back at her.

"For starters I want to know how the Runes first came to be."

"That I'm not sure of," Chance answered honestly.

"Then how are you supposed to trust the interpretation?"

"That's an easy one. The whole premise is based on your own intuition, your own knowing. There is nothing magical or strange, it's not witchcraft or voo-doo. It's not satanic, it's I believe a form of meditation that lets you go within yourself and retrieve information you already know."

"If that's true why do you have this book with the interpretations?"

"It's just a guide, a place to begin. The ancient interpretations have been lost anyway."

"So you're saying these writings, someone made them up?"

"I wouldn't put it that way exactly. I'd say different people have devised different methods using a set of ancient symbols. I believe each person meditated on the answers until they got them."

"Then how can their interpretations possibly have meaning for me?"

"If it doesn't, then don't use it. If it does, then apply the meaning."

"Chance that's a simplistic answer. I would expect that from Sabu."

Chance shrugged his shoulders before grinning at her. "I learned about this from Sabu remember?" His voice turned serious, "But I agree with him, either this is for you or it isn't. It's an extremely spiritual undertaking. It requires nothing less than total honesty with yourself."

Karen was grinning now, her hand covering her mouth. "What?" Chance asked curious, "what did I say that was funny?"

"Oh nothing, you just sound like a convert. I was remembering your reaction when Aisha's mother gave you your first Rune. You weren't talking about the spiritual aspect then."

"I wasn't ready for the total truth at that point. Things have changed."

"Yes they have. Something happened to change your thinking?"

"Yeah," he answered, "something did." But he wasn't going to tell her what he had yet to even tell Blaine. No, his letting go of the woman in his dreams was a personal matter between her and him. Besides, he knew he had yet to face his biggest hurdle.

One day he would speak to Michelle again and he would have to repeat the words he had spoken to her dream image. He wanted to fortify himself so when the time came he wouldn't waver. That was the direction he was heading in now.

"Chance you're day dreaming again, you're supposed to be teaching me about the Runes."

"Sorry," he answered, "I was lost in thought. By the way, I'm not ready to teach you. I was simply sharing with you what I've learned."

"And there's a difference?"

"Subtle, but yes, there's a difference."

"Whatever happened, I'm glad. Everyone can tell there's been a change."

"How?"

"Well for one you don't run from me, neither do you look at me as if I'm about to rip your clothes off. Care to tell me what brought about the change?"

"Sorry," Chance smiled. "If I told you I would have to kill you."

Together they laughed at his use of the corny overused line. Only Chance knew there was a bit of truth in his words. Karen's eyes told a much different story than her lips. If she knew that the change had nothing to do with her and everything to do with Michelle she would be hurt.

There's no need to hurt her, he thought. *Friends are all we can ever be.*

CHAPTER TWENTY-TWO

"You're getting better."

Sabu was preening like a proud parent as he put Chance through his paces. Chance found it amusing.

"I will admit it's getting easier to remember the meanings. Applying them is a breeze."

"Of course, like I told you before—."

"Yeah, yeah, I know, the Runes is but a reflection of our own inner self, letting us know what's right, guiding us," Chance laughed.. I was listening."

"Don't get so cocky, Dr. Morgan."

Sabu was smiling when he spoke, his mood exceptionally jovial. Chance was in the same good mood. He was feeling in a mood to share.

"Will you be attending the lecture?"

"Of course. I wouldn't miss any lecture you're giving, Sabu."

With raised brow and a smirk Sabu walked away shaking his head leaving Chance to laugh.

Chance rolled his shoulders, his thoughts drifting to the people he loved. He thought of Michelle. She was doing her best to be happy, he knew that and in spite of everything, he respected it.

He thought of Blaine his lips curving into a smile as he did the so. The son he loved. He was grateful for his forgiveness and grateful Blaine was living an almost perfect life.

The only thing stopping Michelle and Blaine's total happiness was him. And somewhere within him he knew that was about to change.

He closed his eyes taking deep breaths to cleanse his spirit. Thinking of Michelle didn't hurt. His love had not diminished one iota, but it no longer hurt to think of her living out her destiny.

Unconsciously he rubbed the bracelet he was wearing. There would come a time when he would be reunited with his family, of that he was sure. Now it was all left up to him to find that elusive key. He would find out the thing he had done that had altered the course of their lives and he would change it. He would come to his wife free of any baggage in the next life.

"*How the hell are you planning to do that?*"

Chance's eyes snapped open and he shook his head. "What the hell."

"*Mother Ganges perhaps?*"

"There it was again. The voice didn't last long enough for him to pinpoint. He knew it wasn't Blaine. For a fleeting moment he thought of Sabu, but the voice didn't belong to him either.

It was becoming increasingly clear that maybe he needed to remain in India a while longer. There was something he needed to complete there. It sure as hell wasn't going to be bathing away his sins in the Ganges. He'd have to admit he was now curious about the event.   Perhaps he'd look up the information pertaining to that ridiculous ritual.

Later that night he sat among his colleagues, feeling a part of them, knowing when the time came for him to return home he would miss them. And he'd miss Sabu's lectures. There were always lively debates, all seemed to want to know more. What they wanted to know more of didn't matter. Whatever the topic, they wanted more.

"Was there really an Odin?"

Chance glanced toward his colleague who'd asked Sabu the question. He'd asked the same question of Sabu in their private Rune studies, he wondered how Sabu would handle the question in an open forum.

"I believe there was," Sabu answered without missing a beat. "If you're asking me to prove it, I can't. Just as I can't prove to you the existence of God, except that I don't believe anyone could possibly explain how a construction as wonderful and complex as the human body came into being without the master builder being a supreme spirit."

"Well medical science is making many advances in mimicking the process and a lot of them work."

Chance inched his head over, trying to see who'd made the comment. He kept silent knowing Sabu would have an answer.

"I daresay a lot of them work, and this cloning that scientists are experimenting with, who knows that may work. But, does it negate the fact that man did not by his own inventions of scientific knowledge create himself. And look how many years its taken man to get to this point.

"Still there are more failures than there are successes with these things.

"Take for example the artificial heart, if one works for several years it's considered a success. The original equipment from the original manufacturer is meant to last the life of a person. In many case over a hundred years and when that heart goes out people moan and say his heart just gave out as though there was a defect, a flaw in the plan."

Sabu simply looked around the room challenging anyone to dispute his words. Chance marveled at the conviction he had.

"Now I can only tell you the story of Odin as I've heard it," Sabu continued, his voice smooth, calm and unperturbed. He truly was a gifted teacher, Chance had to admit that.

"Maybe I should dispel another doubt many of you first timers may have about Rune casting. First and foremost the Runes are not to be used as divination, or fortune telling devices. The future is in the hands of God and God alone. Hopefully that will alleviate any doubt or suspicion to where my allegiances are."

"But I thought you worshipped...well, not God."

Oh, oh, Chance thought. He glanced at Karen, at the way her eyes sparked as she too waited eagerly for Sabu to address the young doctor who'd spoken.

"I believe in one God, creator of us all." Sabu answered. The name by which the spirit of God is called varies from culture to culture. I respect the difference and do not make judgment on how others worship. So much has been lost to us. Who am I to make that final determination that I and I alone have taken out a patent on the spirit of God.

"Christians, Jews, Muslims, Buddhist, you name it. Everyone believes they're right and them only. I believe there is only one and we're all taking different paths to get there. But that is only my belief. I may be wrong. Each soul needs to determine what is right for them. No teacher can do that for you. For if it is allowed, he will become master of your soul.

"If there are no more questions on that I'd like to get back to the original question. I only deviated so you wouldn't think I was doing something which would be out of spiritual alignment with the spirit of God. You may disagree with that. We can have a future lecture to deal with that. For now we'll deal with the lesson of the Runes and the question of the existence of Odin."

Great job, Chance thought, *he answered the question without insisting his view was the correct one.*. He settled back to listen, amazed at himself for not having liked the man. Now he couldn't think why he didn't.

"As the story goes, Odin was hanging upside down on the tree of the world. When he spied the Runes he then released himself, picked up the markings and somehow his inner knowing was made aware of the meaning of the markings."

Karen's hand shot up into the air. "Sabu, can you tell me if everyone use the same symbols?"

Chance glanced at her, surprised at her interest. He'd never thought to ask that of Sabu. He'd taken it for granted that there was only one set of meanings. He pulled his long frame upward preparing to hear Sabu's answer.

"Until recently, few people in today's world had heard of the Runes. From what I've learned of the Runes, it was a very ancient alphabetic script. Each of the letters posed a meaningful name and sound but didn't evolve into a language.

"The original interpretation of the Runes are lost to us. The secrets if recorded did not survive. We do know that the practice of Rune casting was used for hundreds of years by warriors bent on conquest.

"You mean the Runes were employed for armies to know when to fight, when they would win?"

"Yes," Sabu answered, "but that's not what we're doing. No, I'm teaching you from the studies devised by others. In fact many of the words and teaching I give you will be taken directly from my studies. I will admit I've taken deliberate literary license as I consulted the Runes on how I should present this to you."

"Okay, so how was it changed for the good?"

"It was mediated on using the Runes. The intent is for the learning of will, of the Spirit of God in our own lives. It's a mean of self help, you might say listening to your own intuition?"

"How can you be sure the meanings you've learned are correct?"

Sabu smiled his face calm and serene. "If it's wrong it's done nothing to hurt me. By using this method I in turn have done nothing to hurt anyone I've taught. This method was mediated upon and came up with meaning stepped only in love, no self recrimination, only a hand in the darkness of our spirit pointing toward personal growth and change."

"But what if someone chooses to use them as the ancient warriors did, to do evil?"

Sabu surveyed his audience. "Would I be to blame if that happen? Would the teachers that I've studied? I don't think so. I'm telling you all here and now how the method I'm teaching you to use should be employed. If you're here to learn more about yourself you will be amazed. Anything else, I'm unable to help.

"But if I'm blamed would that be vastly different from the person who says he doesn't believe in any divine spirit and when you probe you find that it's because some religious person did something to harm that being?

"So the creator is blamed for the actions of his creations, those very beings he imbued with the thing we treasure most. Free will. Still we blame God when things go awry. God is not about hatred or evil, but have people used the bible and other religious items for evil purposes? Yes. All things I cannot prevent. I just attempt to impart what was imparted to me."

Chance mused over Sabu's words. Sometimes it was good to hear the man in an open forum, to hear the things that were thrown at him, things he himself had not thought of. He lay back making himself comfortable not wanting to admit to himself that at certain times he much preferred the solitude of learning with just him and Sabu. Then he was not so quick to point out why the Runes could be wrong. Chance smiled in Karen's direction. As in a lot of matters now he was leaving it to his inner knowing to tell him if he was right.

Karen smiled back at him. He felt the shackle of guilt slowly fall away. It was the first time in a long while that he could smile at a woman without feeling he was committing adultery. His thoughts turned inward. Michelle would be happy with his progress. When it occurred to him what he'd just thought, he realized he still had a ways to go. Michelle would always remain in his heart, soul and mind. He now believed he could live out the remainder of this lifetime. He also believed he knew where he'd made his mistake.

Blaine and Michelle had urged him to let go. He believed the real trick was not in the letting go, but in continuing in spite of not being able to have her in this lifetime.

Sabu entered Chance's room, his bag of Runes in his hand, a tired defeated look on his face.

"What's the matter, Sabu? You're looking tired."

"Those open lectures tend to take a bit out of me. There's always so much negative energy with people wanting to disbelieve, that it takes it toll."

"Well," Chance murmured, "why don't you just make a sign, tell everyone that doesn't believe not to come."

"I would never do that. The whole point is to help people help themselves. Would you tell people not to come to you for medical help if they didn't believe you could help them?"

Chance thought about it for a moment. "No, but I have been tempted on occasion." He laughed. "I'll bet you have too." Sabu's face had a haughty look as if the thought had never occurred to him. Then as he watched Sabu's face changed and he started laughing.

"Yes, Dr. Morgan. I have. In fact you were one of the ones I wanted to say that to."

While laughing Chance knew this was now the moment he'd been waiting for. He glanced at the picture of Michelle with him and Blaine.

"Sabu, this is not the first life we've shared is it?"

"No, it's not." Sabu answered, the laughter that had erupted dying in his throat.

"Who were you? I don't remember."

"I'm not surprised. I was but one of your many students. You didn't know me well, but I was there hanging on the fringes, soaking up every bit of knowledge you shared."

"So how did you know?"

"It was something you'd told me before. We all marveled that you always found your wife and the old Mystic as well. The Mystic filled in for you on several occasions. I remember asking him if it would be possible to find my love ones."

"What did he have to say?"

Sabu took so long answering that at first Chance thought he hadn't heard. The man had a funny look on his face. Chance thought of repeating his question when Sabu finally turned toward him.

"The Mystic told me that not everyone we love will be meant to rejoin us, there are mothers, fathers, siblings and lost loves that will share but one lifetime."

"Did you take that to mean it wouldn't happen for you?"

"It was a long time ago, another lifetime. I understood what the old man told me, what he said and did not say. If there was a real love, a real connection or some unfinished business he thought the souls would again find each other."

Sabu looked intently at Chance. "That was after he'd not been able to find his daughter for several lifetimes. I guess she no longer wanted to be reunited."

"You make it sound as if it were a deliberate act on her part?"

"It was, she had tired of her psychic abilities. The opinions of others were weighing heavily on her, and who could blame her? Remember they burned people alive in many countries and in many centuries for being witches. We're aware those witches were merely psychics."

Chance thought for a moment. "Sabu you're saying that my wife no longer wanted to be reunited with her father. Do you think that's why we didn't find each other sooner in this life?"

For the first time in days Chance felt the stab of pain. He could live with not being with his wife. He didn't think he could live with her not wanting to be with him. He rubbed at his bracelet. If they were not together because of some desire of hers, then how would he find her later?

"I don't believe that's the reason. From everything I've heard from her father she always wanted to be with you, her very soul cried out in love for you. Surely, Chance, you're aware of that. That's how you found her. I don't doubt that you will be together again."

A rush of energy, of knowing filled Chance making him keenly aware of what was going on around him. He'd ignored so many things that should have been clear. No longer.

The voice in his head now had a name. He should have known. The Mystic.

"How long have you been in contact with the Mystic?"

"About ten years or so," Sabu answered for the first time not talking in riddles. In fact it seemed to Chance that he was pleased, as if a heavy burden were being suddenly taken from his shoulders.

"Have you known about me all this time?"

"Not really. I've known of your existence here in this time for about five years. I studied with the Mystic and somehow through my studies of the Runes I was able to perceive things the Mystic may have never told me. I think he may have been in a moment of weakness when he confessed to me that he's been searching for his daughter and that he believed he'd picked up her vibrations."

"How did he do that?"

"It was all because of Blaine. He said he's always known Blaine was his grandson, the soul child of his daughter. He taught Blaine you know."

"Yes I know." Chance answered.

"There were certain things he was able to tell. Don't forget this is the Mystic we're talking about."

Chance rubbed his bracelet again. That sly old coot. He'd known perfectly well when Blaine brought him the jewelry that he was preparing the amulets for us, he'd known all alone.

"Did he engineer my meeting with Dimi? Sorry, Chance corrected himself, "I mean Michelle."

Sabu glanced back at him sadly. "It must be awfully hard to think of her as Michelle instead of Dimi."

"A little. I guess I could get used to any name if she was with me. But I think I continue to slip and call her Dimi, because Dimi loved only me," he said sheepishly.

Sabu didn't answer, he merely smiled at Chance.

"Did the Mystic engineer any of this?"

"I'm not sure, he won't say. But since he's always saying destiny has to take its course, I don't think he did very much."

"I won't take any bets on that," Chance laughed remembering the voice in his head recently. "He can be pretty stubborn when he wants to. Besides, I have to admire him for taking as long as he did to meet us."

"I was with him during some of that. He wasn't the most patient. He kept trying to get Blaine to introduce him to the two of you. I think that was the hardest time for him, knowing you two were so close, yet having to take a backseat and wait things out."

"Too bad he didn't know this before Dimi....oops, Michelle married Larry."

"It wasn't your destiny to be with her, Dr. Morgan. Not in this life anyway?"

"Sabu, since we're on such friendly terms, please will you tell me why the hell you can't always call me, Chance?" He watched while Sabu looked embarrassed. Until finally with his head bent, his voice soft, he spoke.

"I guess all of us came here, into this life with baggage. You can't think of your wife as anyone but Dimi even though she's Michelle this time around. It's the same for me. You were my teacher. I sometimes find it hard to show anything but the utmost respect for you. I would never have called you by your name in the past and sometimes even now it's hard. Though I am getting better." He grinned. "You'll have to admit that."

Chance was amused, his life had taken many strange turns. "Isn't it something, Sabu, that this time around it is you who are teaching me?"

"Not so strange. That is the way of things."

"I think I'll try and reach the Mystic. I just wish it didn't take so damn long to get a call through to the states."

There was a strange gleam in Sabu's eyes. He was twisting his body and for a moment Chance wondered if he were Ill. He looked hard at him, well aware of his mannerisms now when he became excited. There was something Sabu wasn't telling him.

"What is it, Sabu?" No answer. Chance tried again, still no answer. He closed his eyes and mediated on the situation and on Sabu's strangeness. A feeling of supreme peace came over him a nanosecond before the voice said, "I'm here." Chance laughed out loud..

"He's here isn't he, Sabu? The Mystic is in India?"

"Very good." Chance heard and for a moment didn't know if it came from Sabu or the Mystic speaking inside his head.

"I want to see him. Will you take me?"

"Yes, but you don't have an off shift for four more days."

"Don't worry. I'll find a way to switch. You just plan on taking me tomorrow."

"We have to go on Trunk Mile Road."

An involuntary shudder shook Chance, his wide shoulders hunched against his neck. The thought of traveling along that polluted roadway was the very last thing he wanted to do in this life. He thought of the River Ganges and the cremated remains that filled it. He thought of February and the fifty millions bodies that would be flooding the place. If he had to choose his poison, he would much prefer the horrid smell of cow dung, the thick arid haze of the blue smoke and the choking sensation in his lungs and eyes. If that's what he had to do to see the Mystic he would have to find a way to endure it all.

"Sabu," Chance asked almost teasing but not quite. "Is there any possibility that you could persuade the Mystic to come here?"

"*Not on your life.*" The old man's voice sounded in his head making Chance laugh with the sternness of which the man had spoken. Nope, it was definitely up to him. He would have to go to the Mystic. Maybe then more of the pieces would begin to fall into place.

Dr Sands had readily agreed to cover Chance's shift for a later favor. Now all that was left was for him to find a way to survive the trip. Gathering all the supplies he thought he'd need he took them to the truck and waited for Sabu. He grinned when Sabu approached.

"Dr. Morgan what is all that stuff you have there?"

"Call it my survivor kit."

"What's in it?"

Chance looked around as though he was in a very bad spy movie, then he raised the lid a quarter on an inch knowing it would peak Sabu's interest. It worked. He could not keep the grin from owning his face as Sabu came over venturing to peek inside.

"That looks like just a bunch of towels." Sabu muttered confusion showing clearly on his face. "They're wet."

"Bingo!" Chance shouted in triumph. "I'm going to use those to keep some of the soot out of my lungs." He didn't miss the sarcastic look Sabu gave him. Nor did he miss the sarcastic comments.

"You're going to have an awfully lot of laundry to do."

"It's well worth it," Chance answered as he put the large cooler into the back seat of the truck. "Just one more thing, please no windows down today. Agreed."

Sabu muttered something Chance didn't catch, but shook his head in affirmation. It didn't matter if he was still disapproving. What mattered was that maybe with the wet towels and bottled water he'd hidden beneath the towels he would survive a second trip on the congested road and live to tell about it.

Within fifteen minutes they were packed into the truck and heading out, when Karen ran to them. "Chance, don't forget to have a cup of tea.. I wish I was going with the two of you."

Chance smiled and waved but didn't answer. How could he? He didn't want Karen on this trip. As for as the cow dung that fueled the fires to brew the tea, Chance wasn't making any promises that he would try it again.

"She's falling for you."

"What?" Chance asked as he turned toward Sabu, knowing full well what he'd said. Needing a moment to compose an answer.

"You heard me, she's falling for you." Then more sternly Sabu added, "Don't hurt her. It's not her fault that for you there can be only one woman."

"We're just friends, really, that's all we are." Chance wasn't sure if he was saying that to try and convince himself or Sabu. Since his last talk with Karen neither had done or said anything to give the slightest hint that anything other than friendship was what they were after. In spite of Karen's words Chance would have had to been blind not to see her building interest. He felt the mounting tension in the small confines of the truck.

"Don't worry, Sabu, I don't intent to hurt her."

"Harrumph."

CHAPTER TWENTY-THREE

Chance had hoped his irritation had been the culprit in the way he'd viewed his last trip with Sabu. That wasn't the case. It was all as he'd remembered. Taking a look out of the window at the sheer number of people lining the road on both sides was enough to make one stop and think.

It struck him odd that he'd not thought of the level of poverty before. Sure, he'd seen it, though it hadn't even registered at the time. But then, he knew what it had been, his preoccupation with living through the experience.

Trunk Mile Road was indeed an experience. Chance glanced toward Sabu who appeared unaware of the thick layer of blue smoke that hung over everyone and everything in its path.

He was sure if he'd wanted, he could stick his hand out of the window and pluck a hunk of the blue muck to store in a jar. He smiled to himself. This had to be the worst smog on the planet. For a moment he toyed with the idea of actually trying to see if he could capture some of the stuff. But did he dare open the window? His answer was a resounding no.

A closer look and he noticed the population seemed to have swelled from his last trip. There appeared not to be an inch of space uninhabited by squatters in their flimsy metal and cardboard shacks. Everywhere he looked there were animals. Children ran around in wild abandonment while his insides tightened in knots every time one or two ventured a little too close to the unending traffic. Sabu never budged.

"Doesn't it bother you, Sabu, that with all of this traffic people live so close to danger, and take no notice?"

Sabu glanced first at Chance then out the window. "I never noticed."

"You never noticed? How the hell could you not notice?" Chance pulled the wet towel away from his face. He was scowling, and he didn't want the ferocious look distorted by a towel.

"The same way I don't notice the smell you say is here."

With that reminder Chance hurriedly clamped the wet towel back into place over his nose, dabbing at the immediate tears that had gathered in the corners of his eyes. All caused by the pollution.

"You're going to tell me you don't smell that cow shit?"

"That's precisely what I'm telling you."

"How? Just tell me how you can't smell it? It's enough to choke the life out of you."

Sabu was giving him a look that was half disappointment and half amusement. It was apparent with the one raised brow what he was implying. He thought Chance a backwards, rather ignorant child that should know whatever it was he was going to say.

"I don't allow the circumstances to rule me. I'm not trapped by what or how things appear to be. I create my own reality and I have no problems."

"You're telling me the air you're breathing is clean and sweet tasting in your world? You don't have this thick blue soup that's covering everyone else?"

Sabu had slowed —if that was at all possible on the almost none-moving stretch of road. "Look over there," he pointed. "The children you were speaking of, do they seem affected by the things you mention?"

"They don't know any better," Chance muttered, annoyed that they were having this conversation, annoyed that he once again found himself on this road faced with the problem of instant pollution.

"Or perhaps in their individual worlds, their sky is blue."

"Tell it to their lungs."

"How do you know they're all suffering from the pollution?"

"Any fool would know that."

"Any fool would know that if he doesn't like the situation he finds himself in to change it."

For the next thirty minutes Chance ignored Sabu which was good, as Sabu was ignoring him as well. The towel was making it a lot more bearable, and it served as an added function. Chance could pretend to be dozing underneath.

Once or twice as more time passed, he or Sabu made a comment on something insignificant. He mused to himself that Sabu probably didn't want to make the three hour long journey in total silence. Glancing sideways at Sabu, he couldn't help but notice the granite bearings of his chin. The man could be unmovable at times. Maybe he *could* survive the entire trip without talking.

"What are you going to do about Dr. Trammel's offer?"

Now that was a safe topic. Chance moved the towel a mere inch or two. "I've already stayed well past our agreement. I think I may stay at least another month or two, providing I can get someone to continue covering for me back home. I'd like to have a practice to return to."

"Life is not always about material wealth."

"Maybe not, but since I have no desire to live in a shanty alongside Trunk Mile Road, I believe I need to work." He had expected Sabu to at least smile. But when he didn't, he thought how the words he'd spoken so quickly and in jest must have sounded.

"Look, Sabu. I didn't mean to imply that the people.," he waved his hands toward the crowds, "wish to live like this. I'm just saying I don't choose to, and if I have the means to not do so, does that make me a bad person?"

"Of course not. Your wealth is not your doing alone. It is the will of providence. This time around you're given things you lacked before or craved."

Chance didn't buy that. The concept was too damn easy. No way did he totally believe that everything in life was due to karmic choices, or karmic debt. He looked at the hundreds of thousands of people jammed packed into such a sparse piece of uninhabitable land. If Sabu's theory was correct, all of the people were dirt poor and disease ridden because of past life wealth.

That he didn't and would never believe. He didn't have the answer, and maybe it was never meant for him to know, but that sure as hell couldn't be it.

Sure, he'd figured out his own life pattern and he did believe he was a physician in this life because of what happened in his past one. His soul had a need to correct, to find his wife, to help, to not be so poor that he couldn't afford help. Chance sighed. On the surface it seemed that Sabu had a point. Still, Chance doubted.

"Look over there, that nun, she's waving at you," Sabu said.

Chance felt himself being lifted upwards, floating. He felt the towel when it slipped completely from his face. It couldn't be. A strange feeling stole over him, a feeling of lightness and peace He was staring after the smiling nun, the constant burn in his eyes and throat forgotten for the moment.

He foolishly waved after her, like a school boy awed by the

reverence of the moment. How could he possibly meet the same nun twice while on a journey he didn't really want to be on? And how could she remember him? Surely in her work, she came across thousands, hundreds of thousands that gawked at her. He continued staring, the feeling of peace remaining with him, making him speechless.

"Chance, don't you think you'd better replace your towel? The stench and the sting, remember?"

Sabu's voice cut through him like a knife. For until that moment he'd truly forgotten the conditions in which he found himself. He'd been transported for a few moments out of the circumstances in which he'd found himself.

It was too late now, the spell was broken. The smoke just as thick, once again burned his eyes and filled his mouth. The horrid smell of cow shit being used to fuel cook fires turned his stomach, and with a great abdominal wrench, he clutched the towel to his face to keep from puking.

A couple of false starts had him reaching for one of his bottled waters. He drank thirstily before he caught sight of Sabu. He was smirking. The meaning of the smirk had not been lost. Chance had transcended his surroundings.

Once they had begun talking, they drifted easily into their studies of the Runes, everything else forgotten including Chance's momentary lapse from his environmental reality.

Chance glanced at his watch as at last Sabu pulled off Trunk Mile Road and headed for a small village. He could feel the presence of the Mystic long before they arrived at the old man's dwellings. A spirit of peace resided over the place.

Before Sabu could stop the truck completely, Chance was out and running the moment he saw the figure of the Mystic emerge from behind a clapboard door. Two men who appeared even older than the Mystic flanked either side of him.

Chance stopped before the three, wanting to retain a modicum of dignity and proper respect, but his body was twitching with nervous energy, the same as Sabu's had done the day before.

"Hello, Teacher. I should have known it was your voice I was hearing." He grasped the older man's hand and accepted the warm embrace the Mystic pulled him into.

"These are friends of mine," the Mystic answered Chance's questioning look. "They're here to help me. Or rather they're here to help you on your journey."

Chance glanced toward the men realizing at once that they were also Mystics. No wonder the village had such a veil of peace if three such men resided in the place.

"I thought I had to figure this out for myself."

"You've gotten so close. I thought it would be okay for us to help you just a bit."

"Are you going to tell me what I need to know?"

As he'd known he would do, the Mystic smiled at him without answering.

"I'll help you remember. You already know. You just don't want to admit to it. I don't blame you, Chance. You've had a lot of things going on in this life. A lot of guilt. You've done well." The Mystic turned and smiled at the other men, then turned back toward Chance.

From the looks on the faces of the three Mystics, Chance knew they had been communicating without talking. The two men turned and ushered Sabu into the house. While the man Chance had traveled to see, held his hand out, pointing for Chance to precede him to the back of the place.

He had to be dreaming. There was no possible earthly way that, Chance was seeing what he was seeing. A garden, vegetables and flowers were blooming happily. There were several trees, the sweet smell of citrus filled the air. He stared in astonishment.

"How? This is impossible."

The Mystic plucked a fruit from the tree that looked and felt much like an orange, and gave it to Chance. "Bite it," he ordered.

As the sweet juiced dribbled down his chin, Chance still couldn't believe it. There was no possible way the Mystics were growing oranges. The soil wasn't conducive for that, nor for a garden. Not here. Not in this place of nothing.

"Chance, don't you know by now that our lives are what we make of them? We only have to put the thought into action, and it becomes what we want. My friends and I wanted a vegetable garden and fresh fruit. We thought it into being."

"You can't," Chance mumbled low, with the evidence dribbling down his chin. "It's impossible."

The Mystic laughed. "Come, Chance," he ordered. "You didn't drive all this way to talk of fruit. Tell me what it is you really want?"

"For starters why have you been sending me messages? Why didn't you just tell me it was you? Why not just tell me what you wanted?"

"That wouldn't have been any fun."

The old man's eyes were sparkling. He was enjoying this. It was easy to believe he'd done all that he'd done simply for his own amusement. But there was more. Chance knew there was more.

"Ask me the questions you really want answered."

He tried not to, he'd given her up. He'd let her go. His brain refused to think of anything else. Surely there were a hundred questions he could ask this man, but only one he truly cared about.

"Michelle," he said at last. "Is she alright?"

"You mean after her little visit to you."

"You know about that?"

"I know."

Chance opened his mouth to ask why and thought better of it. The Mystic had his ways. They'd all thought he was dead during the battle between good and evil, or damn near death. And all the time he'd manipulated the happenings to teach Blaine a lesson. He suspected that now the old man was going to do to the father the same thing he'd done to the son.

"I want to know how things are with her and Larry." His head went down of its own accord out of shame and guilt for having called her, for having forced her to admit her love for him.

"Did I make it hard for her, for her marriage?"

"You want me to say no, don't you? But I won't. That would be a lie, and we both know it. Yes, your call made a ripple. Larry was not very pleased, not about your calling, but because his wife belongs to you as much as to him."

Chance allowed himself to think of Larry, his imagined nemesis, the man whom he'd been so jealous of. He had what Chance so desperately wanted, yet he was not at complete peace. He too craved more, more than Michelle could give either of them.

"How does Larry deal with this? I mean it's hard enough believing in all this stuff. How can a straight-laced lawyer even come close to understanding?"

"He loves his wife," the Mystic answered. "He loves her truly. And in loving her, he's admitted to himself that you are part of his life."

"That surprises me."

"He can not cut her love for you out of her heart with a knife. To stop loving you, he understands it would not be possible. To demand it of her would mean she's unable to love him as well. Larry understands that Michelle can't separate that love."

"Then if he understands all of that, why are there problems?"

For a long moment the Mystic stared at him until he felt the heat from his gaze burning through him. He wanted to turn away but was caught by the man's gaze.

"My daughter wanted to come to you. Not to bilocate, she wanted to get on a plane and come."

"What did Larry say?"

"He said, 'hell no'! What do you think he said?"

Chance was caught off guard by the Mystic's unaccustomed swearing. "I'm not…well…I thought…"

"You thought what? That her husband was simply going to say, 'go ahead honey, I understand'?" The Mystic cocked his head to the side. "If that is so, you're delusional. Apparently Michelle was delusional as well. She had the same thoughts, or she wouldn't have told Larry of her plans. It took all the energy Blaine and I had to convince her otherwise. I believe she thought you were going to do yourself harm."

"I would never—"

"But you did in the past. We've all been concerned for you. We're aware of the unbreakable bond between you, and my daughter. We know what lengths you'd go to in order to be with her."

"I wasn't going to."

"Your thoughts have taken a very dark turn of late." Shrugging his shoulders, the Mystic smiled gently at Chance.

Chance sighed as a bone deep chill invaded his body. "It was never my intent to make Michelle believe I'd rush myself toward the next life. If that was what she was thinking, how did you dissuade her not to come?"

"We reminded her of the karmic debts she was racking up herself. We told her the futility of our plans to have the three of you reconnect in the next life if she kept hurting Larry. She'd never wanted to hurt him in the first place. But when we convinced her that by coming to you she would hurt you more than help you…well, she agreed with us reluctantly. But she had a condition. If she couldn't come to you, she demanded that either Blaine or I personally check on you. I came in her stead to keep an eye on you."

"Her bi-locating into my room, did she consult with you about that?"

"What do you think?"

The old man was right. Chance knew the answer to that. She'd come of her own accord. "Why do you think she risked everything?" Chance asked at last

"Because you were hurting. Because she was afraid for you. Most importantly, because her soul loves you. I think when she came to you, she no longer cared about what would happen later. She had to assure you that she'd not forgotten, that she loved you as she always had."

"I almost made love to her." Chance's voice was soft with remembering. "She was in my arms, willing. It would have been so easy. She wouldn't have stopped me."

"What did?"

"I knew everyone was right. As much as I hate it, the knowing, I did know. My wife will not be with me until next time around."

"Were there no other consideration?"

"I thought of Larry and how much I'd taken from him already. He'd forgiven Michelle for the affair. Do you know how much I hate that word? I made love to my wife and everyone considered it an affair."

"Chance, don't deviate from your growth. Though Michelle is still your Dimi, this time around she belongs to Larry. Now continue with the reason you didn't make love to her when she came to you."

Locking his gaze with the Mystic, Chance groaned low. "I knew that he wouldn't forgive. And I knew Michelle would not be able to forgive herself. She would not have been able to return to him."

"Isn't that what you've been wanting for almost two years? For her to choose you?"

"Yes, that's exactly what I wanted."

"Then why did you let her go?"

"I had to. I love her. I could read bad karma all over that scene. I didn't want her paying for it."

For at least five minutes neither man spoke. The Mystic was the first to break the silence.

"You do understand though that in spite of your last minute revelation, you're not the only one who's been piling up karmic debts? Michelle has to pay for the things she's done in this life."

"Why?"

"That's just the way things are."

"But she didn't do anything."

"It's not always the things we do. It's the things we feel and think also."

"Can I help her?"

"You're the only one who can. Let her go."

"Damn it, I have."   Chance was angry; he jumped up and stomped about the garden that couldn't exist. "I let her go. Damn you. I just told you."

"No, you think you did."

"Tell me how. I've come half way around the world to let her go. What more can I do?"

"Let go of her."

Slapping his head with the palm of hand, Chance turned back toward his mentor. "You're talking in riddles now. Is that where Sabu gets it? Aren't you listening to me? I let her go."

"Chance, Michelle gives as much of herself to Larry as she can. She loves him. She makes him happy, but always, always she's thinking of you. And she's filled with guilt."

"I can't help that."

"Yes, you can. Open up your heart and allow someone else to love you. You can learn to love someone else. Only then are you going to be able to let her go. Only then will she truly be able to give her husband what he rightfully deserves."

"This makes no sense. My sleeping with some woman is not going to make me stop thinking of my wife. And how it can make her stop thinking of me, you're going to have to tell me the answer to that one, Teacher."

The old man's face crumbled and fell. Chance regretted his harsh tone. "I've tried everything I know to do. When she bi-located to me, all I wanted in this life was to keep her with me, make love to my wife, reclaim her. I didn't. I let her go. What more can I do?"

"Make amends."

Chance was astonished, his head was spinning. He didn't pretend to not know what the Mystic was asking. He wanted him to call Larry.

"What can I say to him? He doesn't want to hear anything from me."

"How about an apology? Tell him you're sorry. Tell him, you know you can never take his place in Michelle's life."

Chance was stunned beyond belief. "You know Larry as well as I do. You know he's not going to want an apology from me. I've made him numerous promises to let her go, and I've broken all of them. What difference would it make to tell him I have no place in her life? I don't believe it, and he will know it for the lie that it is."

"All the difference in the world. You've taken something from Larry that you can never give back, his sense of total trust in his wife. He knows Michelle loves him. That's never been a question. But he's aware she worries about what you think. And as long as she feels that way, it carries over to him. And he can't have the peace he deserves."

The Mystic sighed. "I like Larry. He's a good and honorable man. I like him and he doesn't deserve this turmoil."

"If I talk to him, that's going to do it?"

"It's a start."

"A start, harrumph," Chance snorted. "I thought you were here to tell me what to do to change my karma, to make it easier to find my family in the next incarnation. I know you, and I know this can't be all of it. What else will I have to do?"

"After you make amends with Larry, you need to talk to Michelle. Don't call her Dimi," the Mystic cautioned. "Call her Michelle and Michelle only."

"What do I say to her that I haven't already said?"

"Listen to your heart."

"It's my heart that's got us into this mess." Chance groaned while the Mystic chuckled.

"Don't worry, Chance, you'll find the right words to say to her. You have to help to enable her to forgive herself for not being with you."

The old man rose and plucked another piece of fruit from the tree. This too he handed over to Chance. "Just remember we have the power to change our circumstances. All that's left is the courage to believe this."

The courage to believe. He'd try to remember that. At the moment it would be nice if the teaching could cease and someone would just give him the answer. There was no doubt that with three Mystics present, that they knew what he needed to do in order to erase his karmic debt. They just weren't going to share that knowledge with him. Chance heard the voices from inside the home, the melodic tones of the Mystics blending with Sabu's more formal tones.

"Teacher, is everyone on the planet going to turn out to be someone from my past?"

"It took longer than I expected for you to pick up on that connection, with Sabu."

"Probably because Sabu hated me when we met. How could I think we shared anything?" Stroking his chin he glanced toward Sabu. "I'm still confused about the connection. Why would I have made such an impact on Sabu yet have no memory of him? You, I remember. And my memories of Dimi, sorry, Michelle and Blaine are clear. But with Sabu, nothing other than a tingle, an electrical charge."

Now the Mystic was smiling, looking almost approvingly at Chance. *Why?* Chance wondered. He knew for a fact that he'd done nothing to warrant the man's pride.

"Chance, don't you know it's not always the people you remember that you impact the most? It's not his impact on you, but your impact on him. Even then, in that life, you never knew, but he loved you, practically worshipped you. He wanted nothing more than to be like you."

"Then why did he hate me when he met me?"

"You were not the hero he'd made you out to be. You were a flesh and blood man so riddled with pain you'd become insensitive to the pain of others.

Chance attempted to interrupt. "That's not true. I've always taken very good care of my patients. I care about them."

"Your patients were your mission. Besides, I'm not talking physical. I'm talking emotional pain. Look how you behaved when you first arrived in this grand country. You turned your nose up at everything."

"I had reason to. I wasn't doing it to be mean."

"I think I understand that, but Sabu didn't." The Mystic

permitted himself to smile in Chance's direction. "Sabu thought he was going to meet some highly evolved soul, instead he met a plain mortal man."

CHAPTER TWENTY-FOUR

Almost a quarter of a century of searching had led him to this. Chance laughed at himself and the predicament he found himself in. Turning to the Mystic, he sighed.

"Tell me, Teacher," he began. "Why are you all trying to force this thing between Karen and myself?"

"Is that what it feel likes to you?"

"Yes, frankly it does, and to be honest it's disconcerting and a bit annoying."

"Don't you find her attractive?"

"I would have to be blind not to. She's a very attractive woman."

"Have you had any thoughts of…being with her?"

Chance would not have believed he would be sitting in a garden, in the middle of India surrounded by vast nothing, discussing his sex life with the Mystic. First Blaine, now the Mystic. There had to be more going on than his son and his teacher worrying about his sex life. What the heck could it be?

"I don't give into the whims of my body," Chance answered at last. "Just because I want something doesn't mean I can't say no."

"Ha, tell that to someone else. What about Michelle?"

"That's different. She's my wife."

"Not in this life."

"That doesn't matter." Chance looked out over the fruit trees. "We don't have to continue this. I know what you're trying to do. I will call Larry. Is that what you wanted to hear?"

"It is. Still, I'm curious why you can't see you have much in common with this woman."

"Maybe I don't want to feel as though I've been pimped. If it's necessary that I find someone, I think I can do it on my own."

"But Karen needs someone. She's been hurting for years. She could help you heal, and you could help her."

"If healing is the purpose, where is the love? Where is the passion?" Chance closed his eyes. He was learning to do what he must. But was he to give up everything?"

"There are different loves, Chance, different passions. You both care about people. You want to make a difference."

"There are women in the States who have the same feelings of loss. Why did you orchestrate it to make me believe I needed to come here? Out of almost 300 million people in the US, couldn't you come up with one woman in the country that I would have been compatible with? Beside Michelle," he ended with a smile.

"Do you think that's the reason you're in India? No, Chance. Karen just happened to be a bonus. That was the helping hand of fate. I only wanted you here."

"Why? I still don't understand."

"Seriously? Even with finding me here, you don't understand? I have to tell you, I don't believe you."

"Teacher, I'm not holding back. I don't understand."

Three times the Mystic sighed. And then he began to pace, glaring at Chance, holding his gaze, only to turn away and pace again. "Perhaps I was wrong. Perhaps you aren't ready."

"Ready for what?"

Ready for us to help you in the completion of your search."

"Please, Teacher. I'm at a loss. Help me."

"Very well, if you insist. Besides, this is the reason we sought you out, Chance. It's your learning, for one thing. You were becoming like Michelle had been, denying who you are, not studying, not progressing. It seemed after you found her, you no longer cared about your self-growth. There was so much more you needed to know. I wanted you to learn."

"Are you sure you just didn't want me out of the way? Maybe you were afraid with me in the country, Michelle would become tempted again and come to me. If that had happened it increased the odds you wouldn't get an opportunity to know your daughter in the next life."

Chance peered at the old man. "Tell me the truth, did you engineer this for me, or for yourself?"

The Mystic smiled, not in the least annoyed. "Do you think I would have to descend to such devious means?" He laughed out loud. "If I'd thought of it who knows? But no, I wasn't doing this for Michelle only. True, I knew if you were in such close proximity it would make things harder, too much temptation to stay apart. For both of you," he admonished with a shake of his bony finger. "With you out of the way it is true, she would stand a better outcome, of healing, of having her husband forgive her. And like you, I would love nothing better than keeping her karmic debt to a minimal."

"So, I'm the sacrificial lamb? Karen and I?"

"What you do or don't do with Karen is your personal business. It will in no way affect my next incarnation, or the one after that. It may or may not affect your future with my daughter. I said you need to find someone to give your love to. I never said it had to be Karen."

"Good," Chance answered defensively. "She and I are only friends."

The Mystic was frowning. He paced around the garden once more then scowled some more in Chance's direction before speaking again. "To keep you from avoiding temptation has been a full time job."

Once again something niggled at Chance about his meeting with the Mystic. Something wasn't adding up. He tried with no avail to scan the Mystic's mind only to have his old teacher frowning at him for the trespass. He'd have to come at this another way. He'd have to force the truth out of the man. "Your story is not entirely true. I moved to San Francisco to keep our temptation at bay. There is something else on your mind, Teacher. Out with it."

"I beg your pardon."

The Mystic's voice was annoyed. No doubt, Chance thought, because he wasn't bending to his will. Still, the old man had much knowledge he could give him. He would be a fool if he didn't use it. Since he wasn't making any comments about his San Francisco move, Chance decided to ask him another question.

"George Trammel, do we also share a past?"

"No."

"Are you sure?" Chance was dumbfounded. He'd been certain George also had some link with him.

"I'm certain."

"Then how? Everything about the man is so mysterious. When I first met him, Sabu told me George has been here forever, that he'd only returned home. Now if that isn't a cryptic message what is?"

Now that the Teacher was smiling, some of the tension in the air between the two of them eased. Chance was glad to feel the difference. The energy level was now uplifting instead of debilitating.

With a smile the Mystic spoke. "I agree. Sabu's message was indeed a bit cryptic. But that doesn't mean George has any connection with you. In fact, your only connection with George is that he feels he has lived many incarnations as well. But unlike you, he doesn't have any proof. He can't really remember another incarnation, not even with regression. Nor has he found anyone from any past incarnations."

"Then why?"

"Why the feeling of connection? That feeling just happens with a lot of souls we meet. It doesn't however mean we were in another incarnation with them. George keeps an ear to the happenings in the psychic community. Because of the things that happened to you and your family...our family George had wanted to meet you. He's wanted to meet all of you. When he learned you were coming here he was primed to pump you for information."

"But he hasn't, not really."

"That's because you've had your own personal little guardian angel. Sabu instructed him not to. He informed him you were here on a journey, and to give you the freedom and leeway to discover the things you needed to know. Then and only then was he to raise his own issues with you."

Curiosity was getting the best of him. Arching a brow Chance frowned. "What is it he wants that made you have him back off?"

"He wants what we all want, to know your secret."

"I don't have any secrets"

"There is something, Chance, there has to be. No one has ever done what you and Michelle have accomplished. Somehow it seems stronger in you. We realized it this time around. It was you who began the search for her, long before she was aware of it."

"But she was searching for me in her dreams."

"But you, Chance, you gave up your marriage to find her, without any proof she really existed. So yes, naturally George wanted to talk to you. We all want to know the secret that's buried deep within your soul."

"It must be buried. I have no idea what it is. And if I don't know, how do you plan on retrieving it?"

"With your permission we want...that is my friends and I want to attempt to take you back in time, to the moment of your death. Then we want to take you to the moment you were first created."

Chance winced slightly. Witnessing Dimi's death had been unbearable. What purpose would it serve to witness his own? He was already aware his son was left alone. He didn't need to see Blaine's pain to know.

"Why? I don't see how that can help. I know what it is. My wife's soul was calling out to me to find her. And I did. It's as simple as that"

"Nothing is as simple as that. Are you afraid, Chance? Perhaps you don't want to know of the real damage you did?"

"I already know. Blaine and I have discussed it, and he's forgiven me."

The Mystic looked at Chance, his face relaying that he understood Chance's distress."

"Is it Blaine's pain you're afraid of witnessing, or your own?"

Chance couldn't stop the glare he was directing at the Mystic. "Blaine already showed me some of our past. I'm not afraid of anything."

"Could be Blaine didn't show you enough. Maybe a little more insight and what you learn will be useful to others."

"What difference would it have on my life now?" Chance challenged the Mystic. "I don't seem to have reached the right answer on my own. Reliving something I don't remember can't possibly help."

The Mystic was smiling again. "But you're going to remember, Chance. All of this is about to change. That's why we're here to assist you."

"Weren't you the one who told Blaine and Michelle that I need to learn these lessons on my own?"

"I was."

"What's the matter? Am I taking too long? Are you afraid I might never get there?"

"You would eventually get to where you need to be without our interference."

"Then why are you interfering in my progress?"

"Death beckons."

"For me."

"No."

"Michelle?" Chance asked in a panic. "Blaine?"

"No."

"Is it you?"

"I have no fear of death. My only fear is being cut off from my daughter for the rest of eternity. I need to ensure that will not happen. My friends and I have worked many years on a solution.

Chance was beginning to worry. Three Mystics. Why would it take so many? Was it a regression the men were planning to do? Then he thought of the number of them—— three. Could they somehow be a triad themselves?

The answer was written in the Mystic's face as his eyes glowed with an inner strength that Chance was yet to discover.

"We're not a triad. As far as I know there is only one. And that would be you, Blaine and Michelle."

"Then why?"

"Chance, your future involves so many more than you, thousands of psychics want to know how it happened. We know that it happens. But we want to know how. Time after time your love was strong enough to take you to my daughter."

"I thought that was it. You said it was our love, our soul connection."

For the first time since he'd arrived, Chance noticed that the man appeared to be older than time itself.

"You are right about something, Chance. Part of this, for me, is a purely selfish reason. You've managed to have my daughter love you time after time. But I was unable to get her to do the same with me."

"I don't understand. I thought you couldn't find her for a time."

"That's not exactly true. For several lifetimes I reunited with both of you. Then suddenly she however had no memory of me. I would probe her mind and find nothing. It was as though she was no longer a psychic"

"She was always psychic. I witnessed her passing her powers to our son."

"Yes, I'm aware of that. What I don't understand is why she always knew you, and this time around she knew Blaine. I want to know why she refused to know me."

Chance witnessed the sadness that clouded the old man's eyes, that betrayed his voice and barely hid the quiver of sadness that seemed to overtake the Mystic. He took the Mystic's sadness within himself. He did want to help, if he could.

"Maybe it was just one of those things."

"Perhaps." The Mystic's eyes dropped. "I need to know if it was something I had done that caused this. What could it have been that made her not know me? I was near her as, teachers, shopkeepers, healers. But she never felt a connection, nothing that ever made her look at me for a second longer, not a jolt. Nothing. During those lifetimes I would go to you and you would always know me. It pained me to know my daughter didn't. So I only observed you from afar, making contact with you minimally to avoid suspicion."

The Mystic's gaze held him in place. Chance was confused. He didn't remember every moment of every incarnation. What was it the Mystic wanted from him?

"Chance, the moment you take that final step, everything will work as it should. We've studied the stars and we've mapped everything from the beginning of yours and Michelle's soul connection."

"And?"

"And we need you to let go, to take the step that will bring you back together, that will pave the way for others who want to be reconnected, George, Sabu, my friends," he waved his hands toward the door.

"And you?'

"Yes."

"You want us for an experiment. A psychic experiment? You've manipulated our lives so you and your friends can figure out how to come back and be connected."

Chance was astonished and angry. "How do you plan on doing that? How do you know that what you have planned will even work?"

"It will. We're sure of it. The only thing holding us back is—"

"Me. That's it. I'm not moving along fast enough." Chance walked rapidly toward the Mystic clasping his hand on the old man's seemingly frail shoulders. Where the Mystic was concerned he'd learned nothing was ever as it seemed. He closed his eyes and attempted a link with him.

It worked for a few seconds, long enough for Chance to see a huge body of muddy water. His hand fell away and he moved backwards aghast. "You let me in deliberately didn't you? If you think I'm going to bathe in that water, old man, you're crazy."

"Chance."

"Don't Chance me. It's all becoming clear now. George Trammel asking me to stay on, Karen telling me about the ritual bathing in the Ganges. Sabu, was he in on this too?"

"He knows."

"His teachings, have they all been a lie? Has he been feeding me only enough information so that I would find myself compelled to wade out in that disgusting filth?"

"The information he taught you about the Runes is not false, Chance. He didn't do what he's done to help me, or the others. It was to assist you. His loyalties are with you. He wants nothing more than to make your next transition peaceful. He wants you to be happy. If not in this life, then the next."

Without warning a stab of pain hit him so sharp it had Chance clutching at his chest. He sunk down into one of the chairs, his eyes beseeching. "Tell me the truth. Are Blaine and Michelle involved in this as well?"

"Michelle doesn't know that any of this was planned. She knows now about the woman of course. She loves you enough to want you happy, but she knows about nothing else."

"What about Blaine? Does he know?"

"Chance, he's powerful, and he's learning more everyday. He knows."

Chance felt betrayed. He brushed a hand across his face not believing the tears that were coursing down his cheeks. How could his son do this, use him like this?"

When he opened his eyes, he was surrounded by the three Mystics and Sabu.

"I thought he forgave me," Chance said looking up into the faces of the men surrounding him. "Why?"

"Because he loves you," Sabu answered him.

"It sure in hell doesn't feel like love." Chance squirmed at the uncomfortable look on the faces of the Mystic's friends.

He saw it in each of their eyes. Whatever they'd planned to do to him they were going to do it with or without his permission. He stood to leave. He didn't want any part in their plan.

He attempted to move and found himself frozen in place. Damn. There was no way he had enough power to take on the three of them. One by one they laid their hands on Chance. He wanted to shake them off, yell for them to get back, but he couldn't. His entire body was trembling like a pebble picked up and tossed too and fro by a hurricane.

He felt one of them touch his forehead. He didn't know which one, but it didn't matter. He fell forward, limp and weak. He saw himself hurtling through time and space. Tiny pinpoints of energy pulling at him, at every membrane and cell in his entire body. The electrical energy increased in intensity until his body became transparent.   He thought for a moment he was going crazy. He attempted to scream. In fact he believed he had, but the sound was lost in the vast void of the universe. Still he was being pulled, unable to stop until at last with a tremendous jolt, he found himself in a room. He was laid out on a bed covered with heavy woolen quilts. For a moment he thought he'd hallucinated, then realized the scene wasn't just in his head. It was clear, crystal clear. It was a life past, spent. It was his previous incarnation.

He saw a tall dark haired young man standing at the side of the bed, begging his father, *him*, to snap out of it. To not leave him. That son, he knew instantly was Blaine.

Chance wanted with all his heart to undo what he'd done. But try as he might, he couldn't change the past. He attempted to will the body of his former self lying on the bed to move. He couldn't. He entered Jeremy's mind determined to make him look at his son, and what he was about to do to him. That too was a lost cause. The only thing there was a picture of Dimi. He heard himself saying over and over, "I'm coming for you, my love. It's time. I'll find you. I promise."

The self he was, that was lying on the bed didn't even hear the cries and pleas of his son. It wasn't that Jeremy wouldn't have cared. He just didn't hear. His heart and energy were so set on finding his lost love.

Chance tried again to shake life back into the body of his former self. It was no use, he lost. For the Jeremy of the past had made a choice. He chose to die.

He witnessed the last breath being taken, knowing with full knowledge that no one and nothing could prevent what was about to happen.

Without meaning to, he found himself crammed into the mind of his son. The stench of betrayal threatened to overpower him. To say that his son had a broken heart was an understatement at best.

Chance watched in agony as the pain his son was in consumed him. Never had he felt such wrenching agony. Pain filled his son, tearing him apart, ripping the joy from his soul . Bereavement was uppermost in his mind. His sense of loss unbearable. "No," Chance shouted. "Jeremy, do something. Don't die. Your leaving is killing your son. Our son. Come back." He touched his son, but his touch went unnoticed. He was only an observer in this time. He could do nothing but continue to watch as his son from the past took his father in his arms, sobbing uncontrollably. He sensed his feelings of worthlessness. Still in his son's mind, he felt the love draining out of his son as he lay across the dead body of his father, and gave up.

His son had no desire to live. The father he adored, the father he had been convinced loved him was gone. He had no one, no mother; he'd caused her death with his birth...and now his dear, dear father. He'd been the cause of his death also. His birth robbed him of the two people he loved. He would erase himself from existence. It was decided.

"No, No!" Chance attempted to scream into the mind of his son. He knew what was about to happen and began praying for divine intervention. He was but a spectral. He could do nothing to prevent the unfolding tragedy. "Please dear God," he prayed, "Send someone to save him. I promise I will give up thoughts of Dimi. Save my son."

It seemed that Chance's prayers were in vain. He stood helpless watching as his son gently pushed Jeremy's body over to make room for himself, then he climbed into the bed. The feeling of betrayal growing ever larger within his soul. He closed his eyes and willed himself to die. Like father, like son.

Only it wasn't that easy for the son. He lacked the psychic power or training necessary to make his death a swift one. Chance attempted to push him upward, to make him rise from the bed. But he didn't hear him, and his heart so heavy with grief didn't care.

That was when he saw a man walk into the room, and Chance thanked God, for answering his prayers, for sending help. Now he prayed relentlessly that the man would be able to do what he could not, help his son.

It seemed it was taking his son's possible savior forever to access the situation. Chance wanted to prod him to hurry. He watched as his son's spirit began to rise from his body. Chance was screaming, not caring that he couldn't be heard. With great relief he saw that the man had at last taken in the entire gruesome situation. He knew instantly the moment of clarity for him.

He began pummeling the young boy sharing the bed with the body of his dead father. Chance watched while the man poured water over the bodies of both father and son. The man continued to pour until the bodies were drenched in the water. Still the boy didn't budge.

Once again the man began pummeling his son with his fists, calling for him to wake up. Still, nothing.

"Chance was screaming. "Hurry. Hurry, before it's too late." His son's spirit was looking right at him now. There wasn't much time. "Don't do this," he pleaded with his son. "Return to your body."

He saw the man run over to the fireplace and come running back with a red hot poker. "No, no," Chance screamed at him, "Not that, don't use that on him. You will burn him."

The man laid the poker on the skin of the boy, the hot metal searing the skin of the son, as it also seared the skin of the father.

More people rushed into the room taking directions from the man with the poker. They ran out then returned with pokers of their own. They handed those to the man who jabbed repeatedly at the boy burning both him and the dead man at the same time. It finally dawned on Chance what they were trying to do. They were trying to force the spirit back into the body. God, Chance hoped it wasn't too late. He continued watching as in between the searing they poured water over the flesh of both of them until the bed resembled a river, a river of cremated remains.

"Stop," Chance screamed. In that instant the man's eyes stared up into his and he saw the soul of Sabu staring back.

"Oh my God, stop," he screamed, fighting with all his might to return to his own body in his own time. His eyes remained fastened on father and son, and again he had the thought. They were in a river of cremated remains. The River Ganges, "Oh my God," Chance wept. "That's it, that it."

He'd thought that would be the end of it, that the Mystics would be satisfied, but no. Lifetime after lifetime they took him back. Each time he was with Dimi. But it appeared the Mystics weren't satisfied until they took him to his soul's beginning. He was screaming in agony as he felt something being extracted from his soul, some knowledge. "You're killing me," he screamed out and covered his ears. "You need to stop. My life in this incarnation hasn't finished."

Finally they acquiesced and a voice whispered, "Well done. We have succeeded. We will return you to your life."

CHAPTER TWENTY-FIVE

His hand was trembling, his throat burned with a thousand unshed tears, while the ones he hadn't been able to control still stained his cheeks, the salt drying, leaving a filmy residue.

Chance grasped his left hand with his right and brought both up to his chest, his eyes upturned toward the assembled group.

"Why was that necessary for me to see?"

"Because you needed to," the Mystic answered. "You've been searching for the truth, and we helped. Searching for the truth is easy. Accepting the truth is what's hard."

Chance was angry, more at himself and what he'd done, what he'd put his son through. He'd never known, but this, this, he could have lived a thousand lifetimes without seeing.

"I thought I was to learn it all on my on."

"And you have," the Mystic answered him, a sad smile touching the corners of his lips." It's still in your hands, Chance. You have all the information."

"So, Blaine knows this?" He choked on the words, a sob catching in his throat. Of course Blaine knew. That's the reason for the pain that touched him on occasion. Chance had pushed it away too many times, thinking, hoping, it had to do with his son's work, with the pain of the people to whom he delivered messages. Chance had always known it was much deeper than that.

He thought of Blaine and how many times he'd attempted to make a connection. He remembered vividly the scene of him tickling his son and winced. Compared to what he'd just witnessed, he'd left his son with crumbs.

"Teacher, you didn't answer my question. Blaine knows, doesn't he?" He lowered his eyes begging to be wrong.

"He knows."

"Could he have done this... taken me back I mean?"

"I'm not sure," the Mystic answered. "Perhaps. I tried when we last met but nothing happened."

Chance blinked, he couldn't remember any such thing. He shook his head to clear the still lingering images.

"When?"

The Mystic was looking at him strangely, almost in embarrassment it seemed to Chance. When he noticed his old teacher looking toward the other Mystics, he had his answer. The Mystic had broken some code Chance didn't know about.

"When we were all together during the battle. When you, Michelle and Blaine were the strongest and were using your powers as the Triad. It was then I attempted to enter your mind."

"I didn't feel anything."

"Blaine pushed me out."

This time the man smiled broadly, despite his obvious discomfort. There was pride lurking just under the surface for what his blood had done.

"I would have never known Blaine could over power me in psychic abilities, or would. But I found when it comes to protecting the people he loves, Blaine uses every power he was given."

"But why?" Chance frowned thinking, remembering. "He's been so angry at me. Why didn't he want me to know what had happened to him, what my death had done?"

"Because he didn't want to hurt you. He decided he would bear the pain alone. He never wanted you to find out, never. He kept thinking you would know your sin, know the debt you're paying for, know why you're not with Michelle in this lifetime." The Mystic paused. "You do know, don't you Chance?"

Chance's eyes closed. He felt the sting of the hot poker, smelled the burnt flesh. He embraced the pain his son was in as he saw his spirit once again rising from his body.

"Yes, I know my debt. I cost my son his life."

"No, Chance."

"No?" Chance turned watery eyes toward Sabu. "I saw his spirit leave his body."

"But you broke free before you saw the rest. What we were doing, it worked. Your son's spirit returned to his body. I cared for him. I became his friend, his teacher, his—."

"His father," Chance muttered softly, looking up at Sabu. "You took care of my son. That's why..." He shook his head understanding the instant connection that Blaine had with Sabu when he came to India.

"No, Chance, never his father. The most I could be was his friend. He grieved for you, always."

Chance saw something flicker behind Sabu's eyes. He was trying to hide something. No, he thought, no more secrets it was time he knew it all. "Don't worry, Sabu. I can take it. Tell me about my son. What happened to him?"

"He was never the same. I'm sorry. He spent most of his days attempting to conjure up your spirit, yours, and that of his mother. I scolded him many times on attempting to talk to the dead."

An electrical energy shot from Chance's toes to surround his spine and capture his thoughts. He watched as the energy became visible to those around him. It sparked off an untold energy resembling so many miniature fireworks before diving down into the bracelet he wore on his wrist. Each stone glowed with a brilliance that had not even been there through their battles. The heat from the sparks burned into his skin. He felt as if he was being branded.

With that thought, he fell backwards, eyes open, alert, but paralyzed as he witnessed and accepted the energy going through his entire body with more precision than a laser. He closed his eyes in acknowledgment. He was aware of what was happening. His DNA was being imprinted on the stones. It would work. He would have another opportunity. He would find his family again. Now he knew for sure that the Mystic had been right. He had no trouble believing that in the next incarnation his bracelet would return to him. And in return it would lead him to his wife, his beloved, and his son.

When the last branding sting of the energy ray had vanished, Chance looked at the men, Sabu in particular. "Thank you for taking care of my son." He didn't expect an answer. But the look Sabu gave him said it all. For whatever reason he understood Sabu felt as if he'd repaid a debt to Chance, and for that Chance was grateful.

That should have been enough but Chance had to ask. "Was he ever able to talk to us?"

"Never. But that didn't stop him from trying."

Sabu was half smiling, though it didn't reach his eyes. Those remained sad, Chance noted. He nodded for Sabu to continue.

"His only thought was how to get the dead to communicate with him. He made himself a willing vessel, despite my repeated warnings. But no, Chance, he was never able to conjure you, or your wife."

"Did he get anyone?"

"I wouldn't know. If he had it wouldn't have mattered. He only wanted the two of you."

With a groan Chance looked at the four men gathered around him wishing he was home, in America. "And in this life he's finally able to do what he couldn't in that one. Talk to the dead."

Still, there was more going on here. The men surrounding him didn't take him backward through time just to hurt him, or even to let him view his own karmic debt. If that had been the case they would have stopped at his incarnation when Blaine's soul had first come into existence. Instead, they'd taken him back to the beginning of the birth of Chance's soul. A part of it may have been the old man's selfishness. But there was more, something they wanted.

"You're right, Chance. I didn't lie to you about that. I've lost so much time with my Dharma, and your Dimi. In the incarnation before she met you, she was Dharma."

"Teacher, what are you talking about?"

"My daughter. I have to make sure whatever happened to make me lose her won't happen again. It may seem as if I'm using you, but you're the key. In order to put things to right, I had to begin with you. There was an unbroken connection. Something happened to change that. It changed the course of all our lives. Maybe it's wrong that I want this so badly, but I do. You may think I'm a selfish old man, but it's more than that, Chance."

Chance stared at the Mystic. He had no words, so he only listened.

"We're constantly striving to learn more about the powers of the universe. How to overcome? How to remember? And for the most part, we've made tremendous progress," The Mystic explained, waving his hand in a circular fashion toward the other Mystics.

"You, Blaine and Michelle are, as you said before, an experiment of sort. Your lives have been charted from before. Did you really think I was so brilliant that I automatically knew how to encode the jewelry? Did you really think I didn't know who Blaine's true soul parents were? From the moment I knew of Blaine, I knew you and my daughter were his soul parents. I also was aware he was trying to make contact with the two of you, either in this life or from beyond the grave. Blaine was very angry with me for not revealing that he's my grandson until a couple of years ago. I was probably wrong in keeping that information from him, but I did it with the best of intent. I would never have done anything so foolish as make the preparations for the three, probably the four of us to be reunited if all of my facts about the three of you hadn't been studied and there was no chance of my being wrong. An entire group of Mystics have had a hand in this. But we had to wait until you three were ready, until the alignment of the stars was at the right point. Everything is now in place for us to ensure your next incarnation will be all that you want it to be.

"I'll be damned. Is there no one I can trust?"

"Chance, you and Michelle have such untapped powers, you have no idea. Your love for each other is just the tip of it. These short years that you've been without her, and all the others to follow, they're nothing. Not when you know you will have her again. And this time for always. You know how to fix it."

"In the Ganges?"

"In the Ganges."

"In the Ganges," all three Mystics and Sabu repeated. "Will you do it?"

Revulsion surrounded him, seeped through his skin, and the taste of it was like acid on his tongue. He well remembered the scene from the past. Now they wanted him to repeat it on a grand scale.

"I have to talk to Blaine first."

"So you're considering it?"

"Let's just say that with what I put my son through, if there is a way I can erase it, then I'll have to seriously think about it."

"You're not thinking of doing it just to bring you closer to Michelle, are you?" Sabu asked.

Chance narrowed his eyes before giving the question his utmost attention. Sabu's question had disturbed the flow of his thoughts. He'd not thought of Michelle, either as she was now, or of his Dimi. He could honestly say his thoughts were only of his son, and what he could do to make things right. Since he'd taken a moment to answer, they were all staring at him as though after what he'd been through he'd still think to interfere with Michelle's life.

With a sigh he answered. "No, it's not because of my desire to be with Michelle. It's my desire to heal my son."

The drive back was quiet, Chance was deep in thought, and Sabu was respectful of that. Occasionally the men smiled in each other's direction, more than that seemed too tiring.

The moment they hit the camp Chance went immediately to the computer and booted it up. The moment he had an Internet connection he sent Blaine an email. **Call me. It's important.**

Barely any time had passed after the hurried email Chance had sent. Blaine called him as he'd known he would. Taking a breath Chance allowed it to seep out slowly. "Blaine, it all makes sense now, doesn't it?"

"What part exactly?"

"What you do for a living, what I do."

There was quiet on the line. Chance could feel the pain emanating through the lines from thousands of miles away. He felt the prickly heat of the stones surrounding his wrist.

"You saw the Mystic?" Blaine asked.

"Yes, and a couple of his friends."

"What did they do to you?"

"What needed to be done."

"Are you okay?"

"I am."

For a moment neither man spoke. They each knew what the other was thinking. Still they knew some things needed to be put into words. And eventually they would get around to it.

"How do I make amends for what happened?" Chance started, then paused, overcome by an overwhelming urge to sob. "I never knew you would try and follow me."

"Neither did I. It wasn't planned. I just couldn't see living without you. Just as you couldn't see living without her, without my mother."

"I thought you were old enough, that you would find a woman, marry, have kids. I never knew."

"That there would be no possible way I would ever be able to love anyone. I had nothing left in me to give to anyone. All my love went with you."

"Blaine, I was thinking since I'm here anyway, I might as well stay until February. I'm pretty sure I can persuade a couple of doctors to cover my practice for me."

There was a soft chuckle on the other end of the line. At least he sees some humor in this, Chance thought.

"So, you're thinking of bathing in cremated remains?"

"I've done it once," Chance said thinking of the scene he'd witnessed. "I may as well do it for real."

"You don't have to do it, Chance. You only had to remember, to acknowledge your karmic debt. We both know your innate aversion to doing that. Just between us, we will consider it done. I'm sure this will be enough to have you reconnect with Michelle in your next incarnation."

"I'm not doing this for Michelle."

Silence.

"Then why are you doing it?"

Chance caught the small gasp of surprise. Blaine's words were tortured and measured. He knew what he had to do. He closed his eyes, he'd never tried it before, but the Mystic told him he had the power, had always possessed it. Well, if that was true, he was damn well going to put it to the test. For the first time as far as he knew, he bi-located to be with his son who stood before him in shock.

"When did this power occur?"

"I can't answer that. The Mystic said I've always had it. There was no time like the present to try it out."

"Blaine, link with me," Chance ordered, as father to son. "Enter my mind, find out for yourself."

He once again felt the heat from the stones. He didn't have to open his eyes to view the scene. He knew it by heart. His son was a part of his soul, a part of the psychic triad. He accepted Blaine's gentle probing of his mind and opened himself up even more. This son whom he loved, he had always loved. He wanted no secrets between them, no hurt.

"Chance you still don't have to," Blaine whispered as the last remnants of his probing left Chance's mind.

"But I do, for myself and for you. I have to find a way to forgive myself for what I put you through."

"I promise, you don't have to do this. We're good."

"Another thing, Blaine. There is no longer any need for you to talk to the dead. I'm alive, and I'm here for you."

"I like what I do."

"Seriously?"

"Yes. Tell you what, I'll come, and I'll go in with you."

"No, Blaine, it's something I have to do alone. It's my gift to you. I love you son."

"I love you too, Father."

With that, they ended the conversation. Chance smiled. *He called me father, not Dad or Pop, but Father as he had in the past. And this time it hadn't been because he was trying to persuade me to listen.* Yes, if it took him swimming in that damn polluted water over and over, lap after lap until he rid them both of the horrors of a lifetime past; he was willing to do it.

CHAPTER TWENTY-SIX

Chance watched while Sabu walked toward him, the bag of Runes in his hands. They had not done any studying for a while. Chance didn't know if he had the energy for anymore information. He was already on overload.

"Sabu, I'm not sure if I can handle this right now."

"Why?" Sabu's eyebrow quirked upwards. "Because you now know what your karmic debt is, you feel you're whole?"

Chance rubbed his hand over his body playfully. "I feel whole." He looked down. "I look whole. I know my debt, and I'm resigned to paying it. Yes, Sabu, I think I'm whole."

"What about Karen?"

"What about her?"

"Are you whole enough to accept her into your heart?"

Chance laughed. They weren't giving up. "Listen, it's too soon for that. I admit I like her," he stopped when he saw the sneer on Sabu's face. "Okay, maybe I care a little more for her than just like. But I'm not in love with her. And the last woman I want a relationship with is one that was hand picked for me by a bunch of nosey busy bodies' psychics. There is a chance that in the future, after I return home, I'll find a woman I might enjoy dating. I can promise you now, that woman will not be Karen. As for falling in love, I don't know if I can ever fall in love with another woman."

"Then if that's the case, Chance, you need to tell Karen. She still thinks you can. I'm aware you've told her otherwise, but the fact is she thinks you already are in love with her. She's just waiting for you to solve your problems then come to her."

"But we had an agreement. We both said we only wanted to be friends."

"You forget, she's a woman. She reserves the prerogative to change her mind."

None of this was making any sense. Why was Sabu so concerned with his love life? Why was he determined to have him fall in love with Karen? Then it hit him. Slapping his hand on his forehead he chuckled lightly. "Sabu, you want me to remain in India. That's it isn't it? That's why you're pushing Karen on me. I can't, Sabu. I have a family waiting for me. I have a grandson I've seen much less than I want to. I have to get to know him."

"I'm sorry, Chance. You're correct. My motives are a bit selfish. I didn't want to lose your friendship."

"And you don't have to. We can send emails, call. And, Sabu, there are planes to the States. I would love to have you visit me——my treat. You'll be welcome to stay as long as you please. I owe you a debt I can never repay. I'm sure Michelle would also love to meet you."

Seeing the look that came quickly into Sabu's eyes, Chance smiled and decided to reassure his new friend. "I have no plans to disrupt the course of my family's lives. As for Karen, I'm not in love with her. She will find someone now that she's opened her heart to it." Sabu graced him with one of his rare smiles, then he laid his hand on Chance's shoulder.

"I'm not asking for you to love Karen…not anymore anyway. You're her friend, so I know you will be gentle with her and not hurt her."

Sabu's words burned in Chance's brain as he sat at the table lingering over his half eaten breakfast.. He watched Karen, the way she always positioned herself at his side when he was on duty, always giving assistance when he needed it. The easy way she listened, bringing him out, forcing him to talk when he didn't want to. And always he felt better.

The shift had occurred. He had no way of knowing when, but it had happened. Now she freely talked about her husband, bringing photos to show Chance, telling him of the times they'd spent together. Her laughter now was lighter, and the pain he'd noted in her eyes before, appeared to be receding. Maybe it was time for them to talk.

He accepted the coffee she brought him, but let it sit in front of him untouched. He smiled, not knowing what to say. She wasn't making it any easier for him, the way she was looking at him.

"Chance, is there something bothering you?"

He sighed before taking a breath and speaking softly. "I can't offer you my heart. It belongs to someone else."

"I know," she answered. "So does mine."

He stopped, assessed her for a moment then continued. "Yes, but there's a difference. Your husband is dead." He saw the twinge that caused her lips to tighten and rushed on. "I mean it would be too hard for a woman to live with the knowledge that a man she cared for was in love with someone else, the knowledge that the other woman is just a plane ride away. How could anyone accept so little?" She glanced at him. He'd expected to see tears in her eyes, but there were none.

"I'm not trying to recreate the life I had with my husband. I can't. I will never love another man in the same fashion. I know that and I accept it, but my husband was right. He wanted me to continue living, to do that successfully means I need to find someone to be in a relationship with, someone to love."

"Why me, Karen? You know now that we were set up. Why me, after all of this?"

"God, I wish I knew."

"You deserve so much more out of life."

"So do you, Chance. Maybe that's why? Maybe because we both deserve a second opportunity at happiness."

"I have to call her."

"For her permission."

"No, to tell her goodbye."

"I thought you'd already done that."

"I have."

"So how many times are you going to repeat it?"

"Until I mean it."

"Do you mean it now?"

Chance looked at her, he smiled a little before answering. He'd been nothing less than truthful with Karen from the beginning. He would not do less now. "I suppose I won't mean it until I make the call."

"When are you planning on making the call?"

"When I can say goodbye and mean it. I don't want to hurt you, but I meant it when I said I'd like to be your friend." He wished he could have prevented the sigh that slipped out but he couldn't. "I only want to be your friend, Karen."

He picked up the now cold coffee and took a deep drink. This conversation was over. It had nowhere else to go. He would do what he had to do when he could. He knew it was getting close, but until he made the call there would always be a dying ember of hope. He dreaded extinguishing that. Still, he was aware he knew he would do it when the time came. He had no choice. For Blaine, Michelle, and himself he had to talk to her once more. And to Larry, he thought with a small shudder. He had to make amends with Larry.

It took Chance almost three weeks before he thought he was ready to make the call that would end his twenty year search to reunite with his wife, his years of knowing Dimitra, his Dimi lived and breathed but they would not be reunited in this incarnation. He sighed. It was time to make Blaine proud. And it was time for him to get to know his grandson. Since visiting with the Mystics he was aware enough to know his not being there for Blaine's son had hurt him. With a sigh, he realized one more thing had been added to the pile he carried.

Chance waited for the call to the States to be put through. It seemed for over half his life he'd been waiting on one thing or another. The thought of finding the wife he'd remembered from another time possessing him until at last he found her.

Now here he was waiting again, for the husband of his lost wife to call her to the phone. *"You must make amends with him, Chance."* The old mystic's words screamed out at him. Sure he knew he had to, and was planning on doing it. But so far he'd only been able to ask to speak to Michelle.

"Your business, how's it going?" he finally managed to ask of Larry. *God what a truly ridiculous thing to ask.* That thought ran through Chance.

"It's fine thank you. And yours?"

"Well, I'm not working...not really. What I mean is...I've been helping out in a clinic for the past four months. I'm in India."

Damn. Chance wanted to cut out his own tongue. He was saying the dumbest things. Of course Larry knew he was calling from India. That was part of the reason he was even bothering holding the phone, attempting to make polite conversation until Michelle came out of the shower.

He could do better than what he'd done so far and decided to give it another try. "Larry, thank you for allowing me to talk to your wife."

He thought he heard a grunt, he wasn't sure. Hell, he'd never referred to Michelle as Larry's wife, not to him anyway. He pressed forward.

"I do appreciate it."

He heard a long sigh escape the man holding the other end of the phone. He'd not hit on the correct words yet. "Larry, I'm sorry for all the pain I've caused you."

Chance could sense the moment Larry actually begin to listen to him. He sighed himself. "I never meant to hurt either of you. I was a selfish bastard. I remembered my wife from a life before. And I tried to lay claim to yours. I know now, she isn't my wife." *Not this time.* He thought, but didn't say it. "She's yours, and I want to tell you how sorry I am that I attempted to put a wedge between you."

"She still loves you, you know," Larry muttered darkly, his voice drifting away, the sound of it forlorn.

"I know," Chance answered. "How do you manage to deal with it?"

"Because I love her."

Again Chance heard him sigh.

"And I know that she loves me," Larry continued. "I don't know how to make her stop loving you, or thinking about you. Or worrying that something horrible will happen to you. All I can do is love her."

Damn, Chance thought to himself. *Why did I ever hate him?* He only wants the same_thing that I want. "Listen to me, Larry. You don't need to worry any longer about me. I won't be calling anymore. That's why I'm calling now, to tell Michelle goodbye."

"You've done that before, Chance. But still, somehow, you're in the picture."

"It was harder than I thought to actually do it."

"What's making it easier now? Why should I believe you this time? When my wife comes to talk to you, will I hear her scream out at the end of the conversation, that she loves you?"

Chance cringed. He'd wondered how long it would take for them to get to that. Larry had every right not to believe him. "Don't blame Michelle for that. It wasn't her fault, but mine."

"I don't blame her," Larry answered. "I know that you know which buttons to push to make her feel guilty. It seems we've both done a lot to make her feel responsible for our emotions."

For a long moment they were both caught up in their own thoughts, until Larry voiced the question again. "I want to hear what's changed. How can I be sure that you're out of our lives?"

Chance took a second to answer, wondering what he could say

that would convince Larry that he would keep his word this time, that he would remain out of Michelle's life. He answered in the only way he could. Honestly.

"Because I love her. I'll always love her. I want her happy, Larry. I don't want her worrying about me, dividing her time or attention. She should be giving all of herself to you, and your family."

"Then why didn't you tell her this in a letter?"

Chance couldn't prevent the laughter that bubbled up to his throat from spilling out. "She's your wife," he acknowledged. "Do you think she would have believed it if I had said it in a letter? Besides," he added, "Would you really want her hanging on to a last letter? She wouldn't have been able to destroy it you know." He could tell Larry was thinking over what he said.

"Here's Michelle," Larry said. "Chance, have a good life."

"Thank you for that, and thank you for allowing me to say goodbye to her. You have a good life too. You, and Michelle."

Chance heard muffled voices then the sound of Michelle laughing softly floated out to him, wrapping him in a cocoon of warmth, of love and memories. But that was not the reason for this call, not to remember, but to set things right. When Michelle came on the line, he took a breath then began.

"You sure took your time in that shower," he teased.

"Yeah I know. I thought the two of you needed to clear the air without me in the room."

Deliberate. He should have known. "You know?"

"Yes, I know."

"How long?"

"Long time."

"How?"

Chance knew the answer the moment the question was out. "It was Blaine wasn't it? He showed you?" God how he wished it wasn't true, that she hadn't seen what he'd put their son through.

"Yes, he showed me."

"I didn't break my promise to you. I loved him. Our son was my world. He was all I had left of you. I gave him your name."

"I know you loved him. And thank you for naming him after me. I hadn't known that, neither had Blaine, not until he'd visited with you. He knows he was loved."

"Still, I hurt him."

"You didn't mean to. You didn't know what would happen."

Chance let a sigh escape. She was making this easy for him, too easy. "I'm going to be okay. You don't have to continue to carry guilt for me."

Michelle laughed. "Is that what you think I'm doing?"

"Aren't you?"

"No, Chance. No guilt, not for loving Larry. Not because we're not together."

"Is Larry there, in the room with you? Is that why?"

She laughed again and he remembered every time in every life he'd heard her laughter. He was going to miss hearing that.

"Larry decided he wanted to go for a drive. I think he wants to not be here if we repeat our last conversation."

Chance heard the laughter still in her voice. "Michelle, I'm sorry about that. I'm sorry I forced you to declare your love for me, sorry I made you worry after. After spending a lifetime dreaming about you, it wasn't the easiest thing in the world to just stop. You can't make yourself stop dreaming of who you're dreaming of."

"Don't you think I understand that? From the time I was a child with no way to know what my dreams meant, I dreamed of you and our son. You were in my heart from the moment I was born. My spirit couldn't rest until you found me. It wasn't that I didn't love Larry and our family. It was just that I remembered you and our son, and I loved you too. I don't want you feeling guilty any longer about our being together. It had to happen, Chance."

"God, I've been so—"

"So human, Chance, that's all. You're a man, you're human. You're allowed to make mistakes. So am I."

"Was it a mistake, our being together in this life? I mean for the time we shared, stolen moments really."

"Not a mistake. My marriage is stronger because of it. Believe it or not, Larry and I know how fragile love is. It keeps us on our toes."

"So you don't regret it?" *Why the hell was he pushing?* He was doing it again.

"If it could have happened without my hurting Larry I wouldn't regret a moment of it."

"Of course. I'm sorry. I shouldn't have asked."

"Chance."

"Yes."

"I don't regret a moment of our time together. And that my love, is my karmic debt."

"I'm sorry about that too."

"Why? You didn't twist my arm. I knew what I was doing. It had to happen, Chance. Don't you see that? My God, if it wasn't for you I wouldn't know who I am. I would be hiding the truth. I have a God given gift. I'm relearning how to use it. I've been given an opportunity to love the son I lost. I never got the chance to love him before and because of that I was reborn grieving his loss. And I found you. How can I possibly regret it? And I found out I can't secure my future by living in the past."

"You know I'm not calling again."

"I know."

"I'm going to start dating."

"Karen?"

"No, it will be someone I choose and it will be when I'm ready. Just so it's clear, tell Blaine, and your father, that if either of them so much as comes near a woman, I won't date her. I don't need any of your help in that department. Karen may not fully understand the amount of manipulation that but put us together, but I do. And I may have hurt her by lusting after her and then telling her I couldn't be with her, that I loved only you. I did try to prevent that by telling her from the beginning that I only wanted to be her friend. But she lost her husband a number of years ago and thought I was meant to replace him."

"I feel sorry for her."

"So do I."

"Didn't you desire her, even a little bit?"

"Like you said, I'm human. I desired her."

"Did you tell her?"

"I tried to, but I really mucked that up and ended up insulting her by making her feel she wasn't desirable in her own right. She's a very nice woman. Just not for me. Can you understand that?"

"I understand."

"And, you'll give my message to your father and to our son?"

"I'll tell them."

Chance fought the pain. This had to be done." Can you believe it? I'm actually going to do it. I'm going to bath in that filthy, polluted water, among cremated remains."

"But it doesn't have to be that way if you don't want it like that. Change the reality of it to what you want."

Chance shuddered. "Easy for you to say. You're not the one going for a little dip among the dead." She didn't answer so he pressed on. "I talked to Blaine. He's something else, that son of ours."

"I agree," Michelle answered. "He has a lot of love in his heart, and forgiveness."

"Did you know he tried to reach me...to reach us after?" Chance found it hard to talk about what his dying had cost their son. If he couldn't talk about it with Michelle, he may never be able to get the words out. So he tried again. "Did you know that's why he does it now? Communicates with the dead, I mean. It's from before. It all makes sense now."

He stopped and waited, wondering if Michelle even knew what the hell he was talking about. The way he'd rambled on, he wouldn't blame her if she didn't. He just hoped she wouldn't ask him to repeat it. That he couldn't do. With gratitude, he moaned a low, "thank you," when Michelle answered.

"There is one more thing I wanted to talk to you about," Michelle said. "Blaine happened to mention that you haven't been able to use our grandson's name. He says you always ask about 'the baby.' He said you've always tried to silence him when he tries to tell you his son's name. You do know his name don't you?"

"Yes."

"So why have you never called him by his name?"

"I did so much to hurt Blaine. It's just hard for me to believe he has forgiven me. I love him so much. I always did. But I wonder if maybe he gave the baby the name he did because of you."

"I had nothing to do with Blaine naming his son. He loves you, Chance. Isn't it proof to you that he named his son Jeremy after the father he loved."

"I didn't feel worthy of him doing that."

"Now, how do you feel?"

"I feel we've come full circle. I suppose when they have a girl, he'll name her Dimitra."

"I wouldn't be at all surprised."

"It looks as though I'm finally going to cleanse my karmic debt?"

"The Mystic told me."

"The Mystic," Chance imitated her voice "My God I can't believe how many people from our past we've reconnected with. The charging of the jewelry is going to work. When the Mystic took me back to my very beginning I thought they were going to kill me." He laughed to let her know he was half teasing. "The electrical energy that generated through my body and into the bracelet was so powerful that I screamed out. But even while I was screaming I was aware my DNA was being recorded into the bracelet. We will be together again."

He pondered something he'd wondered about. "Why do you think it is that each life time I've come back as your husband, and not as the wife?"

"Michelle was laughing. "Because we got it right, Chance. We didn't have any questions about our roles, or which we liked better. I loved being your wife. And apparently, you loved being my husband."

She stopped suddenly and he knew she was blushing. "Sabu, you remember me telling you about him, how he annoyed the hell out of me when I first got here. Did you hear he's the one that took care of Blaine after…well after he was alone?"

"I heard."

"Dimi, did you ever wonder why we never connected with anyone else, not parents, siblings or any other relatives?"

"Michelle," she corrected. "Dimi died, remember?"

Chance rubbed the sweat from his upper lip with the thumb of his left hand. "You're right. Dimi died. Sorry, Michelle." It was time to end this conversation, it was becoming hard. He couldn't think of Dimi as being dead when she lived and breathed in the body of Michelle.

"Chance, I know the answer."

He almost asked her answer to what. He'd forgotten he'd asked her anything. "What is the answer?" he asked her, feeling a little foggy.

"We didn't have need for anyone else. That's why we searched only for each other. Our love was enough. Until this time, and then our son was very much on our minds. I may have dreamt of him and cried out for him, but your soul was also looking for him. It was the guilt that kept you from knowing. Look how much you love him. That's no accident, Chance."

"Ahh God. Michelle. You know we're only prolonging this don't you? It's time I did what I said, what I promised your husband I was going to do. It's time for me to finally say goodbye and mean it, to let you go."

"And what about you, Chance?" Michelle asked, "Are you going to be able to be happy, to learn to live again?"

"I'm working on it. I can't make any promises, but I'm working on it."

"That's all I can ask of you."

As they linked he felt her gentle nudging around the rim of his subconscious and opened for her, at the same moment searching out to be with her. There was no need for words. He opened his eyes and saw the prism of crystal light shooting into his bracelets.

"Did anything happen to you just now?" he asked.

"Yes, the same as happened to you. You don't have to worry, Chance. I wouldn't forget you even if I wanted to. And I don't want to." She finished before he could ask the question.

"Larry's a good man," Chance admitted.

"I know.

"He loves you."

"I know."

"You love him too."

"Yes, I do."

"And you love me."

"Yes. Is that enough for you to know? That I love you, that I never made a choice. It was never that I loved Larry more than you. Do you understand that now?"

"It took me a long time to get here, but I do understand. And believe it or not, hearing you say it does help."

Sighing once then again, Chance took in a deeper breath, resolving himself to a present he didn't want. It would be a lie if he said that. He was, and always had been living proof of reincarnation. Why was he so worried? He knew he'd find his family in the next life. "*Let go*," a voice urged. He sighed again. "It's time isn't it?"

"That's up to you."

Chance folded his hands together, bringing the phone from his ear to rest it on his chest. "Goodbye, my love. Have a good life."

He thought she said the same, but he wasn't sure. He hung up as he took in several deep breaths, letting them out rapidly. It was done. He would not call her again, not put her in the position of piling on more debt.

Walking away from the phone, Chance tried to clear his mind. He didn't want to think of what he'd done, or what he was going to do. He sought only peace.

"Chance, is there something wrong?"

He looked toward the voice. It took a moment to focus on Karen. He debated the wisdom of telling her, wondering if she'd read more into his call than he wanted her to.

"Did anything happen?"

She was worried about him, it came because she cared. That made his decision. If nothing else she was his friend. "I called Michelle. I talked to her, and to Larry."

"Was it hard?"

"No harder than I thought it would be."

"So what made you do it?"

"I love her. I didn't want to continue to interfere in her marriage. I want her to be happy." He waited for his words to be reflected in Karen's answer, in her eyes, to see if she really meant what she'd said about the two of them being friends.

"Are you sure you did the right thing?" Karen asked him.

"I'm sure," he answered. "Besides we'll be together again."

"Do you think that I can find my husband again?"

Her question startled him. He'd been unprepared for that. "I hope so Karen. I truly hope so. But, I can't tell you how to go about doing it. I have no idea how Michelle and I have been able to do it time and time again. If I said love, it would imply that I thought our love was stronger than others' love. I don't know if it's because of our psychic gifts, or our promises. I sincerely don't know. But I do hope you find your husband. And at least I also hope you find a man in this life to love you. You deserve that."

The disappointment was evident. Everyone was counting on him making things right, depending on Blaine, Michelle and himself to lead the way, provide the answers. Chance couldn't provide any answers. He knew now why they weren't together, but he could not say why they had always been joined, why they always found themselves in the same role. He liked Michelle's explanation. They'd gotten it right. They had no need to change their roles.

Karen was turning to walk away, her shoulders slumped. He reached out a hand to touch her, tentatively at first, then pulled her closer. Not an embrace, not the touch of a stranger.

"I definitely don't believe we're unique. There has to be others who've met those they've lost in past lives. I believe you stand as good a shot as any at finding your husband again."

"Thanks, Chance."

She was smiling at him, some of the uncertainty leaving, her shoulders rising a quarter of an inch. He'd helped. If only a little, he'd helped.

The weeks slipped by one after the other. As the second week of January got into full swing. Chance could not get the vivid images of his death out of his mind. Now he would be repeating it on a grand scale. He still dreaded the thought of what he would do in February. Planning to bath in the Ganges did not bring a sense of pride to him, but one of trepidation.

His studies of the Runes was almost complete. Whether he wanted to admit it or not, they were right one hundred percent of the time. He was adjusting to that, to everything.

He finished up his last patient of the day, washed his hands, and dipped them automatically in the box of suckers. This time he'd head Aisha off before she came in with her litany of complaints.

Sure enough the child bounced forward as he stepped through the door, her jet black hair swaying as she skipped into the building, holding her mother's hand. He smiled and watched her eyes light as she smiled at him in turn. He held out his hand knowing her reaction would be immediate delight.

For a second she stood rooted to the spot before turning to her mother for permission. With a laugh of supreme triumph she ran to Chance, snatched the candy from his outstretched hands and ran away. A second later she was peeking from behind her mother before returning and kissing both his cheeks.

Chance laughed, signaling the mother, to place her daughter on the exam table, perusing Aisha out of habit, just in case this time she really did have a problem.

"Sabu," he called, "just let's make sure, okay." He endured Sabu's impatient sigh. What did it matter as long as he knew the child merely wanted the candy? He watched Aisha face's as Sabu talked to her, asking her questions. The child slid from the table and walked toward him, giving the candy back to Chance. Two fat tears slithered down her cheeks. She stood before him her head bowed.

"What's wrong?" Chance asked Sabu.

"There is nothing wrong with her." Sabu frowned at the child and her mother. "There never was. She only wanted the candy."

Chance could hear the, 'I told you so,' in Sabu's voice and was grateful he didn't say it. Of course he'd always known there'd been nothing wrong with Aisha. He grinned at the child and her mother while dipping his hand back into the stash of brightly colored candy and increased the supply in his already bulging hands. This he presented to Aisha with a bow and a flourish.

"You take it little one, for brightening my day and my life." He lifted the child in his arms, her head coming to rest on his shoulders. "Anytime sweetie, you come to me anytime." He waited while Sabu translated. He saw the face of the child's mother break out in a grateful smile. Then Chance kissed Aisha on both cheeks before setting her down. He would miss her when he returned home.

When Chance would have turned to leave Aisha's mother stopped him, her hand on his arm. She began making motions on her body while pointing to Chance. At first he didn't get it, then he knew she was imitating washing. He smiled at her. It appeared everyone had heard.

"Yes, I'm going to bath in the Ganges," he grinned. A lot had changed in the few short months since he'd been in India.

A hell of a lot.

"Busy, Dr. Morgan?"

Chance looked up into the smiling face of George Trammel. "Hi, George. No, I'm not busy. I was just going to try and put in a call to the States. Is there something you need?"

"I wanted to thank you for staying on. The extra time has meant a lot. I don't know if I ever got around to telling you how much I appreciate the help. You could have chosen to give your time and service to any of a dozen different clinics. I'm glad you chose us."

"Were you in on this, George?" Chance waited, gauging his response.

"Not from the beginning. I was just grateful for the opportunity to get to meet you in person, to hear first hand what happened. I had no way of knowing what kind of journey you were here for."

"Neither did I."

"You've come a long way."

Chance looked away, over his shoulder. His head swung back to meet George's stare. "I suppose I have." He shook his head slowly from side to side. "You know, George, I find it amazing how a lone incident, one moment in time can shape the remainder of a soul's journey. And when it happens you have no way of knowing the future impact."

"Which moment has that been for you?"

Chance thought about it, "There's been so many, I'm not sure. I guess maybe it would be the moment I chose to hear my wife's voice calling to me. My believing in what I heard led me to her. And that," he smiled, "led me to my son."

"And he led you here."

"Yes." Chance shook his head again. "Blaine led me here. And now it looks like in a few short days, I will be doing something I would have sworn I would never do in a million years."

"What do you mean, would have sworn? You did swear, remember? Every time anyone broached the subject to you. You balked, and your words if I might quote you were, "'hell no, no way in hell will I bathe in that polluted water with cremated remains.'"

Chance found George's imitation of him amusing. "You remembered word for word?"

"Oh yes, by then I knew the plan and I knew you would eat those words. So I wanted to remember them." George grinned at Chance, patted him on the shoulder and said, "Before you leave I have to tell you that the disinfectant was never reused. For the newcomers we use a mixture of herbicides to given the appearance of sludge. Sabu always changed the liquid between uses, and all of the instruments were autoclaved each and every time. We were, you might say, sifting the chaff from the wheat. I'm glad you were part of the harvest. Why don't you go and call your son now?" He glanced at his watch. "This is one of the best times of getting through."

Chance walked away, turning back as George called out his name again.

"Wouldn't it be quicker to just email Blaine?"

"But not as satisfying."

As the operator put through the call, Chance was relieved. George was right. This was a good time for calling. Or it would have been if he hadn't wakened Blaine.

"Chance, anything wrong?" came Blaine's sleepy voice.

"Nothing, I just wanted to check on you and Cassandra and little Jeremy. Everyone okay?"

"We're fine. That's the first time you've called the baby by his name. Are you okay with me naming him after you...well your name from your last incarnation?"

"I'm honored and so undeserving."

"You were a father who loved his son. You deserved the honor. Believe me, I wouldn't have named my son anything else. Since you hadn't used his name I had wondered if I'd upset you."

"Just the opposite. Thank you. And thank Cassandra also." Chance fell silent for a moment. Blaine was waiting for him to tell him the reason for his call, although he was certain he already knew. He would indulge his son's discretion and go along with the game.

"Everything's all set," Chance said at last. "I talked to Michelle, and to Larry. I did it."

"Really?"

"Really. I let her go."

"How do you feel?"

"Strange. I've wanted to be with her for so long. Now to think about doing something different... yeah I guess that's the best way I can describe it. I feel strange."

"What about Karen? Any decision about her?"

"We're friends. I'm going to help her find someone to love, though I haven't told her yet. But I'll do it with her permission, unlike others I know."

"Sounds hopeful," Blaine offered.

"You may have been right about one thing. I do believe we help each other. She's not asking for things I can't give."

"And that would be?"

Chance laughed softly, "Blaine, why are we playing games? I said I let Michelle go. I never said I've stopped loving her. Karen understands. I haven't lied to her. She knows I will never stop loving Michelle. She knows my heart belongs to my wife."

"Then what is it that you have left to offer Karen, or any woman?" Blaine asked.

"I don't know. I guess we'll just have to see, won't we?"

"I'm so proud of you. This is the first time that I believe you. I know it was hard, but it had to be done. You said you talked to Larry?"

"Oh yeah, we talked."

"And?"

"And he probably wishes I would evaporate. But since I agreed to never call his wife again, and I actually acknowledged that she's his wife, not mine---he probably feels a wee bit better about things. Not much, but enough for him and Michelle to let go. She has to let me go also. You do know that, don't you?"

"I know, but I think your taking the first step will make it easier for her. She's going to be alright, and so are you."

Chance found himself grinning for no reason. "I suppose I am. Can you believe it? I'm actually going to bathe in the Ganges. I am going to travel that frigging congested road and bath in that filthy water with fifty million other people. Can you believe it?"

"I can, Chance. I can believe it."

"How can you believe it when I can't?"

"Because I know why you're doing it. You're doing it for me, because you love me."

Chance couldn't argue with that. A warm glow filled his heart. "I'll call you after it's done."

"Would you like me to come? Cassandra and I can hop on a plane and join you."

For a moment Chance toyed with the idea. "Nah, I'm a big boy. I don't need my son to hold my hand. I'm not going to chicken out," he laughed.

"Okay, call me when it's over."

Chance said goodbye to his son, hanging up the phone, laughing softly to himself. He hoped he would be the one to call him after he'd swam in that water and not Sabu, telling Blaine that Chance had caught some horrible disease and succumbed to it.

The day had finally arrived; the entire camp was going to the festival. They were leaving three days early to get there on time.

"Why are we leaving so early?" Chance asked George cornering him as he rushed around surveying the trucks.

"Because the traffic is going to be murder on Trunk Mile Road."

"As opposed to any other day?" Chance couldn't believe the traffic could possibly get any worse.

"You haven't seen anything yet. Just you wait, then you'll be glad we got there and staked out space. Be prepared, there is no room for tents or blankets. If you can find a spot on which to stand, count it as a blessing," George laughed.

Chance's nerves were jangling, a feeling of apprehension skittered down his spine playing havoc with his internal organs. He was going through with it. But he dreaded it just the same. Nothing had been able to prepare him to forget what he was about to do. Not even the Runes.

He'd pulled a stone before he came out to leave. It was the Rune of Wunjo, meaning joy and light. For the life of him, Chance couldn't see how what he was about to do would provide either joy or light.

He did take heart that the stone said his travails were ending, and he was coming into himself. He supposed that meant he was now whole, as the stones had told him in the beginning he needed to seek to become.

He fingered the bag of stones in his pockets, the stones Sabu had given him just that morning as a present. He felt for the book he'd given him with it and pulled it from his pocket, caressed it then replaced it, no longer needing it to read the meaning. He knew them all by heart.

Joyousness accompanies new energy, energy blocked before now. Light pierces clouds and touches the waters, just as something lovely emerges from the depth. The soul is illuminated from within, at the meeting place of heaven and earth, the meeting of the waters.

It's time to get it over with. "Let's do it," he said aloud, as he climbed into the truck with Karen and Sabu.

His well stocked cooler of wet towels almost seemed comical now, considering what he was about to do. Enough pollution to kill several American states should not affect him in the least.

He laughed to himself as he sat back to enjoy the ride. This was the third time he would be traveling on Trunk Mile Road. People always said the third time was a charm.

It didn't take long for the thick blue smoke to creep in on them. But this time there was a difference. This time he looked out at the teeming people living along the side of the road, and for the first time he felt a part of them. Another difference was the frenzied level of activity. He watched as thousands walked today, instead of lying about, the movement itself seemed to spark a kind of gaiety. Everyone was laughing, obviously not minding the even heavier traffic. Chance knew why. They were going to wash away their sins. Why shouldn't they feel light?

He hated to admit it to himself, but it was affecting him also. He could feel his spirit within anticipating the coming event with joy, while his soul felt lighter than it had in decades. He thought of Michelle and Blaine. How could he not? They would be so proud of him. With this one act he was freeing them all.

He laughed and talked easily with Karen and Sabu. There was a rosy glow in Karen's cheeks. He knew it was there in part because of her hope for the two of them. She still hadn't been able to accept his decision. As soon as he arrived home he would began his match making, positive he'd find a good man for her. But unlike what his family had done to him, he'd get her permission. After he was gone from India in time, Karen would adjust and forget about him. Then he'd reach out to her and ask for her permission to help her in her search for love.

A lot was riding on his dip into the river. Everyone was waiting to see what would happen. Chance had to admit to himself that, he was curious. There was no way he could believe he would come out a totally different person. But he was willing to give it a shot. To be forgiven for the hell he'd put his son through, hell yes, he would bathe in it all day if he had to.

A shudder traveled over him and he smiled to himself. Well, he'd have to see about the all-day part. But he would definitely bathe in it.

Looking ahead he spotted one of the sweet tea stands. For once he wouldn't complain about the cow dung that fueled the fire. They all knew where the smell emanated from. He wouldn't belabor the point.

"Sabu, pull over please," he asked." Let's get some tea."

Just then Chance saw the now familiar white van that carried the nuns from Mother Theresa's order. He couldn't believe it, not three times. He pressed his head against the window and was greeted by the same nun he'd encountered on his previous trips. He wanted to talk to her, but feared as in his previous two encounters they would leave.

He saw the nun smiling at him, knew she was looking for him.

Chance watched as she made a hand signal to her driver and saw the van pull over smoothly to the side.

"Stop," Chance yelled to Sabu and was out of the truck the moment it came to a complete stop. He ran up to the group of nuns who were standing in a cluster around a stand to buy the sweet tasting tea.

"Sisters," he pleaded, "Please, may I buy the tea for all of you?"

The nuns smiled at him and nodded in acquiescence. Chance peeled several bills from his wallet and handed them over to the vendor.

His eyes searched for the bright clear gaze of the nun who'd smiled at him.

"Sister, do you remember me?" Chance asked, thinking what a foolish question.

"Of course," she answered coming to stand closer to him. "I remember you. I was looking forward to seeing you today."

That was strange. How could she? "Sister, how did you know I would be here?" Chance asked.

She smiled, and with her smile he felt an even greater lightening of his spirit. He watched tentatively as the nun stepped even closer to him, felt her energy as with her slender, weathered, work-hardened hands, she touched him. Every nerve in his body tingled. He stood still, allowing her to do what she will.

"You have a glow about you," she announced after trailing her hands from the crown of his head downwards. "You're a good man." She smiled. "The first time I saw you, you were filled with sadness, questions. The second time you were seeking answers. And now you're here seeking redemption."

"How do you know all of this?" Chance's heart was in his throat. He felt as if he were in the very presence of the divine.

"I know," she answered simply. "Remember things are not always as they seems." She tilted her head to the side to better observe him it seemed to Chance. Then she made her pronouncement.

"You have great love in this life. Don't worry you will have it again."

With that she patted Chance's hand, thanked him for the tea, and returned to the other nuns. He stood there looking after her until Sabu and Karen joined him.

"What was that about?" Karen asked.

He could feel his mouth opening wide. He knew he was grinning like an idiot. "She's the same nun. She told me that everything is going to be fine."

As the vendor started to hand Chance his change, Chance ordered tea for Sabu and Karen, thought better of it, and got one for himself. Yes, he thought, everything's going to be fine. I have it on good authority.

The rest of the long drive was not only easier, it was downright pleasant. He looked from time to time for the white van the nuns traveled in. He had not seen them since he bought the tea. If they were headed for the Ganges they should be around. He shook his head and smiled at the thought. It didn't matter. He'd gotten his answer. He didn't need to see the nun again to know why she was there. He didn't have to go into the Ganges if he didn't want to. He was already forgiven. But he was still going to do it.

George Trammel had been right. They barely had room for the trucks, they jockeyed for position knowing the others would arrive soon. It didn't matter that they couldn't set up a tent, none of it mattered. Chance looked out over the Ganges. He saw people carrying urns, bottles and jars of all types and makes. Those would no doubt contain the remains of his bathing partners. He smiled, it didn't matter. Everything was going to be fine.

Two days later the entire surrounding rejoiced. Everyone was in a prayer of some sort. Chance may not have understood the words, but he definitely understood the intention. Day had dawned early and bright, swarms of people were heading out as far as the eye could see. Several of his colleagues stripped naked, and half laughing walked toward the water. Others climbed aboard the trucks to watch, not interested themselves in going through the ritual bathing. He looked at Karen. She was blushing.

"Are you going in?" he asked wishing that he wasn't.

"No, Chance, I think I'll wait here for you." She turned her head and he welcomed the privacy. He had no urge for her to see his nude body.

Chance peeled off his jeans and threw them into the truck. He took the rest of his clothing, tossed them in behind the jeans, and covered himself with a huge beach towel.

He walked among so many others, the thoughts of what he was about to do crowding out all other thoughts. He watched as person after person emptied their container into the river and then emerged themselves. He wished for just a small spot for himself. What he needed to do, he needed to do alone.

"Not alone, Chance."

Chance turned in surprise, his eyes growing large. Blaine was in front of him. "How? When did you get here?"

"Did you think I would let you do this alone?"

"But you didn't have to."

"You're my father. I want to be here with you."

Chance wanted to hug his son but was busy holding his towel in place. He looked again at the water and the throng that gathered in, around and through it. "I guess it's time."

"Almost."

At the sound of the voice, Chance turned his head once more. The Mystic was there along with his friends.

"Almost, Chance. Tell me," the old man said as he looked out into the water. "Tell me what you see."

Chance gazed at the water, at the ash colored debris, at the people who'd painted their bodies with ashes of their loved ones, and he thought before he answered.

"What do I see?" he repeated. "I see my salvation. I see the end of my guilt. I see the securing of my future with my son, and my wife. And I see forgiveness."

"Well said," the Mystic answered as Chance turned toward him. "Now look again."

Chance looked at the three men for maybe little more than a millisecond then turned to look back over the water.

In the middle of the chaos, he spotted a clearing. The sun was shining overhead and a rainbow from, where, he had no idea, claimed a perfect section of water. He continued looking, walking forward as he did so. A figure was emerging from the water. His heart soared and raced ahead of his feet. He ran into the water with abandon.

The naked figure stood erect, stretched and her cinnamon colored hair tumbled down her back in wet curls.

"Michelle," Chance whispered in awe, his throat constricted, he looked back toward his son, and held his hand out for Blaine. Blaine smiled at the both of them.

"Now I know what to do," Chance said as he pulled his family into his arms. The three of them locked arms and formed a triangle. And as the radiant rays of the triad shot forth, the murky water they were standing in became crystal blue, clean and pure.

Together they went under the surface and came up again. Three times they did this. Chance knew from the yearning of his soul this was the number of times it would take. They were the psychic trinity, the triad.

He saw the light from their combined auras piercing the few scattered clouds, breaking them apart, showering them in a healing ray of light, and love, yes, and joy.

It was true. He'd truly seen something beautiful emerging from the water. He glanced at Michelle. "Wunjo promised me joy."

"And your soul?" Blaine asked as the three of them continued, linked together.

"It's filled." He looked from the son he loved to the woman of his heart. "It's all been fulfilled. My soul has been illuminated. This is indeed the place where heaven and earth meet; this is the meeting of the waters."

Michelle was glowing, bathed in a golden radiance. So was Blaine. Chance did nothing to stop the sudden rush of tears. It was done. It was over.

"I hope this will be the last time I have to tell you this. I forgive you, Father," Blaine said, his voiced filled with his own raw emotions. "Do you forgive yourself?"

"I forgive myself," Chance answered, and as he did so, the circle surrounding Blaine and Michelle doubled, tripled, quadrupled in size until it seemed they were nothing more than a radiant light. Still Chance remained linked with them.

He didn't attempt to pull Michelle into his arms for one last embrace. That would have been wrong. He knew she wasn't really there, just her soul, hers and Blaine. They had sent their souls to join with him, to give him proof of their never-ending love.

He looked instead at the luminous soul of his beloved and spoke. "For always and forever my love. I'll be waiting for you in the next life."

"And I'll be waiting for you. I promise."

Then to his surprise she embraced him and kissed him on both cheeks. With that she was gone.

"Thank you, Blaine," Chance whispered. "For your love, and your forgiveness."

"You're my father," Blaine answered. "I could do nothing less. I love you." He smiled. "I have a gift for you. I had a talk with Karen and told her I'd gotten a message for her from her husband. He said, that he approves of your friendship, but you're not the man who will make her happy. He advised her that her new love would come to her in two years. He told her to be patient, and that he'd be with her until then."

"Did that really happen? I mean did her husband really give her that message?"

"Do you think I'd lie?"

"Yes."

"This is my profession, my gift."

"And I still think you'd lie."

"Why do you believe that?"

"Because you love me, and you knew I wasn't having any luck with getting Karen to believe I truly meant it when I told her there's nothing in the cards for us besides friendship?"

"I think we all had a hard time believing you meant it. Now I do. And since this was partially my fault, I decided to rectify my mistake."

"So you lied. Don't worry, love makes us do strange things, including lie."

"I didn't say I lied." Both men laughed "But you're right I do love you. On the rest, I plead the fifth. Before you leave India, I will return. Together we need to visit all the wonders and beauty this country has to offer. So far you haven't seen much of that. But there is magic here in this place. I want us to experience it together."

"Will Cassandra be okay with that?"

"She knows how important you are to me. She'll be fine. Let me know when your last day at the clinic will be, and we'll make plans. I can hardly wait."

"And neither can I," Chance whispered to the golden sphere that was the soul of his son. And with those words, Blaine too was gone.

Chance walked out from the water in awe, wonder and love. He glanced toward the Mystics. They were all smiling. "Is that what you were waiting for?"

"It was," they said in unison. "Your journey is complete."

Chance reached for the towel Michelle's father was holding

toward him.

"Nothing is ever as it seems, Chance. Remember, if you don't like the circumstances you find yourself in, change them."

The old man's eyes twinkled and Chance thought instantly of the nun. He smiled, knotting the towel as Karen rushed forward. There was wonder in her eyes.

"I saw...I saw her. And then she just disappeared. Was that Michelle?"

"Yes," Chance answered.

"Did she and Blaine just bi-locate here to be with you?"

"Yes. We'll talk about that later." He walked toward the shore, looked again at the Mystics, back at Karen, and stopped. "Give me a moment to get dressed," he said and raced for the truck. When he returned he held out his hand.

"Come on," he smiled at Karen. "Let's go for a walk. It's time for me to return home. It's time to stop running. I have a family waiting for me. I have a new grandson I wish to spoil. I'm not going to hide out in India waiting for some spiritual reunion. I'm going home in order to be there for my family when they need me. I cheated my son out of one lifetime with me. I won't do it again.

A look of sadness crossed Karen's face, and Chance gave her hand a squeeze. "We're only meant to be friends in this life, Karen. Being friends is a good thing. You will find someone to love, and perhaps so will I in time. If it happens for me, it happens. If it doesn't, that will be fine. You love who you love. I won't apologize for that. As for the two of us, I would welcome the opportunity of continuing to be your friend."

"I thought your bathing in the Ganges was to get rid of your love for Michelle."

"It wasn't to get rid of my love for my her. It was meant to be a symbolic means of acknowledging karmic debt. It wasn't meant to make me forget my wife or my love for her. I can't stop loving Michelle, even though I have no plans to contact her again. I'm not the man for you, but as your friend, I'm going to introduce you to men who just might be perfect for you. Of course I'll do it with your permission when you feel you're ready. In either case, like I said, it's time for me to return home."

Chance's journey was complete. He was whole and he was determined his friend would one day become whole also. As for him, it was time to regain all he'd lost with Blaine and with baby Jeremy. Like he'd told Michelle, he had come full circle. They all had.

The End

ABOUT THE AUTHOR

Dyanne Davis is a Multi-Published, Award Winning author of 20 novels. She has written dozens of articles for on-line magazines. Dyanne lives in a Chicago suburb with her husband of 43 years, William Sr.

She has been a presenter of numerous workshops. She hosts a local cable television show in her hometown, "*The Art of Writing*," to give writing tips to aspiring writers. Interviewing many of her favorite authors has been the highlight of doing the show. You can catch some of the clips on Youtube.

Dyanne also writes a vampire series under the name of F. D. Davis
You can reach her at:
davisdyanne@aol.com
www.dyannedavis.com
adamomegavampire@aol.com
www.adamomega.com

Here is a sneak peek at book two in the Undying Love Trilogy

THE GIFT

Blaine MaDia sat on the jet, his eyes closed behind the dark glasses he wore so often now. It had taken him less than a week to survey the damage in his San Francisco apartment and start the rebuilding process. In the meantime he needed a place to live. So he was heading east to his spacious suburban home forty minutes west of Chicago

Funny when he'd flown to San Francisco he'd had thoughts of staying. Problem was, even with a psychic, life didn't always turn out as planned. For assurance he'd even drawn Tarot cards for himself. Too bad he hadn't asked if he would be burned out of his west coast apartment.

Lifting the glasses a tiny bit from his face to swipe at the sweat that had beaded between his brows, he allowed a deep breath of air to escape. He didn't want to take them off because for the past week he'd taken quite a bit of ribbing, some of it good-natured, some of it mean spirited. Mostly people questioned if he were a true psychic, why didn't he know his apartment was going to catch on fire?

In all honesty he'd answered, 'I'm not God.' Now he was tired of the questions, tired of all the answers. He just wanted to go home undisturbed. If he didn't wear the glasses, strangers would be pestering him with requests for readings. He accepted that as a price for his fame.

On most occasions he handled those requests with a modicum of dignity and humor offering his card to the person asking. He couldn't chance it now; he was in too weak of a state psychically. The fumes from the smoke had wreaked havoc in his body. He needed time to heal. Right now he could ill afford strangers pulling at his energy field. It was all that he could do to keep the barrier of energy surrounding his body, keeping out the thoughts of his fellow passengers.

Sleep was pulling at him when he sat up with a start. He rubbed at his temple feeling the beginning of what promised to be one doozy of a headache. Since the fire, dreams of his mother dogged him raggedly. There were so many questions he wanted to ask. If he could he'd eliminate the dreams, but for whatever reason they continued. *Not now* he thought not wanting to deal with the experience of the fire while sitting on a packed plane.

Trying to push the thoughts from him a searing pain warned what was happening wasn't about him or the fire but about someone entirely different. He closed his eyes in order to better focus his powers, to see who was having such an effect on him. Not since the first time he met Michelle Powers, his soul mother, had he felt such a dramatic reaction. Blaine wanted to know who it was who was having such a strong effect on him. And what was happening to his hard won self-control.

As he focused his energy the feeling became stronger, until at last, he was on his feet, standing, moving forward without wanting to, yet drawn to someone's pain. His hand moved unobtrusively through the air. Since finding his mother he was discovering new powers he'd never known he possessed.

He smiled to himself, the thought that he had only to put out his hand and connect with someone's energy surprising. After a lifetime of dealing with the unexplained, he was comfortable with his gift of clairaudience. He didn't have a name for this newest emerging gift.

The best way he could explain it was mining for energy. He used his hands much the same as he used his mind when speaking to those who had departed this life and were waiting. He focused.

Suddenly he stopped walking, his eyes landing on a woman of petite stature. Even from a sitting position he could tell she was short. He stood over the woman perusing her body in a quick perfunctory manner. She was slender also. His gaze fell on the woman's curly, dark brown hair and a lump formed in his throat.

Blaine stepped back as an irresistible urge to reach out and touch her clutched at his throat. It took all his psychic energy to resist the pull. A tightening began in his groin. Good Lord, not now. He panicked and moved backwards down the aisle. No woman had ever affected him so quickly.

"What is it that you want?"

Blaine stopped his backwards descent and looked down into the biggest pair of chocolate brown eyes he'd ever seen. For a moment he thought his heart would stop. Despite the woman's cold stare he felt drawn to her.

The sadness that had emanated from her to bring him to her now washed over him in waves. He clicked his tongue against his teeth trying to feel the woman's energy.

She'd placed a block to keep him out. Damn. That had never happened before.

"I'm sorry," he stammered. "My name's Blaine MaDia." He smiled at the woman while his skin began a slow crawl of awareness. It wasn't so much her looks as her aura. In looks she was ordinary with the exception of her eyes. It was the woman's aura that held an intense fascination for Blaine.

"I'm sorry, Mr. MaDia. Am I supposed to know you?"

Blaine tried again to probe gently at the woman's thoughts. When that didn't work he tried more aggressively, but still she held out against him, blocking any entrance. This stirred his curiosity making him wonder what it was the woman was hiding so possessively that she'd thrown up a shield against a stranger.

"Mr. MaDia, did you want something?"

Now he was standing there feeling like a fool, his own psyche open for probing, and his defenses weakened. He knew better than to continue with his questions, yet he felt compelled to press on. Never in all the years since Blaine became a professional psychic had he ever used that gift to seek out females, or to impress. He was now embarrassed and could feel the flush of that embarrassment with the next words he uttered.

"I'm Blaine MaDia, the psychic on television." He gulped. The woman appeared unimpressed. "I was just walking, I didn't want anything." Blaine continued. Still nothing. The woman simply stared at him, her deep-set chocolate eyes turning to liquid cocoa. Now besides wanting to touch her, Blaine wanted to stand there and take a long drink from her eyes.

"I don't know you, Mr. MaDia and I don't mean to appear rude, but I'm very tired. I paid for two first class seats so I wouldn't be disturbed." She tilted her head slightly letting Blaine know she wanted him to leave.

"Sorry I bothered you," he murmured and turned to walk back to his seat. He paused and stuck out his hand toward the woman. "Nice to meet you Miss…Miss…"

He waited for an acknowledgment and a name, but the woman looked at him with mere curiosity, ignored his outstretched hand and cast her gaze back on the book in her hand.

Surely the woman had to be a psychic, Blaine thought. In the very least, she was familiar with psychic gifts because she was using them so effectively to keep him out. And he wanted in.

He set back in his seat amused and peeved. He was behaving like a hormonal teenager, trying to impress a girl into giving him her name. Still, knowing something and having emotional feelings about it were two different things.

The very thought of not knowing bugged him, when less than an hour ago all he had wanted was to be able to tune out the emotions and the thoughts of the people around him. Now, more than anything, he wanted to know what the woman four rows ahead of him was thinking. And why she'd thrown up a defense against him.

Blaine took his glasses from the perched position on the bridge of his nose and folded them into the clear plastic container that hung around his neck. He smiled to himself. He loved the three inch case and the glasses that bent like spaghetti to fit into the case. He'd found them at a cheap boutique and thought they were cool.

He gazed around the cabin ignoring an inner command to rest. Sure he knew what he was doing. He knew that soon everyone in his section would recognize him and they would ask for readings. There would be a flurry of activity. Something in his experience no woman could let slide. Then, he thought, the woman with the chocolate eyes would drop her defenses.

He was fully aware his thoughts and actions were wrong. He had no right to violate another person's mind without their explicit invitation. And the code of conduct governing legitimate psychics prohibited such behavior. Still, he found himself smiling at no one in particular.

The need to know this woman was erasing his moral code. It only took a moment and a bit of gentle mental persuasion before the passenger across the aisle turned to him.

"Aren't you Blaine MaDia?"

"That's right I am."

"Wow. I can't believe it. I've been watching you on television for over a year and listening to you on the radio. I heard you wrote a book. Is it out yet?"

"No, it will be out in a month or so. Thanks for the support."

Blaine smiled more deeply at the man, resisting the urge for further tampering. He could easily give the man a hypnotic suggestion to carry the fuss up an octave or two, but that wouldn't be necessary. Nor did he want to cross any more barriers than necessary.

Soon everyone in the first class section were clamoring, begging Blaine for a reading, telling him how much they admired him, watched him, believed him. Everyone that is, with the exception of the lone woman occupying two seats.

Blaine tried again. She kept the invisible fence around her thoughts. In fact she'd fortified it and this time he knew it wasn't to keep out a stranger. This time it was personal. It had been structured to keep him out.

Taking out a small piece of paper from the notepad he always kept tucked in his shirt pocket he scribbled a few words on it and handed the note to the passing flight attendant who wrote on it and gave it back.

Cassandra Boozer. Smiling his thanks at the woman he handed her his card. "Call me. I owe you one."

He didn't care that the woman thought it odd that he didn't just approach his fellow passenger, or as most people thought, his being a psychic he should automatically know the name of every person he met.

Sure that happened on occasion, but most of the times it didn't. Sometimes there was someone with such a strong personality that they would literally shout their name into his subconscious, much like the spirits he preferred to deal with.

There was only one other woman, one other person period that had ever had a draining effect on him. And that woman was his mother from his only other lifetime. This feeling he had for this woman was extremely weak compared to the massive energized connection that had summoned him to his mother's side.

Still as weak as it was, Blaine was intrigued. He didn't feel she was someone from his past, either in this life or the one before it, but

there was something about the woman and for some reason he knew
he wanted to know her.

He stopped the thought as quickly as it had come wondering if it
had anything to do with the cryptic message his mother's shadow-self
had delivered to him. He remembered Michelle's words clearly now.
"You'll find someone, Son."

Could this Cassandra Boozer, the mysterious woman who feigned
no interest in him or his reputation be the one he was looking for?
He thought of her disinterested voice and cold stare. If she was the
one, Blaine sure as hell hoped that her demeanor was just a psychic
front. He had no wish to become involved with a woman with ice in
her veins. No, with a woman like that he would only offer his
professional services.

Again he felt the sudden tightening in his pants and lowered the
paper he was reading to cover the bulge. Oh yeah, he thought, All I
want to give her is professional services. With nothing left to do, he
decided to return to his seat and catch a quick nap.

www.ingramcontent.com/pod-product-compliance
Lightning Source LLC
Chambersburg PA
CBHW071952040426
42447CB00009B/1309